What They Say About *SuperMedia*

"Charlie Beckett provides a serious but accessible introduction to the challenges facing contemporary journalism, intellectually and professionally. Presenting an argument for the importance of journalism in society, whilst also recognising the impact of business and technology on that contribution, *SuperMedia* will be invaluable to media students wanting a cutting-edge survey from an experienced and reflective practitioner."

Adrian Monck, head of the Department of Journalism and Publishing, City University, London

"The idea and practice of networked journalism needs this thorough examination and this manifesto in its favor. And I second Charlie Beckett's contention that we in the news business and in society need networked journalism not just to protect but to expand journalism's future."

Jeff Jarvis, blogger and professor, CUNY Graduate School of Journalism

"Charlie Beckett knows the business from the inside, and in *SuperMedia* it shows. A powerful analysis of the great challenges facing all of us, whether reporters, readers, bloggers, or viewers. Read it, and act!"

Jon Snow, presenter, Channel 4 News

"This important book charts a course through journalism's current crises of trust, economics, and technology and points to a way of reconnecting with a broad social purpose."

Richard Sambrook, director, BBC Global News

This book is dedicated to the people who make up the story of my life: Erika and Roger Beckett, Anna Feuchtwang, and Billy and Isaac Beckett.

SuperMedia

Saving Journalism So It Can
Save The World

Charlie Beckett

Blackwell
Publishing

Blackwell Publishing was acquired by John Wiley & Sons in February 2007. Blackwell's publishing program has been merged with Wiley's global Scientific, Technical, and Medical business to form Wiley-Blackwell.

Registered Office
John Wiley & Sons Ltd, The Atrium, Southern Gate, Chichester, West Sussex, PO19 8SQ, United Kingdom

Editorial Offices
350 Main Street, Malden, MA 02148-5020, USA
9600 Garsington Road, Oxford, OX4 2DQ, UK
The Atrium, Southern Gate, Chichester, West Sussex, PO19 8SQ, UK

For details of our global editorial offices, for customer services, and for information about how to apply for permission to reuse the copyright material in this book please see our website at www.wiley.com/wiley-blackwell.

Library of Congress Cataloging-in-Publication Data

Beckett, Charlie.
    Supermedia : saving journalism so it can save the world / Charlie Beckett.
        p. cm.
    Includes bibliographical references and index.
    ISBN 978-1-4051-7923-2 (pbk. : alk. paper) — ISBN 978-1-4051-7924-9 (hardcover : alk. paper)
1. Journalism—Social aspects. 2. Journalism. I. Title.

    PN4749.B35 2008
    302.23—dc22

                                                                                          2008009038

A catalogue record for this book is available from the British Library.

Set in 10.5/13pt Dante MT by Graphicraft Limited, Hong Kong

01   2008

Contents

Figures

Foreword

First, let's get this straight: No one says that amateurs will or should replace professional journalists. That's not what networked journalism – the concept at the heart of this book – is about. Instead, networked journalism proposes to take advantage of the new opportunities for collaboration presented by the linked ecology of the Internet. Professional and amateur, journalist and citizen may now work together to gather and share more news in more ways to more people than was ever possible before. Networked journalism is founded on a simple, self-evident and self-interested truth: We can do more together than we can apart.

Indeed, pro and am are starting to work together. In the fall of 2007, I held a Networked Journalism Summit at the City University of New York Graduate School of Journalism, where I teach as an Assistant Professor. When I applied for the grant from the MacArthur Foundation that enabled us to hold the event, I thought our task would be to evangelize the idea. But by the time the conference came, it was clear that there were many efforts in networked journalism – most experimental – already underway. And so our job became to share best practices – some of which are in this book – and find next steps. One newspaper in Florida had invited readers to ferret out stories and scandals in volumes of data from a government storm-relief program. A New York radio station had mobilized its audience to find out which neighborhoods in the city were being gouged with prices of milk and beer. A Bavarian startup was publishing profitable local magazines made up of content from local neighbors. And out of the coming together of these best practitioners came more ideas and projects, including a cooperative that is building software to help gather data from the public in crowd-sourced reporting projects. The Internet's power to connect us with information and each other makes all this possible.

But networked journalism is born not only of opportunity but also of need. News organizations – which enjoyed, if not monopolies, then at least protected positions as the proprietors of presses or broadcast towers – now find themselves facing unlimited competition not only for content and attention but also for revenue. They are shrinking. But they don't need to. By joining and creating networks of journalistic effort – helping with curation, editing, vetting, education, and, yes, revenue – these news organizations can, indeed, grow. Newspapers can get hyper-local or international. TV stations can have cameras everywhere. Investigators can have many more hands helping them dig. News sites can become more efficient by doing what they do best and linking to the rest. Reporters can get help and corrections on their work before and after it is published.

The tools journalists can use are constantly expanding. Links and search enable journalism to be found. Blogs allow anyone to publish and contribute. Mobile devices help witnesses share what they see – even as it happens – in the form of text, photos, audio, and video. Databases and wikis enable large groups to pool their knowledge. Social services can connect experts and communities of information.

This, I believe, is the natural state of media: two-way and collaborative. The one-way nature of news media until now was merely a result of the limitations of production and distribution. Properly done, news should be a conversation among those who know and those who want to know, with journalists – in their new roles as curators, enablers, organizers, educators – helping where they can. The product of their work is no longer the publication-cum-fishwrap but instead a process of progressive enlightenment.

So the means, economics, architecture, tools, and technology of journalism all change. What I hope changes most, though, is the culture. I hope journalism becomes more open, transparent, inclusive, flexible. I do believe that journalism will be stronger and more valuable as a component of networks than it was as the product of professional priesthoods. I also believe the amateurs who help in this process will be stronger for learning the standards, practices, and lessons journalists have learned over the years. Both will be better off for realizing that we are in this together, we are members of the same communities. But even with all this change, the essential task of journalism is still unchanged: We want to uncover what the world knows and what the world needs to know and bring them together.

When I began exploring these ideas myself, about the time I started blogging as a print-turned-online editor in 2001 – see www.buzzmachine.com – I called this notion, as many did, "citizen journalism." But I later recanted the phrase for three reasons. First, I believe, it is a mistake to define journalism by who does it, for that implies the certification – and thus risks the decertification – of journalists. Journalism should be defined by the act, and it is an act anyone can commit. Second, I recall a newspaper's online editor approaching the microphone at a conference of her tribe and challenging me as I spoke on a panel: "I'm a citizen, too," she said, tears in her eyes. Indeed you are, I replied, and the sooner journalists act as citizens in their worlds, the better both will be. Third, I came to see that the buzz-phrase "citizen journalism" could by no means capture the full power of collaboration now made possible by the Internet.

That power – the means, opportunities, and implications of networked journalism – is explored most ably in the pages that follow. Until this book, networked journalism has been the subject mostly of blog posts and conference panel discussions. The idea and practice of networked journalism needs this thorough examination and this manifesto in its favor. And I second Charlie Beckett's contention that we in the news business and in society need networked journalism not just to protect but to expand journalism's future.

Jeff Jarvis,
New York
December 2007

Acknowledgments

I would like to thank the following for their help: my researcher Holly Peterson, my assistant Laura Kyrke-Smith, and my personal editor Anna Feuchtwang. Thanks to journalist-professors Adrian Monck and Michael Parks for their feedback. To my new colleagues at the Media and Communications Department at the London School of Economics and the Journalism Department at the London College of Communication for the ideas I have stolen from them. To all the journalists and citizens who have taken part in the *POLIS* debates and research that have informed this book.

Finally, I want to pay tribute to the hundreds of fine journalists I have worked with over the past couple of decades at great news organizations such as the South London Press, LWT, the BBC, Channel 4 News and beyond.

Introduction

"The Dailyplanet.com"

Why We Must Save Journalism So that Journalism Can Save the World

Three scenarios convinced me that my trade had changed forever. The first was standing in my TV newsroom trying to decide whether to show the public a series of cartoons published in a Danish newspaper that had caused riots around the world. It was an acute ethical dilemma that raised profound political and editorial questions that could not be answered in the 45 minutes we had before we went to air. The second was standing next to the River Nile with *Channel 4 News* presenter Jon Snow in the run up to the G8 meeting of world leaders at Gleneagles in Scotland in July 2005. We were broadcasting the program live every night from Uganda in an effort to give the African perspective on world events. We took our state-of-the-art Outside Broadcast paraphernalia on the back of a huge flat-bed truck to locations such as a remote Ugandan village. There we found children were still dying of malaria because of a lack of something as cheap as anti-mosquito nets. I got off the plane from Africa that week and had to rush in to the studio to edit an extended program dominated by the bombing of London by British-born Muslims. The wrecked bus and smoking underground stations were all minutes from where I lived and worked. Three stories: the Cartoons, Africa, and the London Bombings. All with extraordinary resonances and in some way all linked. Something told me that these stories and the way we were telling them were quite different from anything that had been possible or predictable even just a few years ago. When I joined ITN's *Channel 4 News* in 1999 the newsroom had only a couple of Internet terminals and mobile phones were still rationed. When I left to set up a new journalism think-tank at the London School of Economics in 2006 these had become the basic tools of all journalists, including those I met in Uganda. But more important than the change in technology was the new interconnectedness I detected. I was convinced that journalism was at a "tipping point." This book is my manifesto for the media as a journalist but also as a citizen of the world. As a journalist you are constantly being told that the news media have enormous power to shape society and events, to change lives and history. So why are we so careless as a society about the future of journalism itself?

It is very difficult to take anything like an objective view of the news media. People who work within it are prone to fierce opinions about the state of the industry, based on their own aspirations and experience. They have the perspective of their particular sector of the profession: broadcast, print, or online. There is also the distortion of their specialist subject: politics, the arts, sport, or foreign affairs. And a journalist will always be very much of their time: the richly resourced Golden Age of TV in the 1970s, the heyday of tabloid newspapers in the 1980s; or the pioneering idealism of the Internet in the 1990s. And, how on earth, do you compare the experience of a journalist working on a news website in Seattle, say, with that of Galima Bukharbaeva, a journalist in Uzbekistan trying to report the Andijan massacre?[1] Journalists are supposed to strive for objectivity and yet, ask them about their own working lives and their business and you will usually get a partial perspective, a personal view. Possibly even a slightly tired and emotional one.

So why not turn to the people that journalists deal with: the politicians, the advertisers, and the pundits? Or even, why not turn to those people that journalists constantly worry about and yet rarely meet: the reader, the viewer, or the listener? All these groups have very strong and incredibly subjective views of the news media that make the average journalist's opinion look like an unsullied snowfall of neutral and studied reflection. Generally speaking, the public or the audience tends to have a view of the news media based on the last thing they consumed or the last thing done to them by the news media. So a reader tends to talk about the news media based on the paper or magazine she reads (or the dreadful newspapers that she wouldn't be seen dead with on the train), while bankers, politicians, shopkeepers, or artists tend to judge the news media by the way their business is reported. Thus, the financier despairs at journalists' failure to understand why their astronomical profits are for the greater good of the economy. The retailer can't fathom the journalists' incapacity to stand up for the principle of "caveat emptor." The artist despairs at the reviewer's personal vindictiveness and philistine inability to comprehend the truly revolutionary nature of their work. And as for the politician . . . well, funnily enough, they do despise and resent the work of the news media, but they also recognize kindred spirits. Political and journalistic hacks share a lack of time, an adaptable morality, and a love/hate relationship with the public, power, and the truth.

So I am afraid it is back to the journalist this time to try to understand what is happening to our news media. I do not pretend to be objective. I never really have as a journalist. I strive towards fairness, accuracy, and thoroughness, but I refuse to pretend that I am merely a cipher, a neutral medium through which facts and opinions pass unhindered to the public. So let me set out briefly the basis for my assessment of journalism and its future. As will become clear, this is not a history of journalism. Nor is it an attempt to survey its current state in an exhaustive manner. That is a task which, at the moment, is like writing on water. Of course, the past and present shape journalism and its future as well. But what I want to understand is the editorial forces that currently create what I insist can be called "good" journalism. And when we talk about contemporary journalism we mean, in effect, digital journalism. This book is above all an essay about the politics of journalism, its impact, and its potential for facilitating change. What drives this book is a conviction that journalism is at an unique moment in human history.

I hold these truths about journalism to be self-evident:

- News information has never been more plentiful and journalism has never been more abundant.
- Journalists have never had more resources to reach people, anytime, any-place, anywhere – and the audience has unprecedented accessibility to the news media.
- Journalism has never been more necessary to the functioning of our lives as individuals and societies and for the healthy functioning of global social, economic, and political relationships.
- There is the technological, educational, and economic potential for a vast expansion of journalism's impact and for that impact to be beneficial.

This happy set of assertions is largely to do with new technologies, although it is also about other global trends such as political and market liberaliza-tion, the growth in education, and the emancipation of social groups such as women. All this has contributed to an unprecedented expansion of a *relatively* free news media around the world. For all the set-backs for journ-alists in places like Russia or Uganda, the current state of the world's news media and the dissemination of topical information is still better than it was in the past. And, critically, the potential is far greater. However, we are at a crucial moment. There is nothing inevitable about the present superfluity of news information. There is no guarantee that this relatively beneficent state will continue or progress. There is nothing preordained about the virtues that will flow from it. Quite the opposite. There are great threats to the quality and potential of the news media. The values of openness, plurality, and quality are all contestable and contested. Sometimes this threat comes from familiar forces such as commercialization or political authoritarianism. Sometimes it will be new problems such as the fragmentation that choice can bring trailing in its wake. But I do not think that complaints about the passing of some imagined golden age of quality journalism are a sufficient critique. My fears are based on politics, not nostalgia. I strongly believe that in the rush for the digital development of journalism we must retain the values that sustain liberal journalism as a healthy part of a flourishing society. We should not allow fear to determine the future.

Journalism matters. We live in a much more interconnected world where information is ever-more critical to our lives. And it is journalism that conveys that data and allows us to debate its significance. It is always hard to pinpoint exact moments or to detail precise occasions when journalism has altered the course of events, rather than simply narrating them. It is nigh on impossible to separate out media impact from the general conditions of events. Take one example. It appears that the media failed to expose the failings of the intelligence that supported the Bush/Blair case for war in Iraq. Was this because they were impotent, incompetent, or deceived? We do know that if the media had exposed the flimsiness and partialness of that case earlier, it would have been a very different political scenario and possibly a different chain of events. My point is that while it may be difficult to measure, it is hard to deny the growing importance of the media in global events.

Yet at the same time journalism is itself undergoing profound changes for social, economic, and technological reasons. Some of these changes offer an opportunity for journalism to do much more. In fact, these changes offer the potential for a whole new type of journalism. In this book I will outline what I call Networked Journalism. It is a new way of practicing journalism that is already becoming evident. It is a reflection of emerging realities. But it is also an opportunity to transform the ethics as well as the efficacy of journalism. Networked Journalism offers the chance for the news media to enhance its social role. It is a recognition that mainstream professional journalists must share the very process of production. Networked Journalism includes citizen journalism, interactivity, open sourcing, wikis, blogging, and social networking, not as add-ons, but as an essential part of news production and distribution itself. By changing the way that journalists work and the way journalists relate to society, I think we can sustain "good" journalism and, in its turn, journalism can be a greater force for good. It is the only way for journalism to survive the coming storm. Even in this time of plenty there are signs of a change in the weather. Indeed, the clouds have already broken. The immediate future brings a multitude of threats to good journalism, and they are social, political, cultural, and commercial.

This is an "environmental" crisis, which some compare to physical threats such as climate change:

> I want to endorse the idea of the media as an environment, an environment which provides at the most fundamental level the resources we all need for the conduct of everyday life. It follows that such an environment may be or may become, or may not be or may not become, polluted. (Professor Roger Silverstone, *Media and Morality*)[2]

What Silverstone was suggesting here is that journalism could be a catalyst for reform in the way we live that will help address many of the world's problems – like global warming. But it could itself be a victim of developments that could render impotent its power to communicate change. A failure of understanding among people now has never been more hazardous.

Globally the apparently booming news media business is showing signs of ill-health. Some of the symptoms are obvious. There is the decline in the newspaper industry in the developed world. There is the concentration of ownership in mainstream media in the West. There is the increasing facility with which everyone from *Google* bosses to Chinese politicians are controlling the Internet. There is the evidence that repressive regimes and anti-democratic forces from the Russian mafia to Islamist extremists are proving very successful at reducing freedom of speech. And what kind of journalism are we producing in such abundance? Is the world of cyber-journalism going to be about citizen journalism or amateur pornography?

I estimate that we have five years – perhaps ten – to save journalism so that journalism can save the world. Ultimately, of course, issues like climate change and inter-faith frictions are going to be dealt with by politicians and the public, not by journalists. But think of a world where we try doing anything of great consequence *without* an open and reliable news media. Think of an issue, like the heating of our planet, with all its complexity and its essentially global nature. Then think of how much easier it will be to face up to that issue if we have a Networked Journalism that embraces a new compact of mutuality with a cosmopolitan, interactive "audience." This is my vision of a kind of journalism for this century. I know all about the grubby realities of journalism, be it in a sophisticated newsroom in London, in an African village, or the vast cities of India. But I also know that journalism offers great hope for all those places.

This book will first of all set out a way of understanding where we are. Like travelers in a landscape we are familiar with our immediate surroundings. But as the pace of our journey quickens it is harder to see the topography of journalism. The ground is moving beneath our feet and we will soon find ourselves in a strange country. I can't describe everything, but I want to suggest that we have now passed through the first phase of coming to terms with New Media. I will take a more conceptual approach to describing how business models and journalism have adapted. And while I take a Western perspective[3] I want to indicate how other parts of the world also face seismic shifts. For I believe that Networked Journalism is ultimately most important when seen as a global concept that can offer a new paradigm for international journalism.

Key to understanding the potential as well as the process of this change is this idea of Networked Journalism. This is already becoming a fact of life, not just in the digitalized newsrooms of the West, but also throughout the world. New technological realities like mobile phones and forces such as political liberalization are giving the public a greater role in the reporting of their worlds. I will show how the very nature of journalism is changing – again. Not for the first time, the way that we report, analyze, and comment upon events is being transformed. These big moments are often technologically driven. Printing, the telegraph, telephony, television, satellites, and now the Internet all changed the way journalism has been practiced. But it is also about a less deferential, better-educated public. I do not know if this is a cultural change akin to the Reformation or the Enlightenment. But it seems to me that a post-modern, post-industrial, multi-faith world demands a different kind of understanding through its news media.

Networked Journalism is a description and an aspiration. It reaffirms the value of the core functions of journalism. It celebrates the demand for journalism and its remarkable social utility. But it insists on a new process and fresh possibilities. It means a kind of journalism where the rigid distinctions of the past, between professional and amateur, producer and product, audience and participation, are deliberately broken down. It embraces permeability and multi-dimensionality. Networked Journalism is also a way of bridging the semantic divide between Old and New Media. In this book I will continue to refer to New Media and Mainstream Media as useful ways to describe forces that shape the industry. But, in truth, as Tom Armitage[4] has said, a better term is "Next Media," because everyone will be using the "new" technologies at some point soon. Networked Journalism is a catch-all for many types of more connected media practice. But not all journalism will be networked. Some "amateurs" will remain resolutely apart from the "professionals." And much of the news media will appear relatively untrans-formed. However, the way that social and technological changes are open-ing up new audiences, distribution methods and communities demands a new approach. Networked Journalism is one way to describe it and practice it.

The ultimate proof is politics. I will look at the impact of New Media upon the reporting of politics and see if Networked Journalism is having any impact on the way that we relate to the manner in which power is communicated. I will look particularly at the most advanced frontiers in this war between "netroot" activists, journalists, and politicians in the United States. I will then look at the peculiarly intense world of British Westminster political bloggers. But I also want to see whether Networked Journalism and new technology offer a new paradigm for media in places like Africa which traditionally have been seen as still struggling to develop conventional media markets. Of course, that is a relatively narrow definition of politics as being about journalism and governance. There is also a much wider agenda of media and civic engage-ment that future journalism must respond to as well.

And there is no greater global challenge to journalism than its ability to deal with the complex narratives of terror and community. You do not have to believe in simplistic notions of clashing civilizations to understand that ideas are now as powerful as economics in driving conflict and fomenting frictions. What effect is journalism having as it struggles with these hugely difficult subjects? And as these forces are increasingly mediated through dig-ital forums, can Networked Journalism offer a new compact between different cultures as well as between the journalist and the public?

Networked Journalism offers a solution to another challenge facing journalism. If the news media is to be able to communicate these diverse debates and understand these novel stories then it must be more diverse in itself. By that I mean the kind of people who work in journalism, their class, ethnicity and backgrounds. But I also mean the different approaches they take and the variety of styles, subjects, and stories they tell. At present there is a lack of diversity in journalism. This is at a time when improved education levels and easy Internet access to communications platforms means that the news media should be more diverse than ever before. Instead it threatens to be thin and fragmented rather than pluralistic and rich. There is a problem of the diversity of the people in journalism. But there is also the problem of increasingly formulaic, unreflective, uncreative journalism itself – partly as a consequence of technological and economic pressures. Networked journalism offers greater diversity of content and producers if it is thought through properly and imaginatively.

And finally I want to reappraise the idea of Media Literacy. There is no hope for Networked Journalism if the practitioners and the public are not equipped for the task. This is partly about the skills of journalists. This is a particularly big issue in less-developed economies and less-developed civil societies but the need for greater media literacy applies globally. For Networked Journalism to become a reality *anywhere* it is about the public. It is about giving the people – formerly known as the audience – the skills and the resources to be participants in the process. To teach people how to take part in the news media, and to understand how it works. This is much more than the practical task of media studies. It is also about giving people the resources to adopt a critical engagement with journalism. And it is a political education, too. Journalists and the public need to have a sense of their responsibilities, as well as their rights. I firmly believe that, ultimately, journalists – including Networked Journalists – must have a sense of what is objective and what is the truth. This means that while they will be more engaged with society in the process of journalism, they must retain the final, inner arbitration of the ethics of their work. It will be a very difficult balance to strike. It will be much harder to define boundaries and draw up codes of conduct. In the end journalists don't have a choice. Their work will become more networked whether they like it or not. Our task as news media practitioners is to think through the consequences and work harder and more imaginatively to exploit the opportunities. That way, the public, politicians, and journalists can realize the potential role of the digital news media in promoting good governance and development across the world. Then we will have a media with "super" powers. But before journalism can save the world, we must save journalism.

1

"Help! Help! Who Will Save Us?"

The New Media Landscape

1.1 Introduction

> We all are caught in the greatest upheaval our industry and the institution of journalism has ever faced. (Robert Rosenthal, Managing Editor *The San Francisco Chronicle*, resignation memo)[1]

Journalism is being turned upside down. It is on a roller-coaster ride that can be exhilarating but rather scary. Across the world thousands of journalists are losing their jobs. Hundreds have lost their lives. It is not a "safe" career in any sense now. So what? Detroit automobile workers have lost jobs, too, and aid workers don't exactly have an easy time of it in places like Darfur or Iraq either. I think it matters because journalism has a social and political role. It can do something for you. It also matters because it is a global business that represents a huge amount of wealth generation. It is vital for the efficient functioning of economies, especially the financial markets. And without good information how are you going to run your complicated lives? How can you choose your children's school or your next car? So, even if you don't pity the poor hack, please think of your own interests.

What's wrong with the news media business? Surely it is riding a wave of technological innovation? How can all these blogs and websites and clever gadgets threaten journalism? Why did the online editor of a massively successful British paper tell me this, off the record:

> Over the next few years our shareholders are going to have to consider not taking a dividend. Or our owners will have to consider whether they can go for a few years without a profit while we restructure the business.

What we are witnessing is not the impending obsolescence of a defunct industry. Even mainstream media such as newspapers cannot be compared to, say, the canal barge industry on the eve of the train age. But neither is it simply a step up in efficiency, from a typewriter to a word processor. Business models will have to be re-structured in a profound and thorough-going way that introduces a huge amount of risk into their economic strategies. Advertising revenues are disappearing far faster than new ones are appearing. Competition is swallowing up the gains of efficiencies. Consumers are transforming their tastes and habits and redirecting their purchasing power. And the producer, the human capital, will have to be completely over-hauled. This is not just a question of investing in new technology and new systems, because no-one knows which technology will be relevant in a few years time. It is about a revolution in the way that one of the planet's most important cultural and economic forces is going to operate. And as we all know from our history, revolutions have a habit of being rather nasty and often end up going horribly wrong.

Since *Polis* (the new forum for debate and research into journalism and society at the London School of Economics and the London College of Communication)[2] was founded in the summer of 2006, I have been talking to media leaders and practitioners about how their business will survive and thrive in the new media landscape. I like the metaphor of a journey through a landscape because it suggests how different the trip will be according to where you start from, the direction you take, and the scenery you pass through. Different media markets are moving at varying speeds. Individual journalists, news organizations, or audiences will take different routes and have different views.

During *Polis* sessions I have heard some highly innovative ideas for new ways to make money out of journalism by repackaging it in forms that just wouldn't have been technically possible, let alone profitable, a few years ago. Some are directly derived from new technology, such as the local newspaper journalist who is turning an online soccer fanzine into a franchise for sports websites paid for by advertising.[3] Other ideas look like "old" media but still profit from the new economic and consumer conditions that are emerging. For example, in an age where online news is cheap and plentiful there might be a market for a product that combines the tactile joys of old media with some good old-fashioned high-quality exclusive journalism. Why not sell a daily super glossy, star-writer-filled publication to the mega-rich for $10 a day? Or why not spend billions on taking over your nearest rival in a bid to overtake a global competitor? OK, so the last idea is hardly new. It is a traditional reaction by boardrooms to preserve thin margins, but it will be interesting to see which kind of strategy works.

Not all changes in the business models for journalism are made because of technological change. Take the rapid growth in "Lads mags" in the UK and their subsequent decline. This was as much about editorial, cultural, and economic changes in the make-up of a social sub group as it was about new technology.[4,5] Magazines like *GQ* and *Loaded* exploded on to the market in the UK in the 1990s because of the growth in a post-feminist, cash-rich group of young men. They fell away recently partly because there was a growth in easily accessible pornography online, but also because they became a stale format. It is possible that they can rediscover some editorial verve. But the real problem is that their content and their audience has gone online. This is something that has not happened yet, in such as striking way, to the women's magazine market, but that might just be a question of time as women increasingly go online. Women have always been put off by the Internet's geeky image. But, to be stereotypical in the reverse direction for a moment, surely shopping and social networking are web strengths?[6] My point is that it is about people, not programming. What is undeniable is that the fundamental shift in the economics of journalism is about the way that the technology is facilitating these changes in the consumption model for news.

And there is a parallel revolution occurring in the business models for news production. Look at how much easier and cheaper it is to be a journalist now then it was five or ten years ago. With a mobile phone, a hand-held video camera, and a laptop with Internet, journalists are now exponentially more productive than they were five years ago. A broadcaster like ITN in the UK reckons it has cut costs by 40 percent in the past five years, mainly by cutting people. This is how the man behind those savings at ITN describes the process:

> The prime driver of this process has been digital technology, which has allowed journalists to do many of the tasks that were currently performed by specialists such as tape-editors, researchers, librarians – even cameramen. This process will continue but I see the next big quantum reduction in costs coming from easier delivery of picture: all the infrastructure associated with satellite picture delivery: satellite paths, technical coordinators, SNG vehicles, Master Control centres . . . are likely to reduce as file-based picture transfer takes hold and becomes common place and easy.
>
> Having said all that – it's just as well costs are coming down, because the requirement to have flexible budgets that can be used to cover any news

eventuality, from going live from melting icecaps to purchasing the latest schlock-horror video of a jailed LA temptress, has never been greater. The breadth of what constitutes news is wider than it has ever been. (Guy Ker, Chief Operating Officer, ITV News, ITN)[7]

As Guy Ker says, efficiency savings have been partly eaten up by the new demands upon journalism. But it is now much easier and cheaper to deliver that journalism. Traditional media such as newspapers are now hugely more sophisticated but at a lower price thanks to new technology. It allows rapid edition changes, color printing, and journalists laying out their own copy. This has allowed old titles to survive and new ones to arrive.

The reduction in satellite costs and the expansion of digital spectrums means that the old oligarchy of the main terrestrial channels has been blown apart by a plethora of 24 hour and other digital news channels. And the Internet and other technologies now allow a panoply of platforms for the public to access news information. Newspaper, radio, and TV journalism is now distributed via computers and mobile phones. And that is before you start to count the ever-expanding array of blogs, web forums, and social networking sites that create their own news online.

This book will not go into the specifics of technological change, mainly because the pace of change will make anything written this month outdated by next year. I want to stress that this is about the dynamics of the journalism as it relates to the technology. This is essentially an economic question, but it should not be reduced to finances or management. In the short term news-media businesses will survive if they make the right decisions about staffing and marketing, but in the long term they will only thrive if they understand the larger social, political, and editorial dynamics at work. They have to know what kind of journalism is needed and wanted and how to deliver it.

The rise of online journalism presents a fundamental challenge to the present economic organization of the news media. But what form that challenge will take and how fundamental it will be is still very much up for grabs. Journalism is not a static resource like copper which depends on our ability to extract it from the ground. It can be made profitable simply by better manipulation of existing resources. But that is for the short term, at best. Investment in new technology and the efficiency gains that brings will not be enough for strategic success beyond the next few years. There have been heroic efforts made to get more for less from journalists over the past decades. It's an imperative that drives any business. What we are witnessing now is a more fundamental shift in the whole relationship between the news producer and the consumer. So anyone who wants to ensure that their news media business has viability beyond the next five years must attend to the fundamental shifts in the very nature of journalism and its usefulness and attraction to the audience. Just a few years ago *YouTube* and *Google* didn't even exist, now one has taken over the other in one of the biggest media deals of recent times. They are among the most powerful players in media and increasingly influential in journalism. If you concentrate too much on the structure of the business as it is or the profit projections in the short term you will fail. It will be the idea of journalism, and in the future the idea of Networked Journalism, that will pay. And that idea is a good one.

The business of journalism promises relevant information that people can use to construct their lives. In increasingly affluent societies people will pay a premium for good information. They need it to make the myriad decisions that Governments now want to leave to the individual or family. From cradle to grave the news media helps you decide. Which maternity hospital? Which vaccinations? Which mortgage? Which college course? And there are all the lifestyle and recreational information that you need to plan holidays, change your diet, or choose your entertainment. People also appear to want to make their politics more personal and to decide for themselves the part they are going to play in issues such as climate change. Journalism helps people make those calls. This is a global phenomenon. Everywhere that incomes rise we see that people are expected to do more for themselves. Generally they seem to enjoy that freedom. But the best choices are informed ones, and journalism at its best helps provide the independent facts and analysis to do just that.

But people want more than just consumer journalism, important as that much-belittled form is to individuals and families. They also seem to want more opportunity to debate their world. And they also want a more varied and informed level of commentary upon it. They want to know more about the rest of the world as well as much more about themselves and their immediate environment. There is a global feeling that formal politics or politicians are held in disrepute, but this doesn't mean that people are not interested in politics. The number of people active in community, interest, or pressure groups has risen as the membership of traditional parties has fallen. And in less developed societies, where political opportunities for engagement are offered, people take them. Look at the queues for elections in South Africa or Iraq. So while there is a decline in demand for formal coverage of politics, such as the reporting of parliaments and congresses, there has been a growth in the interest in the reporting of all the other aspects of civic society. Much of this is cultural and social in subject matter but it has political consequences in that it still mediates morals, material decisions, and social organization. Conventional news media have been slow to recognize this shift in the interests of the public. So much of the media that talks about these issues is now generated by the citizen. *Google* and *MySpace* and *Facebook* have built vast business empires largely on the basis of that proposition.

So with all this demand for information and debate, why are the business models that deliver journalism in crisis? Why are the media business pages in the West full of talk of declining revenue and job cuts? And why are so many pessimists convinced that underdeveloped media markets such as Africa will never deliver?

I think this is partly because there is a tendency to look at the journalism business from two extremes. One says that we must defend the fine state of journalism as it is. The other evangelizes about the potential of New Media to obliterate the old guard and bring in a new dispensation. It may be that neither is correct.

1.2   The New News Media Landscape

The fundamental premise of this book is that it is impossible and undesirable to separate out New from Old Media. Take the example of print versus electronic news in the US. It is clear that most news websites get much of their primary information from the country's 1,400 newspapers or from agencies such as Associated Press. In the last century we lost more than 1,000 of those titles in the US alone. That is still a lot of journalism resource but we will all suffer a diminution of the amount of journalism available if those "conventional" newsrooms continue to decline at the same rate. "New" and "Old" Media are already intimately linked and, as we shall see in later chapters, this is something that needs to be accelerated, not resisted. But it is important to try to understand the *degree* to which journalism is happening online and to begin to understand the *way* that it is happening.

The figures in the West are stunning. The last time I checked, *Technorati* was tracking around 100 million blogs. Some analysis suggests that 3 percent are consciously about politics.[8,9] I make that 2.4 million political editorial voices that weren't there before and those numbers are increasing all the time. There is no precise definition of a weblog so it is difficult to describe exactly when they become news journalism rather than personal discourse. This is how *Technorati* attempts to define the difference:

> Weblogs are different from traditional media. Bloggers tend to be more opinionated, niche-focused, and partisan than journalists, who strive for editorial objectivity. Blogs encourage dialog with readers, which is why many traditional journalists now also have blogs. The relationship between blogging and journalism can be characterized as symbiotic rather than competitive. Bloggers are often sources for journalists, and many blogs contain commentary and riffs on what journalists wrote that day. Frequently newsmakers use blogs to respond to what journalists write about them. And by linking to traditional media, weblogs can introduce new readers to journalists and their publications.[10]

As journalism goes online I think that distinction becomes increasingly blurred. I think it is more useful to think in terms of Personal Bloggers and Journalist Bloggers, who are in effect, Networked Journalists. Recent research[11] indicates that about 40 percent of blog subject matter is "my life and experiences." But even if you don't want to include that within a definition of news, there is about 20 percent of the subject matter which is explicitly concerned with politics, business, and current affairs.[12] As we will see in the next chapter, the debate is not whether this is journalism, but whether this kind of activity redefines journalism itself. But for now, never mind the semantics, just take note of the numbers. More than 1.1 billion of the world's estimated 6.6 billion people are online and almost a third of those are now accessing the Internet on high speed lines.[13] Mobile phones are seen as the next platform after TV and PCs. Mobile phone ownership is up to 3 billion around the world and it is expected that one billion handsets will be sold each year by 2009. The evidence is that the little hand-held screen is set to become a vital portal for Internet access.[14] And while you can have that mobile phone for just a few dollars a week, so the cost of delivering the services to it is falling as well. The cost of delivering Internet and satellite services is plummeting, which means that the price of starting up a digital channel in the UK has fallen to as little as £100,000. And online TV is, of course, even cheaper. The cost of starting an IPTV channel like *CurrentTV*[15] is not the cost of spectrum or licenses but mainly the cost of content. And the cost of making the actual programs has plunged. Even on terrestrial stations it has fallen by about a third in real terms in under a decade.[16]

This means that the little guy can get involved in production much more easily. However, that doesn't mean that the business is not still dominated by the Big Guys. It's just that they are different Big Guys. The largest media corporations in the world are now not just BBC, NBC, or Reuters but include Disney and Google. All the world's previous media giants had journalism at the heart of their histories, however small a role it eventually played on the balance sheet. This is not true of New Media, where media outlets are often owned by massive holding companies, such as GE, focused on light bulbs or heath-care rather than journalism. At the grass-roots level, purely journalistic New Media ventures are much rarer than the millions devoted to retail, social networking, pornography, culture, or sport.

Wholly online news sites were originally often very specific blogs or forums, usually devoted to a particular community and its needs. In the early days of the Internet this usually meant news *about* the Net. So Internet businesses devoted to news which are in direct competition with mainstream news media have been relatively unusual. They are now emerging. Some are very highbrow, such as the academically inclined *opendemocracy.net*,[17] which publishes high-fiber analysis and reportage. Or they serve an informed elite group, such as the stylish and well-informed US political online magazine *Slate.com*,[18] which targets political obsessives. Others are political with a small "p" such as the online video site *Current TV*,[19] which is a moderated user generated content site with liberal backers. Some, such as *Digg.com*,[20] act as user-controlled recommendation and linking portals rather than producers of content. These "pure" online news operations are still a tiny part of the overall news offering. There is far more news produced online by mainstream media groups who have taken to the Internet, such as the *New York Times* or the BBC. So there is a bigger threat to traditional offline journalism from non-News websites than there is from journalism originated online. But this will change. To ignore the journalism that works most innovatively online is to ignore the future. That is why "mainstream media" are right to take its fight for survival to the Internet.

1.3   Mainstream Media Fight Back

Much of mainstream media around the world have been relatively successful at coping with technological change. People are still reading newspapers, even in high-tech cities like London and New York. And they are still sitting down to watch evening bulletins in front of TV sets in the new media metropolises like Seattle and Los Angeles. Global newspaper sales were up 2.3 percent in 2006, and rose nearly 10 percent over the past five years, with advertising revenue up almost 4 percent and 16 percent over the same two time spans. Of course, this has been helped by a boom in China (up 15.5 percent since 2002) and India (up 53.6 percent). But even in Europe, paid-for daily titles sold 0.74 percent more copies in 2006. Add in free dailies and it gives a 10.2 percent circulation rise.[21] The figures are similar for TV. Take China. In the early 1980s, there were only 20 TV sets for every 100 households, but by 2005 there were 30 percent more sets than families.[22] All that may give some comfort to those who do not want to abandon Old Media certainties. But what about those markets where the Internet is most prevalent?

In the US there have been dramatic drops in viewing figures for the main TV news shows, but recently it appears the decline may have at least slowed, according to the *Pew Report* for 2006:

> Despite new anchors, millions in promotion, press attention and more, network evening news lost another million viewers, roughly the same number it has lost in each of the last 25 years. As a percentage, of course, the number is growing . . . The number of people who go "online" for news or anything else has now stabilized, confirming something we first saw last year. In all, about 92 million people now go online for news.[23,24]

So Mainstream media in the West are in part being sustained by the stickiness of the market. Not everyone has deserted traditional journalism overnight. There will be a place for mainstream news on mainstream platforms for some time. Surveys show that a majority still prefer getting news on TV or on paper.[25] Not everyone wants to watch the news online or on their mobile phone. Not all wheels will need reinventing. If you are a commuter on a train then the newspaper can still be a very good way of consuming information in a pleasurable and efficient way. If you have just spent a hard day at the office then a half-hour news bulletin can be a much less arduous way to update yourself on the day's events then having to sift through your RSS feeds online. Look at the way that radio has thrived in the modern world. The "wireless"[26] is that most old-fashioned of broadcast media, redolent of the pre-computer age. And yet it is radio that is proving most adept at fitting in with our time-poor lifestyles and our multi-tasking leisure schedules.

Another reason for the continued strength of traditional platforms is because mainstream news media have the skills and the experience. The people that have been delivering journalism for the past 20, 30, or 40 years have got rather good at it. The "inventions" of formats for delivering journalism to a mass audience, such as the tabloid press, the TV presenter, or the radio phone-in, have all been honed over decades of increasing editorial and technical competition and development. As Martin Fewell, Deputy Editor of ITN's *Channel 4 News* said: "My difficulty with the Internet as the tree of knowledge and the blogger as journalist is how good they are at finding things out. The greatest threat to mainstream media is not technological advance but the threat to our ability to provide a high-quality news product."[27]

Indeed, my old employers at *Channel 4 News* are a good example of how mainstream journalism can adapt and thrive. *Channel 4 News* is, in a sense, a very old-fashioned format. One hour of daily live studio-based news and analysis with live interviews and packaged films produced largely on the day in the UK and around the world. *Channel 4 News* has been at the forefront of presentational developments such as the use of standing presenters and a huge video screen in the studio. But it is basically the same kind of format that a presenter of the BBC's *Tonight* program would recognize from the 1960s. And yet during the past decade of New Media revolution, this program has put on ratings alongside increased critical acclaim. This is partly because all concerned have worked very hard, with great imagination and dedication, to maintain standards. It has targeted and grown a niche audience of around 1 million people who want high quality news with an alternative twist. But it has also exploited new technology to slash costs and deliver new services.

When I joined, the program staff still had to do background research for stories by walking across the corridor to get yellowing newspaper cuttings out of paper envelopes stored in the "Information Library." Since then a slightly larger editorial team has added two daily half hour programs to its output alongside an online operation that has video, podcasts, and blogs by the team. Soon it will deliver radio news as well. Certainly, there were downsides. Many non-journalism jobs were lost. Some journalists and technical staff complained about the increased workload and pace and felt that they didn't have as much time for investigative research or creativity. However, it has also given journalists the freedom and variety that was lacking under the old divisions of labor. *Channel 4 News* continues to win awards. And, crucially, it has allowed *Channel 4 News* to build the sense among its viewers that it is a community. When I joined the program it received about a dozen viewer letters per day (and strangely enough, some *were* written in green ink). Now it receives hundreds, if not thousands, of emails, often before and while it is on air. And where before the letters were usually pedantic or cranky complaints, now they are often a vibrant part of the news gathering process. Instead of just asking for viewer opinions, *Channel 4 News* recognizes that it has a very committed, intelligent, and informed audience who can often help create the news itself. The *Channel 4 News* website already publishes blogs, podcasts, and Jon Snow's daily *"Snowmail"* email newsletter. It runs a popular online *Factcheck* tool that monitors and checks claims made by political organizations during election campaigns.[28] New content will include user surveys, and a TV news service for mobiles. Interactive Flash bulletins will be introduced which will link stories to relevant maps, background information, and timelines. All this is free content as *Channel 4 News* acknowledged when it abandoned its paid-for Real Video service.

> There is so much free video out there – from the BBC in particular – that there's simply not a great commercial future in trying to charge people, however good or original your video is. Essentially this is an environment where people are used to getting most of their news for free on the net, and to get the traffic you have got to compete on those terms. (Martin Fewell, Deputy Editor, *Channel 4 News*)[29]

So *Channel 4 News* has made it to the end of the first decade of the new millennium in great shape, but that issue about monetizing content is why it *may* not exist in another ten.

I am not suggesting that mainstream news media are about to be wiped off the face of the earth. As I will make explicit in the next chapter, I am convinced that there is a growing market for the core functions of journalism. Indeed, in an age of information overload, I will argue that there is in fact a growing need for the way that journalists can filter and package that information. Martin Fewell says that it may be that the programs that stress their journalism and their "live"-ness that will thrive:

> Content is king. Our view of the future is built on a belief that we need to develop and enhance our reputation for original, distinctive television journalism – content – in a digital market that's increasingly saturated with generic news. Live television news is better-placed than most forms of linear TV to cope with on-demand viewing. Research shows it's less likely to be time-shifted than any other genre of TV. If we can maintain our originality, our impact, we'll continue to stand out and be successful.[30]

I am a great admirer of my generation of editorial leaders who have sustained journalism in all its forms. But there are fundamental forces at work which mean that the ability of mainstream news media simply to adapt at the margins is not enough, however excellent the core product. *Channel 4 News*, for example, which is made by ITN, has secured its immediate future because of its contractual arrangement with its public service-regulated commissioners at Channel 4. But the threat to advertising revenue on TV and the failure to monetize online platforms pose a medium-term threat. There is a technological tide and a generational shift of such magnitude that those of us who wish to perpetuate the best values of mainstream news media journalism will have to do more than simply reform the existing model. The heroes of the first wave of New Media assault have to realize that it is time to prepare for another onslaught. But this time they must get out of the trenches.

1.4   The New Threats to the News Media Business Model

The fundamental problem facing the mainstream news media is that its audience is declining. This is not just the problem of it simply migrating to online news platforms. The deeper threat is that the audience is disappearing and it is not always turning up again elsewhere. Not all readers who stop buying newspapers, for example, transfer their attention to the newspaper's online version. Indeed, they may not even stick with conventional news at all. And even if a journalism business can provide the online platform for its audience it can't be sure it will still make money. First, there is a problem with the old methods of generating income such as advertising. Online banner or video adverts get in the way in a physical manner that interferes with the Internet experience. It is far less tolerable to the online reader than newspaper adverts or TV commercials. Second, there is a historic cultural problem with the Internet. After people pay for their broadband connection they don't want to pay again to use the services online. With the exceptions of pornography and some sport, there is a universal expectation that, like the British National Health Service, the Internet should be free at the point of use. The third problem is that as people go online they have the audacity to provide much of the journalism for themselves. They use search engines to find information and RSS feeds to organize their own news consumption.

Some of them even do their own reporting or commenting on blogs. And a large number, especially young people, seem to go online and forget about journalism completely in the face of other attractions such as gaming, social networking, and sex.

1.4.1   Loss of audience

First let's have a look at the reality of that loss of audience. This is how one former UK newspaper editor describes the dynamic:

> Online consumption of news is absolutely galloping ahead with a 200 percent growth since 2001. An interesting fact that astonished me was that as broadband adoption goes up, there is a pretty sound scientific correlation to newspaper circulation. For every 1 percent of broadband growth, newspaper circulation goes down 2 percent, which would in turn see the death of newspapers by 2090, assuming a steady rate and that there are no more advances. (Richard Addis, *Shakeup Media*)[31]

Here we are looking at a US/Western model because obviously the greater the Internet penetration, the greater the threat. The numbers change all the time but broadband homes are seeing big falls in the consumption of old media news, especially among young people. The audience of yesterday is thinning while tomorrow's audience is simply not turning up.

So this is not just about the numbers. It is about losing a whole culture of paying attention to conventional news, it is about losing the audience's interest. It has now become a badge of honor among some young, self-styled intellectuals not to use popular media, particularly television.[32] Many parents – especially those in their 30s – brag about how little television their kids watch, and these parents now turn away from the "mainstream" networks to "spoof" programs for their own news. In the US it's now a measure of your "cool" factor as a young urbanite not just to say "Did you see *Jon Stewart* last night"[33] but also to say "I was listening to the podcast of *Wait, Wait, Don't Tell Me* from NPR this weekend."[34] This may be a small elite in the US, albeit a trend-setting group of opinion-formers. But there is a wider shift in the way that the next generation is assimilating news information.

Young people in connected communities are getting their news from online news aggregators, friends, and social networks, as opposed to newspapers or television. We know that those who are online watch less TV

– that would seem common-sense. A third of all *YouTube* users, for example, said they watch less TV. And about 80 percent of US males aged between 18 and 24 say they use *YouTube*, so that's a significant loss of eyeballs.[35] The growth in wireless connectivity can only enhance this trend. If people can go online through mobiles, PDAs (personal digital assistants like *Blackberries*), and laptops then they will have fewer reasons to go to the TV. The evidence is that they become increasingly frustrated with conventional TV news because it lacks the accessibility, interactivity, and flexibility of online news platforms. They enjoy the new ways of handling information and sharing in its creation and distribution. This coming generation is using social networking sites like *MySpace* or *Facebook*. On top of the practical virtues that other platforms offer, they are fun, and provide a sense of community that transcends anything offered by mainstream media. They are, quite simply, redefining the way that a new generation communicates. And most frighteningly, we can't predict where they are headed:

> Flying blind is the unavoidable consequence of coming to terms with today's most important demographic group: the tens of millions of digital elite who are in the vanguard of a fast-emerging global youth culture. Because of smartphones, blogs, instant messaging, *Flickr, MySpace, Skype, YouTube, Digg,* and *De.lic.ious*, young people scattered all over are instantly aware of what's happening to others like them everywhere else. This highly influential group, many of whom are also well-heeled, is sharing ideas and information across borders and driving demand for consumer electronics, entertainment, autos, food, and fashion. Think of it as a virtual melting pot. As the population of the young and Web-savvy grows into the hundreds of millions, the pot is going to boil. (Steve Hamm, Media Journalist)[36]

More on that in the next chapter, but suffice to say for now that it is a social shift that is reinforcing and consolidating that loss of audience and the loss of attention for mainstream media.

1.4.2   Loss of revenue

Even where mainstream media have innovated, they can still suffer. In the US some of the most innovative work has been done by local papers. Newspapers like the *Miami Herald* have worked hard to reach new audiences online, for example, by running a Spanish-language edition, something that might have been prohibitively expensive on paper. Sometimes this helps keep up sales and means that when readers go online they stick with the brand. But the revenue doesn't follow. As this media analyst suggests we just do not have the data to justify the value of online journalism to advertisers.[37]

> Newspapers are hard-pressed to find concrete evidence of the benefits of online ventures. Despite optimistic claims, the Web brings in only 7 percent of revenue, and there is little documentation on the effectiveness of online advertising and the local reach of newspapers' websites. (Mica Sawyers, *The Editor's Weblog*)[38]

Revenue generation is made harder because with some rare exceptions people do not want to pay for online news. So it is not surprising that so far online advertising does not replace lost revenue. Local newspapers in the US, for example, have been particularly badly hit by free online sites, such as *Craigslist*, which have competed with them for classified advertising. So even where they have been able to hold up circulation, their revenues have plunged. *The San Francisco Chronicle*, in the Bay area where *Craigslist* first began, has had more time than most to reshape its business model and so far it has failed and could disappear as a newspaper and even as an editorial entity within a few years.[39]

TV has the same problem. People who watch video online watch much less conventional TV. That's bad news for the Networks. Nearly as many people watch video on US TV Network Websites as watch video on *YouTube*. That's good news for the Networks. But they are not making money out of it because there are fewer adverts and they charge less for them. So even when they chase the audience they lose the revenue.[40]

Online advertising revenues are growing rapidly but they are still a relatively small part of media sector income. TV revenues in countries such as the UK and the US may have stalled rather than plunged, but in a dynamic market economy, a lack of growth coupled with cost inflation is a recipe for medium-term financial disaster. It is the margins that make the difference. This is particularly a problem for journalism. While media is big business, news has rarely been a source of easy profits in itself. On mainstream TV, for example, news is a core part of network branding but does not often compete successfully for ratings with soap operas, films, or sport. It is helped by its relatively low production costs, but as margins are eroded there is intense pressure to both cut outgoings and improve ratings. That is usually a lethal combination for quality journalism. In the past, media organizations cross-subsidized their news divisions. But increasingly, the major media corporations are losing their spectrum monopolies. And in a world of fragmented consumption patterns, news can be seen as less important to defining a brand. In the UK, for example, BSkyB sells itself through its films, sport, and entertainment channels. Its excellent 24 hour *Sky News* channel gives it respectability but is not a growing part of the business.

1.4.3   Fragmentation

So we can see that the same diversity that has allowed thousands of new media businesses to grow also threatens profit margins. But choice has another impact on news in particular. Choice can also be described as fragmentation, the separation of audiences or communities into diverse and often distinct parts.

There is more choice than ever before in mainstream media as they go digital and online. Even before you consider the range of purely online activity there is no doubt that people have more news sources in their lives. The advance of digital transmission systems means that there is more airspace for more broadcasters. The reductions in printing costs have made newspapers much easier and cheaper to set up. Of course, many of these new outlets are owned by the same people, but, compared to 20 years ago, we now live in a genuinely multi-channel, multi-text news world. From the birth of CNN in 1980 to the launch of *Aljazeera English* in 2006 we have witnessed an explosion of "choice." And that is before we look at what is available via the Internet.

But more outlets do not always produce greater editorial plurality. In the UK the main commercial channel, ITV, has reduced its specialist religious and children's programming significantly.[41] If the pressure is on those public service elements of broadcasting then surely news will face reductions, too. We have seen the figures for the way that young people are using different media but it is particularly worrying for news. Have a look at the figures for news consumption in UK multi-channel households, which reflect trends in other countries. The viewing of young adults has been disproportionately affected by multi-channel television. Viewing of the main terrestrial channels by 16- to 24-year-olds fell 16 percent from 2001 to 2005, against an overall fall of 10 percent. Given young adults' historical disengagement from news, this means that some key genres now have very low young adult reach:

- 24 percent for current affairs programming (44 percent overall);
- 12 percent for regional news (33 percent overall); and
- 34 percent for national news (60 percent overall)[42]

Ed Richards, the boss of Ofcom, the organization that regulates British broadcasting, recognizes the key questions go beyond media economics:

> The drift away from news consumption, whether in broadcast or print media appears to be a secular trend that is accelerating, particularly among certain groups. Many get their news from other sources – notably online. But are they also changing the way that they absorb news? In other words, getting specific information about single issues that interest them as consumers rather than following news more widely as citizens. If so, how far does this matter for a healthy civic society?[43]

Ethnic minorities are the first to abandon traditional news for a diversity of satellite and digital offerings. The evidence seems to be that they are technologically adept at finding material that is most relevant to their cultural needs. This is good news for ethnic minorities, but bad news for mainstream broadcasters. It raises deeper questions about how society communicates with itself when groups within it are increasingly not watching the same news. We shall return to this issue in Chapters 2 and 4.

It is not just about social groupings going off in search of their "own" media. There is a more fundamental divide, which Markus Prior describes thus:

> The new fault line of civic involvement is between news junkies and entertainment fans. Entertainment fans are abandoning news and politics not because it has become harder to be involved but because they have decided to devote their time to content that promises greater immediate gratification. As a result, they learn less about politics and are less likely to vote at a time when news junkies are becoming even more engaged. Unlike most forms of inequality, this rising divergence in political involvement is a result of voluntary consumption decisions. Making sure everybody has access to media won't fix the problem – it is exactly the cause. (Markus Prior, Princeton University)[44]

Prior is certainly right to identify the problem, but to blame choice or access is defeatist talk. People have always had the alternative of being entertained rather than informed. It is just that now it is much easier to get much more entertainment. As Guy Ker said above, news needs to define itself more broadly. It also needs to create a sense of why it matters to people and to show that it actually cares about and listens to its audience. One of the key challenges for the news media in the future is how it creates and sustains online communities around their work. We will deal with this in greater detail when we look at Networked Journalism, Editorial Diversity, and Media Literacy.

1.4.4 Loss of diversity

At the same time that there is a growing multiplication of the audiences, there is a danger of a lack of diversity in producers. All industries go through periods of change and retrenchment. Look at the car industry. But journalism is different. I would argue that we need a strong and plural news media market for a healthy society. So any decrease in the amount or plurality of journalism because of financial factors is worrying for more than economic reasons. New technology is saving time and so leading to job cuts. That is called efficiency. But it is clear that journalists are now being sacked, not because of innovation, but because of revenue reduction. Can a great newspaper like the *LA Times* really cope with a cut of 20 percent in editorial staff without cutting standards?[45] And it is not just jobs that are going. The number of independent mainstream media outlets in the US is falling. There has been a trend for some time in the US of greater media conglomeration, partly driven by other forces, but certainly accelerated by the threat of New Media.[46-48] Journalism is a highly competitive culture. It is an unusual business in that to produce a rarity (a scoop) helps build a mass audience. Having worked in both the subsidized and private news media sectors, I am convinced that it is vital that there is as much competition between news media organizations as possible. Market forces in journalism tend to increase the propensity to freedom. At the newsroom level, healthy competition makes journalists strive for exclusive and impressive stories. At the business level they encourage journalists to compete to build community with their readers, a role in society and a critical distinction from their rivals. Mergers, bankruptcies, and downsizing all reduce this healthy competition.

In The US we have already witnessed the reduction in choice through consolidation, although there is some evidence that the process is slowing. Globally we have seen Thomson take over Reuters,[49] and although they are primarily financial market reporting organizations, that has also reduced competition in global news gathering. In the UK I would argue that with the 2012 switch-over from analogue to digital TV[50] we are coming up to a watershed.

Greater digital choice should encourage greater competition but in practice it will mean the end of the public service subsidy for ITV and Channel 4, Britain's main two private sector alternatives to the publicly funded BBC. That puts a question mark against their ability to continue to provide diversity.

I would suggest that similar processes are at work across continental Europe. Mainstream news organizations are being undermined by the drift online. In France, for example, the circulation of the premier newspaper, *Le Monde*, has fallen over the past seven years to a low in 2006 of 350,000 a day. The newspaper and its sister publications are expected to have a shortfall of €40m in 2007.[51] And on the left of French news media *Libération* is losing millions of Euros and, some say, it's Gallic soul:

> It's like the last days of the Titanic . . . or . . . something else tense and very unpleasant with possibly terrible consequences. The final hours have come [for *Libération*] – though they might last a very long time. (Claude Moisy, Media Analyst)[52]

1.4.5   No such thing as a free lunch

This loss of revenue and loss of healthy competition has other consequences.

We see already how UK newspapers are abandoning journalism in favor of free handouts of old movies on DVD. Increasingly, the newspapers deal in features and lifestyle because, as one editor told me, they leave telling the basic news to the BBC and the Press Association. In the short term this has had some unexpected consequences.

In London there has been a forest-felling, tube-train-filling explosion in free newspapers. Around 1.5 million copies of four main free papers are handed out to commuters every day, and that's just in the capital. Across Europe and the US independent and free versions of paid-fors are being given away.[53]

For someone like me who started his career on a free local newspaper this is a potentially positive trend. I have no cultural hang-ups about a cover price. Thousands of people who didn't read a newspaper now do so on their way to or from work. Hundreds of mainly young journalists have been employed to fill these newspapers. And if they are to survive and thrive then these newspapers will have to fulfill a demand. Their editors tell me that they will have to improve the product they make if they are to continue:

> We will take on the readers of any of the paid for papers over any of our stories. We grab the time of the readers and provide information that matters

to them quickly, and we do it well. It is the delivery method that has changed, be it free papers or online video, audio, interviews, interaction, and the like. You still need to go out there and find and break a story. There is still an audience to take it in but the major difference here is that there is a bigger world to market it to. (Kenny Campbell, Editor, *Metro* (London))[54]

However, I think they are essentially a stop-gap measure. They are a way of delivering advertising to a certain audience with some limited journalism. This may be a marginal answer to the challenge of online media, but it is not the saving grace of the newspaper sector overall. From the evidence of the free newspapers so far, they have not yet answered the question of one veteran newspaper journalist turned academic: "How do you subsidize the cost of good journalism if the 'paid-fors' go free? The free papers are full of gutless, bloodless editorial that is lacking in good, investigative journalism" (Paul Charman, London College of Journalism).[55]

1.4.6   Loss of quality?

All these trends would suggest a loss of quality. The former British Prime Minister Tony Blair spoke about it in the context of political coverage:

The media are facing a hugely more intense form of competition than anything they have ever experienced before. They are not the masters of this change but its victims. The result is a media that increasingly and to a dangerous degree is driven by "impact". Impact is what matters. It is all that can distinguish, can rise above the clamour, can get noticed. Impact gives competitive edge. Of course the accuracy of a story counts. But it is secondary to impact. It is this necessary devotion to impact that is unravelling standards, driving them down, making the diversity of the media not the strength it should be but an impulsion towards sensation above all else. (Tony Blair, MP)[56]

This speech got most attention for what I felt was an ill-judged attack on "feral beasts." It came badly from a politician at the end of a career that had depended to a remarkable degree on adept and, some would say, dishonest, handling of the media. But few denied the general point: that journalism is under more pressure because of tightening profit margins and multiplying deadlines.

However, journalism is always accused of lacking quality. It is intrinsic to its production. It is the art of the possible, not a profession for perfectionists. There will always be a tension between the desire to reach as many people as possible, and the need to invest in the best possible product. The very act of journalism is to debase or dilute reality. It is impossible to represent the world in all its rich complexity when you are up against a deadline. But the question is whether the pressure to protect profit or meet budget cuts is reducing the overall ability of journalists to tell stories well and to find things out.

Talk to experienced journalists and they will say that if you reduce resources – especially time – then editorial corners will be cut. This is something that has been ever-present in my working life, in print, public service TV and commercial broadcasting. Every year there have been fewer journalists creating more product. The managers would argue that it is a result of the efficiencies of new technology. They are right. But there does come a point where journalists are so efficient that they do not have time for the kind of networking, background research, and speculative effort that brings long-term rewards in terms of editorial quality. That is especially true in the context of the contemporary high-speed 24-hour news cycle. I think journalism is changing into a multi-skilled but layered process. Like a modern army, there are the front-line troops dealing with the constant combat, and then there are the reserves who are supposed to bring an extra dimension to the fray. Increasingly, those functions of immediate and then "quality" journalism are being separated out. There is a danger of it being lost altogether.

Some critics blame the culture of the media itself. People like John Lloyd, of the *Financial Times*, now at Oxford University, feel that the media's competitive disregard for wider values has poisoned the well of public discourse:

> Good journalism, of which there is a great deal, may be in danger of losing out to a journalism which pays little attention to facts, which insists on an underlying story of public degradation and political bad faith, and which encourages among its readers and viewers an attitude of either contempt or distrust – all the while excoriating public officials and politicians for presiding over a period of "voter apathy." (John Lloyd, *Reuters Institute*)[57]

Often these critics of current journalism are skeptical of the power of online news to do anything but worsen the situation. The theoretical assumption underpinning this critique is sound. It is based on ideas like that of the political philosopher Jürgen Habermas[58] who believed that the media helped make up a structure of social discourse, a space for public democratic debate. Interestingly, Habermas has himself expressed ambivalence about the Internet:

Use of the Internet has both broadened and fragmented the contexts of communication. This is why the Internet can have a subversive effect on intellectual life in authoritarian regimes. But at the same time, the less formal, horizontal cross-linking of communication channels weakens the achievements of traditional media. This focuses the attention of an anonymous and dispersed public on select topics and information, allowing citizens to concentrate on the same critically filtered issues and journalistic pieces at any given time. The price we pay for the growth in egalitarianism offered by the Internet is the decentralised access to unedited stories. In this medium, contributions by intellectuals lose their power to create a focus. (Jürgen Habermas)[59]

More on Habermas later and his fears about the dumbing down effect of the Internet, but one ex Silicon Valley entrepreneur is much more certain that the Internet is to blame. Andrew Keen is a one-man campaign to warn us of the evil impact of the Internet upon all that is civilized:

Old media is facing extinction . . . The monkeys take over. Say good-bye to today's experts and cultural gatekeepers – our reporters, news anchors, editors, music companies, and Hollywood movie studios. In today's cult of the amateur, the monkeys are running the show. With their infinite typewriters they are authoring the future. And we may not like how it reads.[60]

Keen's argument is that we rely upon journalists as professional gatekeepers to maintain the veracity of news. We simply can't trust the Internet. Digital images can be faked, bloggers are biased and unaccountable. Citizen journalism is unverifiable and obsessed by the personal and the banal. They are:

An army of mostly anonymous, self-referential writers who exist not to report news but to spread gossip, sensationalise political scandal, display embarrassing photos of public figures and to link to stories on imaginative topics such as UFO sightings or 9/11 conspiracy theories. (Andrew Keen)[61]

And his case is supported by some senior figures in the journalist establishment. Nicholas Lemann spent a lifetime writing for the US's finest intellectual magazines and newspapers before becoming Dean of Journalism at Columbia University School of Journalism. His lofty disdain is tangible:

The more ambitious blogs, taken together, function as a form of fast-moving, densely cross-referential pamphleteering – an open forum for every conceivable opinion that can't make its way into the big media, or, in the case of the millions of purely personal blogs, simply an individual's take on life. The Internet is also a venue for press criticism ("We can fact-check your ass!" is one of the familiar rallying cries of the blogosphere) and a major research library of bloopers, outtakes, pranks, jokes, and embarrassing performances by big shots. But none of that yet rises to the level of a journalistic culture rich enough to compete in a serious way with the old media – to function as a replacement rather than an addendum.[62]

These criticisms have some validity. It would be amazing if a vast public space like the Internet was only occupied by deep-thinking people making profound and revelatory journalism. Why should the Internet not reflect humanity in all its banality as well as its glory? What these critiques have in common is a curious nostalgia about the history of mainstream news media. Most of these accusations could and have been made at any time over the last century or so against the mass media.

Since journalism began there have been people lamenting its tawdry nature and the inevitable descent into trivia and sensation. The chronicler of post-war Britain, Anthony Sampson, was a critic from a classic elitist, albeit liberal, position. Yet he himself cites people going back to the age of Swift regretting the decline of the news media. He quotes this wonderful lyric by the nineteenth-century Romantic poet William Wordsworth written in response to the novel use of engravings within newspapers and magazines:

> A backward movement surely have we here
> From manhood – back to childhood, for the age –
> Back towards caverned life's first rude career.
> Avaunt this vile abuse of pictured page!
> (William Wordsworth, "Illustrated Books
> and Newspapers")[63]

Goodness knows what the Poet would have made of blogs. Writing back in the 1970s Sampson laments what he sees as the decline in classic, intelligent reporting: "Investigation has been almost abandoned. There are no new Orwells or Priestleys, to inspect the rest of the country . . . instead there has been an explosion of columns providing comment without facts."[64]

Sampson rails against a "retreat from the world" by the news media and complains that parliamentary speeches are no longer recorded at length in *The Times of London*. He fears that while the media used to battle against the Establishment, the media has now become the nearest things we have to an elite governing clique itself. Contemporary critics of the Internet, such as Andrew Keen, share this world-view of a vibrant liberal civilization imperiled.

Just because they are nostalgic doesn't mean the doom-sayers are wrong. I would argue that it is the very nature of journalism to be continually struggling to define and maintain editorial quality. In that sense, journalism does reflect society. One person's progress is another person's decline. But those people who have examined media history in a more systematic way have found that it is possible to argue that journalism has improved in quality as well as quantity. Stuart Purvis is someone who has been at the top of broadcast news for a few decades now, before becoming a media commentator and professor. He gathered research that compared journalists' output between 1965 and 2005. He found that the contemporary output of TV News and newspapers is much more in-depth and diverse and certainly more attractive:

> Golden ages often look a bit tarnished when you look back at them later. And 1965 is no different. For instance a flagship TV news programme with one presenter, one interviewer, one voice-over, one pundit and one reporter is not much to get excited about. Peter Snow [the presenter] did very well to keep it all together. And the newspaper equivalents are similarly uninspiring by today's standards. Viewing the programme and looking at the paper from '65 frankly I found much of it boring in content and presentation. The "long view" must surely be that the technical revolution in production has made the news media more accessible, and yes, more attractive, too . . . rather than dumbing down, there's a sector of the market in television and print that has smartened up in order to appeal to those post-war generation that got access to higher education for the first time in their family's history. (Professor Stuart Purvis, City University)[65]

A similar exercise found that two contemporary quality US newspapers were at least as good on "measurables" as they were in 1972.[66]

There is as much "quality" journalism around today as there ever has been. Indeed, as news organizations invest in online services I would argue that there is far more. This is partly about the success of outfits such as *The Economist*, the *International Herald Tribune*, *Channel 4 News*, *The New York Review of Books*, the *Financial Times*, and, of course, the BBC. But as Purvis warns, we may see the glass as half-full now, but we are at a crucial moment: the pessimists may *become* right. And soon. I fear that we have already reached the "tipping point," that crucial phase in the adoption of a new technology when its applications are determined for the immediate future, the moment when society chooses how it will shape its effects. The examples I have given of high-quality journalism are from organizations that can satisfy an information-hungry elite who have the resources to fund more labor-intensive journalism. Most of them are also the ones that are best exploiting digital and online possibilities to build their brands. A world where good journalism is only available to them is not one that will spread the benefits of an informed public. The US has some of the finest magazines and periodicals in the world which help satisfy the intellectual cravings of America's vast educated elite. But what about the Network News shows? There is more than enough pressure upon journalism to fear for the future.

1.5   What Is Happening to the Public Sphere?

This all matters because the news media landscape helps to define the world we live in. Changes in the media have social impacts and in turn social changes shape our journalism.[67] The recent changes in the news media are not determined by technology in a simple mechanistic way. Technology changes as much in response to societal changes as it causes them. We won't understand the future of journalism without realizing that this is more than a change in gadgets and gizmos. It's not just that a new generation is using strange new games and websites in new ways. It is the fact that society has been changing radically for the past 30 years for a lot of other reasons. And so people want a different kind of media, which new technology can help produce. That means we have to understand that not only is the business model up for reformation, but so is the very reason for journalism itself. So when we talk about the "dumbing down" or "decline" of the media, we are talking about a moving target.

Another way to express this is to say that the public sphere is changing. This is not the place for a detailed engagement with Jürgen Habermas' central concept, but it is useful as way of understanding what we mean by the space that media and society share:

> By the public sphere we mean first of all a realm of our social life in which something approaching pubic opinion can be formed. Access is guaranteed to all citizens. A portion of the public sphere comes into being in every conversation in which private individuals assemble to form a public body. Today newspapers and magazines, radio and television are the media of the public sphere. (Habermas, The public sphere: an encyclopaedia article)[68]

Of course, the point about Habermas' public sphere is that he thinks that the ideal has deteriorated since its original state of virtue in the London coffee-houses of the late eighteenth century. There, he argued, matters of public interest were debated, not just by the landowning gentry, but by merchants and regular citizens. The aim was consensus, and the focus was on the power of the argument, rather than the social status of the speaker. Newspapers played a role as informers of the debate, publishing information that informed readers so they could participate in debates on the topics of the day. Habermas argues that this ideal public sphere was lost early in the twentieth century when newspapers stopped being vehicles for reporting and debate and become mere commercial interests. I don't entirely accept this rather selective and almost naïve version of society and media. But I do share his aspiration for the role of media within politics. I agree that the idea of a public sphere that is both mediated through journalism and socially or politically constructed helps us to understand what we are going through now.

I do not want to pretend that somehow all this new information technology has reshaped the world on its own. I want to stress broader social changes. In the past 30 years we have witnessed global political realignments. And these have been accompanied by a more general shift in the way that people live their lives as individuals and communities. Any description on this global scale will be inaccurate in some places and contain sweeping generalizations. Well that's journalism for you, so here goes. How about this for a list?: The End of Apartheid; The End of Communism; Privatization; Climate Change; Water Scarcity; The Rise of Political Islam; The Return of the Asian superpowers India and China; Growth of Asian incomes to Western levels; HIV Aids; Avian Flu; Immigration; DNA technology. All these have remade our world in the past 20 years. People are less deferential, they consume more globally, they live longer, are better educated, starve less, are less poor, and have much more control over their reproductive lives. This is simply not the same people or the same world that it was a generation ago, so why should the public sphere remain the same?

The concept is still very useful as theory but the media's place in any understanding of the architecture of that sphere must change as the sphere changes:

> The idea of the public sphere, preserved in the social welfare state mass democracy, an idea which calls for a rationalisation of power through the medium of public discussion among private individuals, threatens to disintegrate with

the structural transformation of the public sphere itself. It could only be realised today on an altered basis. (Habermas)[69]

I believe that the Internet is fundamental to that "altered basis." I will argue later in this book that a new Networked Journalism is the inevitable, or certainly the most desirable, response to this changing dynamic. As the public sphere is threatened journalism must change to sustain its core functions and value. So when we judge what is in decline and what is thriving, we must not assume it is a static object. Society is changing, so journalism must change too. Journalism is changing so society should pay attention.

1.5.1 Public service is in retreat

One measure of the threat to the positive role of journalism in the public sphere is the attitude to the public service element in journalism. Up to now states have been prepared to accept responsibility for helping to deliver social value through journalism, especially through broadcasting. Where private enterprise in its rawest condition does not deliver a sufficient amount of quality news journalism then the state or public bodies step in to subsidize it. This has been done on the basis of both "market failure" and cultural policy. In this I follow the definition of Gavyn Davies, economist and former Chairman of the BBC.[70] He defines what he calls "Reithian" [after Sir John Reith, first Director-General of the BBC] broadcasting as a public good, or product. He says that ideally it should be provided by the free market but it isn't. This is partly because there is no wholly free market in news media. Spectrum is limited by analogue technology, for example. He also points to the distributional failures of the private sector. By pricing the way it does, in a free market some parts of the population will not receive the services because they can't afford them or they aren't prepared to pay the price. As Davies says, the advent of digital technology means that many of the technological arguments for market failure are removed.

However, as Davies explains, there are other kinds of market failure that public service broadcasting must address. In the UK he says that is best done by the BBC but he does not exclude other models, if they can address his analysis of market failure. Fundamentally, he says, people want public service broadcasting in the same way they want a fire service or an army. Even if they don't use it every day they believe it is a good thing to have around for the common good. This is a political and cultural question. And as those social values change alongside technological change, surely the market conditions are also subject to review? Put simply, as market forces strengthen, current public service structures are threatened.

One thing is clear: the meaning and delivery of public service has changed. Take the example of *Schoolhouse Rock*,[71] which taught millions of US schoolchildren about everything from government to grammar. This series of cartoon public-service announcements was shown on the ABC network during the ubiquitous Saturday morning cartoon shows in the 1970s. If you sing the words, "I'm just a bill" to nearly any American adult between 30 and 40, they will answer back: "sitting on Capitol Hill."[72] This particular episode had a singing and dancing US bill, explaining the congressional process through which he becomes a law. "Generation X" Americans remember this process, not because it was taught in school, but because it was part of the media landscape in which they lived. The Schoolhouse Rock motto was "because knowledge is power!"[73] So a generation of Americans grew up believing that knowing about news, politics, and grammar was important, because they saw it on TV. This sort of public service spot is largely gone from American television these days, replaced by heavy-handed "do the right thing" announcements that media-savvy young people ignore. This apparent failure could be because young people have become too sophisticated or because not enough resource or thought goes in to the messaging. Either way it is symptomatic of the fact that delivering pubic service has become a whole lot harder than it was in those pioneering days. In the US the public service sector has never been strong. National Public Radio's audience is small and its budget is getting smaller.[74] The US possesses some of the finest newspapers and magazines in the world, but, as we discussed above, they are becoming more isolated.

Elsewhere, there is evidence of similar pressure upon public service. This is not just caused by competition from New Media. It is partly about new technology and deregulation. Digitalization and liberalization have allowed the proliferation of broadcasting outlets in countries such as Italy, Germany, France, and the UK, where governments have not continued the privileged position of the subsidized state media. In Britain the deadline for revolution is 2012 when public service TV effectively ends in its present form. The UK market is unique in that the Labour Government that took power in 1997 chose to reinforce rather than reduce the dominant position of the BBC with a long-term settlement that has enabled it to expand its digital services in preparation for the analogue switch-off in 2012. At that point the public service remits for Channel 4, Channel Five, and ITV, the BBC's main competitors, effectively ends. The semi-commercial companies will lose their spectrum "subsidy" which allows them to broadcast universally with little competition. The implication will be that if their revenue is declining then the regulators will not be able to insist that they maintain public service elements such as children's TV and local news coverage. Of course, the BBC will continue, but it will not be able to replace the amount of public service journalism that will be lost. And as we discussed above, the quality of the BBC's journalism very much depends on quality competition from other broadcasters. Plurality relies on having a number of broadcasters who share in some measure the public service values that are subsidized directly by taxation at the BBC. And with the competition gone and the BBC alone, the danger is that the public may question its uniquely privileged position.

In the UK Ofcom is considering a long term solution in the shape of a Public Service Provider (PSP), a fund that would finance public service broadcasting regardless of the producer, outlet or format. It could even transfer the resources to online journalism. This has sparked predictable outrage, which reflects the degree to which public service providers feel that the carefully constructed edifices that uphold the best values of broadcasting are being laid waste in the name of competition. It is difficult to imagine the genius that will create a PSP that manages to be fair, creative and clever enough to find the money to bridge the gap between the declining independent public service broadcasters and the yawning chasm in their accounts.[75] This matters way beyond the shores of Britain. The challenge for the future of public service journalism will in part depend on establishing models like the Public Service Provider that can correct market failure and invest in socially useful news media.

There is a danger that public service journalism will effectively become a rump financed by the world's more Welfarist governments, like the railways in post-war Britain or the postal service in Italy – dull, inefficient, out of touch with the latest technological developments, and servicing an ageing sector of the public. We will look again at this in the next chapter. But for now, let us go to another world, a happier world, a futuristic world, where start-up costs are tiny and anything is possible. It is a place where everyone from Reuters to Rupert Murdoch is looking for a second chance.

1.6   A Second Chance in *Second Life*?

As we have seen above, there is a real danger that the next generation will not learn the news habit. There is also a danger that journalists will not learn the New Media habits that make their information palatable to the next generation. This is partly about the way that people communicate when online. It is much more individualistic and personal process than it is with traditional media. Our experience of communication online is a mix of the global and the immediate – often at the same time. We can create social networks that are not bounded by the usual confines of an office or family or even of reality. People use mobile phone texting, MSN messaging, and email alongside traditional methods such as speech or phone. They no longer privilege traditional communications platforms. They are as likely to watch a movie on a plane on a portable DVD or a laptop as they are on TV, let alone at the cinema. I am convinced that this is affecting the way that people consume news. So if you can't beat them, join them?

It can go to the extreme that people are now getting their news through virtual reality. *Second Life*[76] is a continuous social online game. You pay real money to join up and are given in-game resources to create a second life for yourself online. So far, so *Sims*. But what makes this different is that the persona you create is not off the peg. You can develop your career, your personal life, and your lifestyle in a community with millions of other real people playing the same game. And it is not pure fantasy. There are conditions, one of which is money. *Second Life* has currency. You can exchange the *Second Life* currency on *Ebay* for real US dollars. By the end of 2007 it is estimated that *Second Life*'s GDP could rank it above Granada, Gambia, and Samoa.[77] And where money goes, so do politicians. At least three candidates for President in 2008 have a presence in *Second Life*.[78]

Another condition of *Second Life* is information. It is an information-rich society where you play in public (or at least with other subscribers). Now Reuters and other media organizations are opening up a bureau in *Second Life*.[79] The US online magazine *Salon.Com* has even embedded a reporter in *Second Life*.

Figure 1.1   *Second Life*: A second chance for journalism?

Wagner James Au has an impressive looking avatar which he is modest enough to put alongside a real photo (see Figure 1.1). Recent assignments have included covering the latest in beachwear fashion in this virtual world, a review of the first *Second Life* "novel" and running commentary on *Second*

Life's first music festival. He tells me that being a journalist in Second Life has significant advantages over real world reporting:

> You're able to interview people from all over the world through their avatars, which gives them a level of protection and anonymity, and assuming you're not already Jeremy Paxman, it encourages you as the reporter to ask provocative and potentially rude questions that would be difficult to pose in the real world. Of course, there's an additional level of fact checking required, if you need to ask for specific real world details of the person behind the avatar, but that's not insurmountable. (Wagner James Au, *Salon.com*)[80]

Wagner James Au says that apart from the practical differences there are three different types of reporting that you can do on *Second Life*:

> First, treating it as another channel for real world reportage, another tool alongside instant messaging, Skype, etc. For example I've interviewed a US Marine about the siege of Fallujah, Israelis during their last battle with Hezbollah, and Venezuelans regarding Chavez's closing of a rival TV station, all within *Second Life*.
>
> The second level, of course, is reporting on *Second Life* itself, as a noteworthy and emerging platform of user-created content in a 3D space with its own internal economy, which should have a million active users by the end of 2007.
>
> The third level is less explored, which is sad, because it has so much potential, and there are so many stories in there: journalism by allegory, writing about the conflicts and dramas in *Second Life* as illustrative of essential human issues. That's what excites me most, frankly, seeing how themes of politics, sexuality, religion, and so on, are recast in an alternate world. (Wagner James Au, *Salon.com*)[81]

This is all delightful stuff. It may well have lessons for us that we can pick up on in the next chapter on Networked Journalism. But hold on just one minute. *Second Life* is a fake world. It is a virtual concoction. Reporting on *Second Life* is only really definable as journalism if you put it in a specialist category such as sports or the arts or describe it as creative writing. While Wagner James Au may have created an interesting online piece of journalism, the presence of news outfits like Reuters is more of a marketing move than a solution to their real world challenges. While there is evidence that more entertainment companies are turning to the Virtual World market[82] there are also signs that it is not a goldmine for real world media businesses. It seems that people go to *Second Life* because it is an escape from commercialism and so they are simply not spending enough real money while they are there.[83]

The idea that *Second Life* offers anything but a metaphor for the rejuvenation of journalism is simply escapist fantasy. The news media is clinging to the edge of the window ledge of a burning building. It can't jump and it can't hang on for ever, shouting "Help, help, who will save us?" It is time for SuperMedia to come to the rescue.

Chapter Summary

- Journalism is going through a revolution of historic proportions.
- Journalism is as good as it has ever been but it has to change and it has to do that while coping with huge political and economic threats.
- There is a massive threat to the current business model for journalism.
- The audience is changing in its nature and its behavior.
- Production costs are falling but competition is increasing and so profits are threatened.
- Mainstream media has historic resources and a recent history of innovation but must reform itself again.
- There is a danger of audience fragmentation and a loss of diversity in production.
- There is a danger of a major loss of public service journalism and a drastic fall in the quality of mass journalism.
- Simply taking journalism online is not the answer.

2

"Is It a Bird? Is It a Plane? No! It's SuperMedia!"

Networked Journalism

To live up to its billing, Internet journalism has to meet high standards both conceptually and practically: the medium has to be revolutionary, and the journalism has to be good. The quality of Internet journalism is bound to improve over time, especially if more of the virtues of traditional journalism migrate to the Internet. But, although the medium has great capabilities, especially the way it opens out and speeds up the discourse, it is not quite as different from what has gone before as its advocates are saying.

(Nicholas Lemann, 2007)[1]

There's never been a better time, I tell students, to be a journalistic entrepreneur – to invent your own job, to become part of the generation that figures out how to produce and, yes, sell the journalism we desperately need as a society and as citizens of a shrinking planet. The young journalists who are striking out on their own today, experimenting with techniques and business models, will invent what's coming.

(Dan Gillmor, 2007)[2]

2.1 Introduction

It seems to me that both the arch-skeptic and the Internet evangelist can be right. In fact, both Nicholas Lemann and Dan Gillmor *have* to be right. If it is to have any value then journalism must retain its core ethics and its vital skills. But if it is to survive then it must adapt. It must go further than that and offer something more. In the previous chapter I set out the structural problems for journalism now and going forward. I have suggested that it simply has no alternative but to embrace new business models if it is to thrive over the next period. Not many media people would disagree violently with that. But I have also made the case that the way journalism works will have to change profoundly. In this chapter, I will give the newsroom perspective on these changes. I will put journalism back at the heart of this debate. And I will explore some of the practical, moral, and political challenges it poses.

I want to use the idea of Networked Journalism to describe a way that journalism can change to meet the challenges of the digital era. In later chapters we will look at how Networked Journalism will address the key issues such as politics, terror and development. We will then look at how Networked Journalism can offer creative opportunities for the news media. We will look at the idea of Editorial Diversity and finally the need for greater Media Literacy to sustain Networked Journalism.

But first let me set out what I mean in the wider context of the conceptualization of journalism. This will not be a history of journalism or a survey of the theoretical or sociological literature that has sought to define the term. But to know where we are going it is important that we refer to the past, the present and the ideological debate around the nature of the beast.

First, we need to realize that journalism is not a given. It has changed over time to adopt different forms and procedures. What we have at present in the West – and it is still the Western model that predominates – is a comparatively recent cultural and economic form of the industry. While there are aspects that are grounded in nineteenth-century mass communications, most of the conventions and structures are drawn from the mid to late twentieth century. Journalism is like the motor car with its roots in the late nineteenth century. It was pioneered in the early twentieth, reached its heyday in the late twentieth but is now being questioned. And, like the automobile in the age of global warming, it is being questioned not for its technical performance but because it simply doesn't meet the needs and aspirations of the *coming* age.

Then we will look at what it is like to be an online journalist or a journalist who has to deal with the new realities of multi-platform media. We will take some classic journalistic problems and see how they might change through networked journalism. What impact will Networked Journalism have upon the following:

- the temporal nature of journalism;
- the distance / representation tension;
- the cycle of newsroom sensitivity;

- the role of the audience; and
- trust and authority.

These issues sound almost philosophical but they are the bread and butter of journalism. If the idea of Networked Journalism can't stand up to the daily battering of these practical tests then it is irrelevant.

I am not suggesting that all journalism must be Networked. Much media production will continue to look pretty familiar to a mainstream journalist. Some will remain resolutely apart from connectivity. There will be great differences in the degree to which a particular journalist or news organization is networked depending on the actual story, the market, the national or local circumstances and the resources available. However, my definition does seek to go further than the narrow definition of networked as meaning someone who uses a particular network for a specific journalistic act. There is a larger purpose to the idea of Networked Journalism. It could just be the description of what will happen. It could just be a novel approach to journalism. But I hope that it can be much more than that. Ultimately, I hope it offers a contribution to the reformation of the global public sphere. Networked Journalism is a return to some of the oldest virtues of journalism: connecting with the world beyond the newsroom; listening to people; giving people a voice in the media; responding to what the public tells you in a dialogue. But it has the potential to go further than that in transforming the power relationship between media and the public and reformulating the means of journalistic production.

2.2   Where Does It Come From? The History of Networked Journalism

In the past journalism has been a cult, a fraternity, a guild. Its members have evolved rituals, a language and customs that define their trade and mark out their territory. The literature of journalism is heavy with the claustrophobic culture of the newsroom. From the tribal behavior of the hacks in Evelyn Waugh's *Scoop* chasing false leads across Africa[3] to Michael Frayn's bathetic soap opera *Towards The End Of The Morning*,[4] the British media is rightly represented as a cross between a Public School and a Public Bar. And in the US, Hollywood's unerring sense of reality and illusion has captured US journalism's earnest melodrama, eternally enacting a moral pageant through *Citizen Kane*,[5] *His Girl Friday*[6] to *All The President's Men*[7] and *Broadcast News*.[8]

These are the myths that men cling to when drowning in seas of quotidian compromise. Journalism likes to think it is a superhero when it is really Clark Kent. Proprietors and editors like to hobnob with the great and the good but journalism as a trade is not comfortable with a permanent place at the top table. And yet the fact that journalism is not as institutionally powerful as it might like to think it is has allowed the news media a unique place in politics. This relative autonomy has given it a role and space in society somewhat apart from both the people and other institutions. One of the defining characteristics of journalism is its unstable relationship with authority. On this I am with the British commentator, Simon Jenkins:

> The British media does not do responsibility. It does stories. And stories tell better when they are about individuals, not collectives. The media is unconcerned with what people like me find decorous or important. It kicks down doors and exposes the hidden corners of the human condition. It fights competition, plays dirty and disobeys the rules. There is nothing it finds too vulgar or too prurient for its wandering, penetrating lens. The press does not operate with any sense of proportion, judgment or self-restraint because it is selling stories, not running the country. The unshackled and irresponsible press sometimes gets it wrong. But I still prefer it, warts and all, to a shackled and responsible one. (Simon Jenkins, Journalist)[9]

This sense of a cultural practice with an internal logic apart from society is core to understanding what we mean by journalism, and how that might change as Networked Journalism.

I take the basic activities of journalism to be to report, analyze, and comment on the world from one to many. Both the producer and consumer recognize the act and the nature of the process as journalism. "Selling stories," in Jenkins' phrase, has been going on for some time. And there is still much in common between early variants and even the most cutting-edge of current practitioners.

It could be argued that seventeenth-century pamphleteers in England were an early form of blogger.[10–12] There was a rapid expansion in the production of printed material of a topical and political nature during the English Civil War and the Interregnum. The public and political elite used it as a weapon in their ideological warfare. These pamphlets were a mix of propaganda and reportage and had an audience that was acutely conscious of the code and language used to make specific and general points. It all sounds very much like a wood-cut version of today's political blogs.

The Swiftean scribes in the eighteenth-century coffee houses so beloved by Habermas can also be seen as analogous to New Media journalists. They worked in such small geographical and cultural confines that their relationship with their audience permeated every moment of their work, from commission to dissemination.[13] I do not claim that this period of journalism was some primordial paradise, although it has some pleasing resonances with the idea of Networked Journalism. My point is that historically, what was being produced was recognizably journalism but it was also fundamentally different to what was to come next. Journalism changes. That is very much where we are now. The eighteenth-century topical writer enjoyed a similar contiguity with his readership as that between a blogger and his or her readers, albeit in the Square Mile of Georgian London rather than in cyberspace, one keyboard speaking directly unto another screen. And they had the same loose relationship with classical objectivity that bloggers demonstrate, switching from reportage to propaganda and back again with ease. But they also pioneered the communication of important facts, such as stock market reports, and helped the evolution of political debate through the media, in a way that has definite parallels with contemporary online journalism.

The industrialization of journalism from Dickens'[14] time onwards changed that relationship into the commodified structure that underpins mainstream media today. Journalists became 'professionalized' through training, trade association, and specialization. New technology such as the telegraph, trains, and mechanized printing made the mass media possible. A tremendous increase in personal wealth, education and free time meant that there was a mass market for that journalism. Thanks to the genius of entrepreneurs like Lord Northcliffe[15] in Britain and Joseph Pulitzer[16] or William Randolph Hearst[17] in the US the product was "democratized" into an item of mass communications culture. The way it was produced and distributed changed so much that although they were still recognizably news-sheets, they had little else in common with their eighteenth-century forerunners.

Where before it was cliques talking within or between themselves, now the media could claim, with some reason, that it was a national popular conversation. Indeed, great papers like Northcliffe's *Daily Mail* or Pulitzer's *New York World* frequently claimed to speak *for* the people. They certainly appealed *to* the people who bought them in their millions. These organs of mass media production appeared to represent general attitudes and aspirations. Ultimately they were owned by individuals or boards, and they were produced by company employees. Broadcast journalism did very little to change this hierarchical, Fordist construct.

This type of journalism reached its zenith in the period between 1950 and 1990. It brought an extraordinary variety of journalistic formats and platforms. It has given journalism an almost universal reach, even throughout restrictive or under-developed societies. From the appalling viciousness of the Nazi paper *Der Stürmer*[18] to the campaigning zeal of Cudlipp's *Daily Mirror*[19] to Walter Cronkite's CBS Evening News,[20] mass "industrialized" journalism has helped report and influence history. Journalism has become a major global industry and a cultural institution in its own right. And its representations of reality have become integral to the way we mediate our lives and recollect our histories. The exponential growth of public relations in political, commercial, and civic organizations is itself a testimony to the way that journalism is seen as a force in economic and social affairs. This was simply not the case before industrialization and not remotely to this extent until the middle of the twentieth century.

And yet in all this time, journalism was not "networked." Now it can be. What the digital revolution represents is another deep shift in the nature of journalism, at least as momentous as the move from coffee shop to newsroom.

2.3   Networked Journalism – A Definition

Good journalism has always been about networking. The image of the lone reporter piecing together facts through pure observation, like Sherlock Holmes with a deadline, was always a myth. The best journalists have always listened, conversed, and researched. They have always followed stories up and understood the coverage of an event or issue within a wider context. They have adjusted their reporting in response to feedback from colleagues and consumers. But the idea of Networked Journalism takes this in to a new level and in to a new paradigm. This is the definition of Networked Journalism by blogger Jeff Jarvis:

> "Networked journalism" takes into account the collaborative nature of journalism now: professionals and amateurs working together to get the real story, linking to each other across brands and old boundaries to share facts, questions, answers, ideas, perspectives. It recognizes the complex relationships that will make news. And it focuses on the process more than the product . . . I believe that the more that journalists behave like citizens, the stronger their journalism will be. In networked journalism, the public can get involved in a story before it is reported, contributing facts, questions, and suggestions. The journalists can rely on the public to help report the story; we'll see more and more

of that, I trust. The journalists can and should link to other work on the same story, to source material, and perhaps blog posts from the sources. After the story is published – online, in print, wherever – the public can continue to contribute corrections, questions, facts, and perspective. (Jeff Jarvis, media commentator)[21]

This is a pragmatic definition that I accept as far as it goes. As Jarvis himself recognizes, the term has deeper roots in communications theory and analysis. I believe that for Networked Journalism to mean more than just interactivity it must be considered in the much broader context of changing technology and social behavior. This is how one group of communications scholars describe the new flow of ideas:

> With the advent of the multimedia Internet, publics can traffic in both professional and personal media in new forms of many-to-many communication that often route around commercial media distribution. Personal media and communications technologies such as telephony, email, text messaging, and everyday photography and journaling are colliding with commercial and mass media such as television, film, and commercial music. (Annenberg Centre for Communication, USC)[22]

So where does journalism fit in to this New Media landscape? In principle, I believe that it is difficult to separate it out. That is an important characteristic of Network Journalism. It is very much part of all the other communication that happens digitally. The war between Old and New Media is ending. It is becoming a false distinction. But let us start by trying to look at some of the factors that have changed in the transfer from one to the other, for journalism, before we consider Networked Journalism further.

Here is a list of differences that I will then try to unpack. In each case we can see how New Media technology offers opportunities to tackle problems that journalists labored with under with Old Media. New Media also brings threats and problems of its own. But first I want to explore how these changes can meet the needs of the twenty-first-century media consumer:

Old Media Problems	New Media Solutions
Barriers to entry	Permeable
Unresponsive	Interactive
Crude technology	Infinite technology
Expensive	Cheap
Deadlines	24/7
Single platform	Multiple platforms
Linear	Multi-dimensional

2.3.1   From barriers to entry to permeability

In the past the journalism industry has had high barriers to entry. By this I don't particularly mean at the individual level. Generally speaking, in terms of recruitment, journalism has always been fairly open to all talents (and sometimes to those with none). Veteran political journalist Andrew Marr notes in his history of journalism[23] how in the modern era there has been a tendency towards graduate-only entry to the business with the expansion of higher education, media studies, and professional training. But in practice a Higher Education degree remains non-compulsory or less of a hurdle in an age of expanded higher education. However, starting a journalism business, especially broadcast or mass media, has until recently been very difficult with a whole series of legal and regulatory obligations. In most countries, until recently, the creation of news media enterprises was regulated largely for political reasons. Broadcasting was especially controlled as a way of rationing limited spectrum width. In a digital age the idea that government would spend its time and taxpayers' money trying to close "pirate" radio stations seems absurd. But for most of broadcasting history in many countries that has been the reality. Despite protestations of support for freedom of expression most societies have made it difficult to create journalism enterprises. The capital costs were relatively high. Apart from the staffing costs and equipment there are the ancillary costs of marketing and distribution systems. It is all relative, of course. I once asked a rural Ugandan radio station what investment they needed to transform their busy but basic output. "Another microphone so that we can conduct interviews and have live debates" they said. Now you can launch a new website with a few clicks of the mouse. That may not be enough to compete immediately with a major media organization. But if you do have an idea and a customer base then the venture or cooperative capital will follow. The obstacles to entry and growth are now much reduced.

2.3.2   From unresponsive to interactive

In the past Old Media was responsive only in terms of sales, viewing figures, and advertising. In other words, it was only concerned with commercial imperatives and secondary contact was highly limited. Apart from the cash–price exchange, direct contact with the consumer was typically through cross-word competitions and letters pages. Now every mainstream media outlet has an email address at the very least. Most have forums where the consumer can comment and many encourage user-generated content. Where before the

Figure 2.1 The new *Daily Telegraph* newsroom with its "spoke" design to reflect the new reality of multi-platform production (Photo Matt Brown/Nature Network, London)

news media produced its goods in glorious isolation, now the consumer can provide information and views that contribute to a network of editorial production. The BBC has its User Generated Content Hub while newspapers like *The Daily Telegraph* and the *Houston Chronicle* have their own online area for hosting reader's blogs (see Figure 2.1).[24,25]

This has helped shift the balance of power between the media and the consumer. Where before journalists or editors decided and you listened, the consumer is now becoming an intimate part of the process. When this happens in a positive way then it is Networked Journalism in action. Partly, this is driven by greater commercial sensitivity. Old Media audiences are declining so news organizations have to get much better at measuring what consumers want and then giving it to them. If done in a crude way this can simply mean DVDs handed out free with newspapers or reality TV shows instead of news. A more sophisticated version means creating a tailored output and a raft of different ways of keeping in touch with the customer. Technology now allows consumers to choose their own RSS feeds, to channel hop or record an almost infinite variety of digital offerings. The news media organization and the journalist have to chase the consumer. News media organizations now have to recognize the resource that the public offers. Now every time there is a serious incident, media organizations appeal for viewers to send in mobile phone pictures and video. This is the start of Networked Journalism.

2.3.3 From crude technology to infinite technology

Old Media news communication now seems incredibly crude. Imagine a reporter on assignment before the advent of the mobile phone. I remember hunting down phone-boxes to file copy. My colleagues remember waiting for film stock to be developed. In the US the phrase "film at 11" in broadcast news refers to this phenomenon. TV news stations had to develop film for broadcast, and they could not get this done in time for the 6pm news. So anchors on the 6pm bulletin would entice viewers to the later broadcast by promising them "film at 11." Journalism was physically constrained by technology, distance, and space. There were strict physical limits on the capacity of journalists to transmit information or to package it. Newspaper journalists bashed away on typewriters with duplicating paper that was handed to sub-editors who then passed the copy on to printers who laid out bits of metal to be banged onto sheets of paper by vast heavy machinery. The whole process was laborious and prolonged. Now thanks to better transport, the mobile phone, satellite, digital cameras and digital editing and rapidly increasing server space and broadband speeds, new communications are almost as fast and as big in capacity as the journalist's ability to fill it. Peer-to-peer interactions allow media organizations to access the server power of all their customers. Of course, there are production limits, but compared to even a decade ago they are far less constraining than the self-imposed limits of deadlines or budgets.

2.3.4 From expensive to cheap media

All that old technology was incredibly expensive. Flying out a reporter to cover a story with a crew is so much more resource intensive than a multi-skilled journalist. The communications costs of transmitting that story have plummeted thanks to optic fibers and silicon chips. Ultimately, what could be cheaper than a website? The reduction in production and transmission costs means that it is easier than ever to spread the product across platforms.

Digital material is easily replicated, reworked and redistributed on to mobile TV, podcasts, and online video. It all means that, dollar per minute, news is getting cheaper.

2.3.5   From deadlines to continuous news

All of the above means that journalists no longer have one deadline to work to. It's not just the 24 hour news channels that work around the clock. Recently, many national daily newspapers have decided to start breaking their own stories on their websites. Understandably, newspapers want to keep editorial value back for their hard copy platform. But in a world of online news and 24 hour news channels there is always the danger of an exclusive being scooped by a rival. Even a journalist working primarily to one outlet and one deadline has to consider contributing to a blog about the work, recording a podcast, or going online to respond to audience questions. "Appointment-to-view" television news shows and newspapers that you buy at a certain time of day will not disappear, but they will find it impossible to stand alone.

2.3.6   From a single platform to multi-platform journalism

The 24/7 journalist now has to service a variety of platforms. This is partly a function of the change-over from Old to New Media. So typically a newspaper will keep printing but will also have a website. It is partly a function of the fragmentation of audiences. As we are able to use a greater variety of communications devices the provider has to put their content onto those platforms. Evidence shows that this is not just a question of "cut and paste." One survey of how people will consume news on mobile phones,[26] for example, showed that the material had to be radically different. Video packages that worked online or on TV were physically unwatchable and unattractive on mobile TV. At the same time there is the Holy Grail of convergent technology. This can be exaggerated. Certainly it makes sense for a computer and a TV to do the same things, but I do not foresee a single-device world any time soon. People are increasingly enjoying the differentiation that separate platforms provide. Journalism has to show the creativity to cross technological boundaries in a way that plays to the consumer's enjoyment and employment of differentiated functionality. Networked Journalism is the way to exploit that increased connectivity.

2.3.7   From linear to multi-dimensional news

"Linear" has a variety of meanings[27] in news media terms. In the context of production it means the media organization starting with a story idea and going through a linear process of putting research, material, and presentation together to create a product. In consumption terms it means the idea that the viewer or reader will start at the beginning of that product and go through to the end. New Media means that where stories were static before, now they are multi-dimensional. They are now a process rather than a product. They have a different character depending on which platform they are on. And yet they may be created by the same person in all those forms. Where, before, the public consumed passively, now it can intervene *at any stage* of the process. Multi-dimensional Networked Journalism will deliberately engage with the public at all stages. It will invite contributions to the editorial selection process, to news gathering and to reworking the product according to audience responses. The public will help choose, research, produce, and disseminate the journalism.

2.4   What Networked Journalism Looks Like

So that is how New Media journalism is different from the past. Networked Journalism exploits those new conditions. Networked Journalism is about working with the grain of New Media. But there is more to it than that. It is about the journalist becoming the facilitator rather than gatekeeper. But that is just to view it as a production process and from the news media point of view. Increasingly in the New Media world we have to understand that the public is using this information and relating to it in ways that we are only just starting to map, let along understand or explore. At this point we are entering the territory of the "imagineers,"[28] the people who are trying to understand how our use of new technology will change the way we communicate. This isn't science fiction, as it often draws upon existing models. As *Daily Telegraph* technology blogger Shane Richmond points out:

> Social networking, as well as being fun, addictive, diverting and so on, meets a basic human need: it allows us to feel part of something. The challenge at the moment is ensuring that people stay with your platform, rather than moving on when the next fad comes along. It's not a challenge that news providers can avoid either. Young people are increasingly getting their news

from within social networks. (Newsflash: they always did, it's just that we didn't label *offline* social networks.) In the past, those people eventually found their way to newspapers and print media. What about in the future? (Shane Richmond, *Daily* Telegraph)[29]

The Networked Journalist has to become comfortable with the idea of this social networking. The way that individuals form small communities online, and at the same time have access to a much wider group, is very much an echo of the way that people used to relate to old media. In the past we shared our experience of news by talking about what we had read in the newspaper or seen on TV. Now increasingly people will do that online and the best news producer will have to become attractive to social networkers. They will also have to become a social networker themselves. This means doing things like the *Daily Telegraph* has done with *My Telegraph*[30] where it provides very easy and attractive weblog hosting with a ready-made community of bloggers and blog-readers attracted by the Telegraph brand and by its wider editorial input. And the *Telegraph* itself has become a blogger with its mix of newsroom commentary and news reporting on its newsroom blog. Beyond blogging, however, the Networked Journalist has to find new ways of intervening in or creating a wider range of social communication networks.

Something as simple as the comments posted on a *Facebook* profile wall have validity as crowd-sourcing mechanism. Have a look at the sites set up by US Presidential candidates and it is possible to see a flow of interesting (as well as fatuous) comment from young people, a group notoriously hard to reach by conventional media. Networked Journalists have to be aware of the potential resource this kind of platform offers, both in terms of information gathering, but also in building a consumer community.

The journalist's job will be to ensure every opportunity to have "amateur" input at every stage of the process. There is no reason why the public can't contribute, they are doing it already. RSS feeds allow us all to select which data we want to import directly, for example. Links and email allow the public to "edit" information by selecting and referring on bits of information. And as *YouTube* and any number of online video sites testify, the public is perfectly capable of using cheap and easy recording equipment and software to package and broadcast their own information. Of course, we may have to apply the 1 percent rule that Professor Jay Rosen of New York University uses for citizen journalism. Only 1 percent is of a high quality, 10 percent is acceptable and the rest is poor or banal. But it can all contribute to Networked Journalism.

This is already happening. Look at the way that the public used mobile phones to capture images of the demonstrations in Burma in late 2007. Some were posted on personal blogs but many more were sent to news organizations which couldn't get their own staff to the protest locations. They were not the same as a journalist sending a report. It meant that the news organization had to be conscious of the partiality of the people sending the material and the difficulties of establishing provenance. Much of it was out of focus or grainy. But does anyone doubt for one second that the citizen journalism from Burma enhanced our understanding of what was happening?

Another example of imaginative and effective engagement with the public was demonstrated by the Florida newspaper, *The Fort Myers News Press*. It is a great example of what is called "crowd-sourcing," exploiting the public as a journalistic resource. After Hurricane Katrina *The Press* took legal action against the US Federal Emergency Management Agency, (FEMA), to obtain all the data on relief payments to local citizens. It generated a massive data-set which the newspaper put online. It then asked its readers to comb through the information. Within 24 hours 60,000 searches were made. These produced hundreds of stories for journalists to follow up of anomalies in relief payments. Neither the journalists nor the citizens could have achieved that editorial output on their own. It was a tremendous example of Networked Journalism in action. These are all great individual instances of innovative connectivity. But I believe they can add up to something that offers a much more substantial benefit to the news media.

2.4.1   The networked newsroom

In Chapter 5 I will look at the way that networked means editorial production and training will have to change. But as part of the definition of this more connected or "distributed" journalism I want to imagine a different kind of "newsroom." Of course, the idea of a newsroom as a physical place becomes increasingly redundant. As news organizations go online they have moved their desks around to reflect the change in production methods but the shift from linear to multi-dimensional goes further than that. I want to avoid the mistake of replacing one set of models for another, so what follows may be schematic but it is not prescriptive. And while what I will describe appears to be complex, we must always remember that topical news journalism, in general, and breaking news in particular demands simplicity, speed, and executive expediency. Sometimes the Networked Journalist will have to cut to the chase. Not all the elements I will describe will happen all the time. In my attempt to give some sort of conceptual structure to this process I am indebted to the work of Birmingham City University's Paul Bradshaw and his "Model For A 21st Century Newsroom" at his website, *Onlinejournalismblog.com*.

2.4.2   The warehouse fire – Networked Journalism in action

In the following simple example I show how a variety of new media technologies can work alongside traditional reporting (see Figure 2.2). We take a city newspaper which has full online facilities and see how it responds to a warehouse fire. What is different about this networked piece of journalism is that it is continually subject to public input from the moment the story originates to its aftermath days and weeks later. With this practical event-based piece of journalism there is a degree of complexity, but the processes are all directed towards fast and focused news gathering and reporting. It does not include other elements of potential networked input such as the audience contributing to story selection. It takes us through the different stages of a story, which in practice will not be clear cut. It moves from the Alert, to early Draft versions which are little more than newsflashes, to more sophisticated Packages of information. Then as the facts emerge the story takes on Analysis and finally Consolidation and Interactivity. Beyond that the story continues as a longer-term issue and a prolonged conversation between experts, residents, and politicians mediated in part by the journalists.

Of course, real stories do not fit so easily in to such diagrammatic form. But what is important to note is the high degree of communication between the journalist and public. And this is not just in terms of information. As the story is "published" it is made up of public-generated material put up in relatively unmediated fashion. This means that the story is not stable. The first impression of a straight-forward incident develops in to another story about risk which in turn is challenged as more people join the narrative's network. It is the journalist's job as a facilitator to bring the participants in to the network, not to act as a gatekeeper to guard the media version of reality.

2.4.3   Networked sourcing

The Networked Journalist will continue to have "conventional" sources such as other media, agencies, public relations, and government. But increasingly

The production stage	What the journalist does	What the public does	The narrative
Alert	Fireservice tells newsroom that they have an incident in a downtown location	Residents text newsrooms that a large downtown warehouse is on fire in Hill Street	Newsflash: a large downtown warehouse is on fire
Draft	Newsroom sends out email and text alerts, newsroom blog activated, website alert posted, expert and public networks activated. Public blogs and social networks monitored.	Residents send in text and email descriptions, mobile phone stills and video. Public active on Twitter, Flickr, Facebook and personal blogs	Developing story: warehouse on fire is near homes
Package	Online text, audio and stills compiled with graphics and maps that link and use widgets to public generated content and to both public and expert websites	Resident feedback along with local representatives using email, phone and blog giving witness accounts of incidents but also commentary and analysis	Story takes on new analytic dimensions as it emerges that residents had complained of proximity of firework warehouse and experts had criticized safety standards
Analysis	Packaging shifts to include series of viewpoints of residents complaints and experts statements with timeline, links to comparable incidents and references to online reference material. Crowd-sourcing exercise underway with residents to map proximity of homes to warehouse. Political correspondent gets reaction from City Hall officials and politicians	Residents join in crowd-sourcing exercise on proximity while Twitter, mobiles, and email used to track missing people with information linked directly to news website page	The story turns in to a political row as the City Hall politicians claim that funds were not available because a previous budget proposal for tax hike to cover costs had been rejected by local residents. Crowd-sourcing and social media reveals no-one is missing or injured and no homes are damaged.

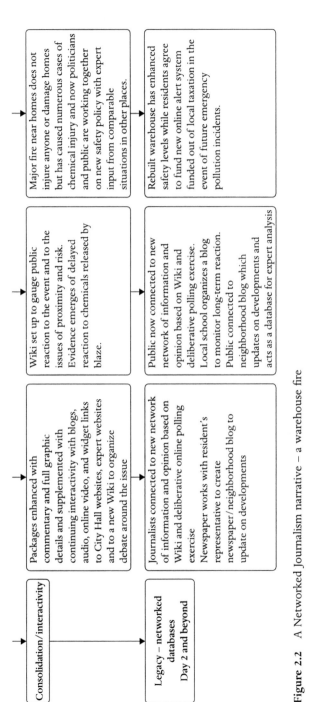

Figure 2.2 A Networked Journalism narrative – a warehouse fire

Consolidation/interactivity

Packages enhanced with commentary and full graphic details and supplemented with continuing interactivity with blogs, audio, online video, and widget links to City Hall websites, expert websites and to a new Wiki to organize debate around the issue

Wiki set up to gauge public reaction to the event and to the issues of proximity and risk. Evidence emerges of delayed reaction to chemicals released by blaze.

Major fire near homes does not injure anyone or damage homes but has caused numerous cases of chemical injury and now politicians and public are working together on new safety policy with expert input from comparable situations in other places.

Legacy – networked databases
Day 2 and beyond

Journalists connected to new network of information and opinion based on Wiki and deliberative online polling exercise

Newspaper works with resident's representative to create newspaper/neighborhood blog to update on developments

Public now connected to new network of information and opinion based on Wiki and deliberative polling exercise.

Local school organizes a blog to monitor long-term reaction.

Public connected to neighborhood blog which updates on developments and acts as a database for expert analysis

Rebuilt warehouse has enhanced safety levels while residents agree to fund new online alert system funded out of local taxation in the event of future emergency pollution incidents.

they will benefit from what their communities of interest are able to contribute. Instead of occasional forays in to the public sphere they will be intimately connected to that network on a perpetual basis. In this world the Networked Journalist will be doing all those online things. They will be connected to RSS feeds, members of social networking sites, interactiving with other blogs, linking different parts of their network to each other. But as journalists they will also have the skills to reach out to the offline world and engage with the parts of society that were ignored by conventional media. The point of the *Fort Meyers Press* example given above is that while it exploited a network of online citizens to enhance its journalism it also reached out to a lot of people beyond the digital network.

And what comes "after" the story is nearly as important as its sourcing and production. The continuous relationship between the journalist and the public is what is going to sustain Networked Journalism as a community and, therefore, as a business model. So that means that every piece of editorial must be lodged in a structure that can perpetuate its value. It will be inserted in to social networking sites. It will be properly annotated so that anyone using tagging and bookmarking will come across it. It will be linked to the relevant subject databases and digital mapping systems. And at each point it will offer anyone using that data a route back in to the journalistic network. By referencing or linking back it retains the value and builds the community of interest.

So that is what Networked Journalism looks like. I think it is a credible series of possible models. It is not the only form that journalism will take, but as way of working it offers a practical and creative approach to journalism in the new media environment. It is also a valid response to the current challenge to the deeper problems facing journalism. Let us now examine how a more connected form of news gathering and distribution could address some of the systematic and constituent problems that face any form of news mediation but especially at this moment in history.

2.5   How Networked Journalism Can Save the Media

We have already described above how New Media technologies are providing Networked answers to journalism's limitations in terms of process, the way that journalism works. We have seen what Networked Journalism looks like in principle and practice. In Chapters 3 and 4 we will address how Networked Journalism might improve journalism in practice in specific subject areas. Then in Chapter 5 I will give some training, education, and production ideas for fostering its development. But first of all let us see how New Media technologies and a more networked journalism can address some deeper editorial problems. These are the eternal quandaries of journalism, but they are made more acute by today's increased pressures of economic and social change. I would label them as the problems of *trust, time, place, humanity,* and *audience*:

- How do we keep public trust?
- How can we tell stories with accuracy and context when we only have a limited time to gather information and publish it?
- How do we connect people in different places?
- How do we put humanity at the heart of journalism?
- How do we retain the audience's attention?

2.5.1   The problem of authority and trust

So how can Networked Journalism address the crisis in authority that threatens the news media? Journalism is utterly pointless if it is not trusted. If the information is not believed then it becomes something else: fiction, polemic, or propaganda. In the digital era the Internet will provide vast amounts of communication and informational data and activity. But if it is not trusted then it is not news journalism.

This is not to say that traditional journalism has a history of being greatly trusted either. One of the fundamental reasons that I am so passionately committed to finding new ways of producing news is because I realize that journalism is subject to increasing skepticism and cynicism. Along with politicians and most authority figures and institutions, journalism is questioned to a greater degree than ever before. I welcome that. Too often in the past journalism has been partial, inaccurate, and downright false. It has been arrogant and complacent. A questioning approach by journalists is a job requirement, but the distain for their subject and audience that some in the media have shown in the past is a disaster for its long-term credibility.

There are "good" and "bad" reasons for this. Journalism has always been subject to the limits of time and resources. It gets things wrong because the full facts have not always emerged. In the phrase of 24 Hour News channels: "Never wrong for long!" But there have been other, less acceptable pressures on Old Media journalism.

Journalism has to make money or provide value. Even where it is supported by subsidy, it still needs ratings to justify its existence. This competitive drive means that all journalists construct their work to maximize what Tony Blair decried as "impact."[31] There is clearly pressure from advertisers to maximize audiences, which means that popular subjects and treatments will always be more attractive to management. Many privately owned media organizations have owners who frame the agenda of their companies. This does not mean that they bestride the newsroom like Charles Foster Kane.[32] But inevitably the world view of a proprietor or major shareholder will be a factor in the editorial considerations of their staff. News organizations have political characters, as well. Until recently broadcasters tended towards centrist views or were balanced by regulation. Of course, "centrist" can mean becoming a lackey of the state. This was demonstrated by the BBC when Reith helped deceive the nation during the British General Strike of 1926.[33] There are plenty of organizations who believe that mainstream broadcasters continue to show an institutional bias. While the TV Networks in the US are accused of being corporate stooges, the BBC is seen as a liberal conspiracy.[34] Many media organizations are very political. They campaign on specific issues, back political parties and hold to explicit or covert ideological positions. Media organizations also have a cultural bias which means that they can get stories out of proportion or perspective. It wasn't just the White House that was slow to realize the human disaster that Hurricane Katrina brought to New Orleans. US news organizations, dominated by middle class metropolitan managers driven by Washington or West Coast agendas were also slow to realize that this massive and iconic story was happening and what it said about contemporary America. As Pulitzer-prize winning writer David Shipler wrote, this was a structural failure in US journalism, not a one-off mistake:

> There is no more telling indictment of reporters and editors than the surprise felt by most Americans in seeing the raw poverty among New Orleans residents after Hurricane Katrina. In an open society, nobody who had been watching television or reading newspapers should have been surprised by what Katrina "revealed" to use the word so widely uttered in the aftermath. The fissures of race and class should be "revealed" every day by the US's free press. Why aren't they? (David Shipler)[35]

As Shipler writes, it is very often what the media fails to report that undermines its authority, as much as when it gets things wrong.

Finally, the way that we do Old Media journalism sometimes just isn't up to the job. When issues get complex, journalism often fails. In the build-up to the war in Iraq, I do not believe that the media in any country really got to grips with what was happening, what we were being told, and the Intelligence that was provided. This is not a political point. Whatever you think about the virtues of going to war, the public were not well served by journalists who failed to give them all sides of the debate and all the facts.[36] Some of the reasons for this were about the media itself. The news media, and television in particular, are very suited to war because it produces a dramatic narrative and compelling imagery. There was a particular political situation post 9/11 that meant the western media especially were much less critical than it should have been about the Bush administration's policy in its so-called "War on Terror." Others would argue[37] that there is a more fundamental long-term problem with mainstream media in that it is too subject to "group-think." This is the herd mentality which means the news media allows itself to follow an agenda which is too easily framed by the authorities. In the chapter on Editorial Diversity I will deal with these issues in more detail, but for now I hope I have made it clear that Old Media journalism has no monopoly on authority, no unsullied reputation for telling the unvarnished truth.

We must be careful not to follow fashionable cynicism in dismissing the public's trust in journalism per se. If you look at the figures it seems clear that the numbers are on the way down. They are also medium specific. People declare a higher degree of trust in TV newsreaders but don't seem to believe what they read in the newspapers. They find public service organizations such as the BBC and American NPR more credible than their commercial rivals, although even the most respected are treated with more suspicion than in the past. Generally, they put journalists in the same snake-like category of trust as politicians and real estate agents.[37–42]

But before we assume that journalists are all seen as pathological liars, we have to put this in a historical and social context. First, we should recognize that despite the fashion for cynicism, the trust percentages for some mainstream media can be reasonably high. While people claim not to believe the media, they do seem to share the media's views quite closely and recycle the media's versions of events. In this respect I would say that the public are not skeptical enough. But if we do accept that there has been a relative decline in trust we have to ask who is at fault. I have already outlined some of the fundamental flaws with mainstream media but that is not the whole picture. When one looks at the loss of trust in politics, for example, I do not blame the media to the degree that John Lloyd[43] or Lanny Davis[44] do. With the increase in Higher Education and the privatization of so many functions to individuals, the public has much higher expectations of politics and much greater personal investment in the economy than before. Politicians encourage us to aspire. In contrast, the media constantly reminds us that politicians are human and that the world is not perfect. Contrasted with our desires, this is bound to lead to disappointment. When asked in a public opinion survey whether this means you have lost trust, it is easy to blame the messenger. Now if that sounds complacent, then you are right. There is no way that either politicians or the media can or should accept this even if there are "reasons" for it. But they should not blame each other; that is a zero sum game. They should both put their houses in order. Journalism has to justify itself and it must change to do so. To be sure, there must be wider social changes if we are to rebuild trust in politics, but the media can begin by acting with greater humility, self-awareness and the assertion of the more positive values it claims to uphold. Networked Journalism can help the news media address the crisis of trust in journalism as a way of re-building its relevance and authority. By sharing the process with the public it offers a new relationship of greater transparency and responsibility. Its primary function is still to chase the stories that dominate our public agendas, but stories that are more honestly told. And by involving the public it also forces the consumer to take responsibility for their part in the news media market.

2.5.2   How Networked Journalism can rebuild trust

One of the defenses of the Old Media approach to journalism was that by separating out the producer from the public you inculcate a sense of objectivity. This would be reciprocated by trust from the public. Networked Journalism does not mean sweeping away those ideals. I do not think that striving for fairness, accuracy, and thoroughness is inhibited by sharing the process with the former audience. In fact, I am sure that it can strengthen it. What is objectivity anyway? In the mainstream news media it is continually compromised by the pressures of commercialism, competition, and cultural bias, even among the most honorable and self-aware journalists. Without delving too far into philosophical theory it is clear that objectivity is relative. It depends on the prevailing political norms. It is constructed socially. So what makes journalists think that they have a unique insight in to its essential nature? Well, quite rightly, it is because journalists have the experience and skills to strive towards objectivity. They have editing ability. In other words they are relatively proficient at judging sources, evaluating competing arguments and representing a version of reality. But Networked Journalism can make them much better at it.

Citizen journalists or amateurs are often able to claim the high-ground on trust. Generally, they are doing it for a good motive – they believe in what they are doing or they are enthusiasts. They are not usually in it for the money. And they are part of a community – often quite a small, self-regulating community – that polices itself. Some, like the British political blogger "Guido Fawkes,"[45] have tried to remain apart from scrutiny with limited success. But on the whole bloggers have gone a long way to try to be transparent and ethical. This is not the same as being objective or accurate, but it is a strong claim to greater accountability than mainstream media. The bloggers online currency is their trustworthiness and the other bloggers are ferocious at maintaining its values. The untrustworthy or irrelevant blogger tends to be ignored. It seems to me that bloggers don't want to replace mainstream media, but they are an alternative. In turn, the more creative professional journalists want to use citizen journalists – almost as if they are creating embeds in the real world. There are practical and principled grounds for cooperation.

Take the case of the faked Reuters photograph of an Israeli shell hitting Beirut during the 2006 conflict with Hezbollah. A freelance photographer had enhanced a picture of the city's skyline by adding more plumes of black smoke. It was a pretty crude *Photoshop* procedure but it wasn't spotted by the normal Reuters editorial checks. It took a journalism watchdog website called *Little Green Footballs*[46] to highlight the mistake. Reuters responded by pulling the photo, suspending the photographer and reviewing and then publishing their policy of the processing of photographs. It was a short-term blow to their prestige but a learning experience which they embraced. Reuters made it clear that they welcome correction like this because they recognized that it can only enhance their reputation for trustworthy reportage. *Little Green Footballs* is a right-wing website with some particular political obsessions. I would always go to Reuters rather than *LGF* for my news. But networked together they make for a more objective news process. Reuters and other news media should be building in this kind of outsider oversight into their production processes.

The *Washington Post* is another media organization which is attempting to take New Media seriously. Although, like Reuters, it is not diving all the way in yet. It has now published ten commandments, or rather "principles,", for its web journalism.[47] In it they make some unexceptional assertions:

"Accuracy, fairness and transparency are as important online as on the printed page. *Post* journalism in either medium should meet those standards." But they also make a firm decision to put their quality journalism online: "We will publish most scoops and other exclusives when they are ready, which often will be online." And they recognize that the online medium is different in style and substance: "We recognize and support the central role of opinion, personality and reader-generated content on the Web . . . We embrace chats, blogs and multimedia presentations as contributions to our journalism." And they recognize that this is going to mean changing the habits of a lifetime in the practical daily routines: "The newsroom will respond to the rhythms of the Web as ably and responsibly as we do to the rhythms of the printed newspaper. Our deadline schedules, newsroom structures and forms of journalism will evolve to meet the possibilities of the Web."

It all builds up to a rallying cry for any news organization facing up to the implications of the digital era. They appreciate that it is about more than creating a website alongside the newspaper – the two have to become one: "Publishing our journalism on the Web should make us more open to change what we publish in the printed newspaper. There is no meaningful division at *The Post* between 'old media' and 'new media.' "

But as blogger Jeff Jarvis has pointed out, this doesn't really mention the "former audience." *The Post* is still seeing the public as an adjunct to its work rather than an integral part of it:

> To me, they leave out a vital 11th principle: They should be committed to working in new and collaborative ways with the people formerly known as readers. They should be recasting their relationship – and institution's and each journalist's relationship – with the community. (Jeff Jarvis, Media Commentator)[48]

To be fair to the *Post*, the memo that contained the ten principles also recognized that they are not on tablets of stone and that the paper has to keep an open mind about the future: "We must continue to evolve the content and forms of journalism that we publish in the printed newspaper, partly in response to and inspired by journalistic evolution on the Web."[49]

But when the memo then talks about how they are going to go out and search for their fragmenting audience *The Post* turns not to bloggers or wikis but to a group of internal practitioners. The ultimate irony is that rather than shout about their principles from the rooftops they were leaked – by a journalism website. In truth, the ten principles may be more about the internal politics of the *Post* where the paper and online divisions need this kind of road map to peaceful coexistence.

All media organizations should publish codes like this. Not because they need to solidify policy, but to enhance institutional commitment and to send out a message to their audience that they are now welcome in the newsroom. This would be a significant step forward to creating a better relationship of trust.

2.5.3   Journalism and temporality

Journalism is topical. It is about telling people something as quickly as you can. Everything else is history. The temporal nature of journalism means that deadlines and physical limits impose a restriction on how journalists work and what they can produce. We have seen how New Media means that these restrictions are being relaxed. Now journalism becomes a non-linear, multi-dimensional process. Networked Journalism embraces that potential and builds it in to the whole system.

New Media allows the Networked Journalist to draw upon multiple sources. Internet search is the basic tool, but there is a whole range of links and feeds, tagging, and email alerts that can cast the net wider. Reuters has now set up a partnership with the blogging network *Global Voices*.[50] This allows Reuters to draw upon a world-wide network of bloggers who can add personal perspectives. Reuters also hope that they become an editorial resource feeding in to their own coverage. At the time of writing there were no plans to pay them, however. Reuters Foundation has also created *Alertnet*,[51] an emergency news mapping tool which gives information on everything from storms to wars to pandemics across the globe. This is multi-dimensional sourcing in action compared to the old ticker-tape or news-feed model where periodic updates of pre-selected material were the only ingredients for news production.

The Networked Journalist can still have a deadline. The discipline of a target time remains a useful motivational tool. And consumers will still want to know what stage a piece of journalism has reached. There will continue to be newspapers and TV news shows that are "appointment to view." But generally, the journalism will have two new temporal dimensions. First, it will become active immediately when the Networked Journalist begins work. From the moment of the commission there is no reason why the journalist should not "go public." This is in effect what the conventional journalist does by talking to experts or contacts. Increasingly, it will be a blogger, for example, who contacts a "professional" journalist to activate a story process. The journalist will be the facilitator who alerts a network about the emergence of the story and begins a process of building, testing, and linking the information. This is already happening with political blogs in the UK, where journalists often run stories through the bloggers to see who reacts. And bloggers will take stories from the mainstream press and dig deeper or find alternative angles. This is an entirely positive development which gives the story process greater temporal reach.

With Networked Journalism, stories then have life beyond the deadline, because online reaction can become part of the significance. This is, of course, rather embarrassing if you are a US Senator like George Allen who made an injudicious remark that had a prolonged life on *YouTube*.[52] But it does mean that stories that have resonance will, indeed, reverberate for as long as the audience is interested. The more that people relate to a story the more it will be perpetuated through online interaction. The journalistic effort that may have ended up in the garbage can or disappearing into the ether can now live on through time-shifting and the Internet. I am convinced that the Networked Journalist who deliberately uses that new technology in the creation and dissemination of their material and who engages with the public most fully and directly will be the journalist whose work lives longest. Instead of a small traditional media clique deciding that a story should be pursued ad nauseum, the public will have a direct role in perpetuating particular lines of inquiry or analysis. The danger is an agenda set by the crowd but in practice it will remain a collaborative and mutually directed process.

2.5.4   Journalism and geography

The other great limitation on Old Media journalism was distance. This compromised both reporting and publication. This was and is a practical problem but it is also a philosophical issue. Distance is physical but it is also moral. How we understand and represent other people has consequences as to how we treat those who are remote from us. In the concluding chapter of this book I will examine these ethical and political aspects of Networked Journalism more deeply. But here I want to stress how Networked Journalism allows us to make contact, share information, and communicate across distance.

The world is shrinking, thanks to new technology and other factors, such as burgeoning bargain air travel and low satellite costs. Digital journalism allows us to make the links. Let's go back to Reuters. On its Africa website[53] there is now a complex range of bloggers, both Reuters staff and in-country "amateurs." This is a sharing of the news media with the mainstream giant carrying the independent voices. The bloggers add depth and value to Reuters' professional coverage. Some of the blogs are media critiques such as this acidic judgment on a *Time* magazine story implying that Guinea Bissau is the next "narco-state":

> Imagine if *Time Magazine* did a story about New Jersey being the car theft capital of the USA, and then half of the pics were taken in Massachusetts. Would that make sense? No. Would people in Massachusetts have the right to be offended? Yes. *Time*'s editors are just assuming there's little chance that their audience will notice or draw the distinction between the various countries in deep, dark, scary Africa. Furthermore, they print a picture of a pile of alleged cocaine cash, all in Liberian dollars, and I guess the reader is supposed to think it's a huge stash of filthy loot. But to the educated eye it looks like an amount of LD worth about US$8. Come on! I have that much LD on my dresser after changing a ten dollar bill! ('Liberia Ledger' blogger)[54]

This is just one example of how Reuters has given an African a chance to answer back to the West, not through a random blog but through one linked directly into the mainstream media network. But for this to be genuinely Networked Journalism the bloggers have to be more than online stringers. It is important that it is seen as more than a bolt-on added feature.

Distance is already being bridged by citizen journalists in unexpected ways. It is not just about blogging. We should remember that the images of Abu Ghraib were in effect user-generated content, although it took the US TV program *60 Minutes* and journalist Seymour Hersch to bring them in to the mass media public realm. *Aljazeera* then took it to an Arab audience which was able to engage through that channel's phone-ins and website. And, of course, the pictures themselves had a million further media lives on blogs around the world providing the material for further journalism. The story of Abu Ghraib and the way that it was interpreted and performed differently around the world with extensive interaction between amateurs and professionals was one of the biggest examples of Networked Journalism that we have seen so far.

This is not just about the media organizations. If governments and other bodies such as NGOs (non Governmental Organizations) want to reach out, then they must facilitate greater access for people to use New Media platforms to communicate beyond their borders. The BBC World Service

Trust (WST), for example, is enabling Pashto and Dari speaking audiences, inside and outside Afghanistan, to listen to their favorite radio programs using the Internet.[55] A similar WST project called *Zig Zag*[56] is aimed at young people in Iran who use a secret language to communicate. It gives them a chance to hear each others' voices, and to engage online with figures such as religious leaders. I will examine the potential of Networked Journalism to cross boundaries like this in Chapter 5. But it is clear that through social media or news media the new technology is able to cross both physical as well as social barriers.

2.5.5 Journalism and the cycle of newsroom sensitivity

Networked Journalism can allow the journalist greater engagement and more reflection upon their subject. This is the paradoxical goal of any good journalism.

I describe it as the cycle of newsroom sensitivity. With Networked Journalism, we are able to take this process beyond the newsroom.

In a conventional news production process and particularly in a conventional newsroom, the journalist goes through a cycle of sensitivity. By sensitivity I mean their interest – emotional and intellectual – in their subject. At one level most professional journalists go through this in terms of the progression of their career. They go in to the job because they are curious about the world. They are often politically or personally engaged and often have an ability to see things from other people's point of view. They are interested in what other people think and they are open to understanding the thoughts and emotions of others as a way to understand the world. In this sense they are sensitive. But a journalist's experience and training turns a subjective approach in to an objective discipline.

For a newsroom to work it has to have individuals who perform generally in accordance with the norms of that organization and who strive for similar editorial goals with shared editorial values. Ideally, the journalist gets space and time and resources at points in their career to reconnect with their "sensitivity" and renew those original motivational drives. In practice that rarely happens.

A similar cycle occurs on a daily basis. The journalist enters work fresh from their real world, full of openness and interest in the world. Then the journalist has to deal with a subject and impose their journalistic discipline. They have to subjugate their personal feelings and individual intellectual perspective to the effort of striving for an objectified product, a communicable representation.

They must make sure that their journalism is as thorough, critical, and accurate as possible. And yet, their journalism then tries to connect the subject with the viewer. One way is through "human interest." The journalist tries to tell the story in a way that the audience can relate to, even when the subject is remote socially or geographically. At that point in the production process the journalist is attempting to reintroduce the human element and produce an emotional reaction. On the day of the London bombings, for example, the journalists I worked with went through that cycle. We went to work as usual leaving behind our normal lives. We then had to deal professionally with a story that was an extreme example of a disturbing and emotionally engaging event. But of course, we wanted our coverage to reflect the human dimension of the day. We did this by taking extra care to allow victims to speak with great emotion about what had happened, so allowing the viewer to connect directly with the emotion of the events. After transmission the journalist is able to re-engage with the real world. They may take with them all sorts of emotional reactions of guilt or distress or compassion about the days reported events.

The negative aspect of this cycle is that it can produce a kind of false consciousness in the way the journalist works through stories. In its most sterile manifestation it leads to formulaic journalism. It creates the tired clichés where presenters ask victims "how they feel," or reporters show starving African children with fly-blown eyes. It can open up a distance between the journalist and the subject that is never closed. I believe that this makes for less fulfilling journalism for all concerned.

These cycles of sensitivity are not exclusive to journalism. One could argue that doctors have to perform a similar cycle. But Networked Journalism allows the possibility of turning this in to a much more virtuous cycle. Beyond that, it gives the opportunity to turn the circle in to a network. Networked Journalism, where the "amateur" and the subject are allowed into the whole process, allows the journalist to maintain the connection without resorting to formula. Journalism will still be about representation – how else can it perform the core functions of filtering, editing, and packaging? But the whole multi-dimensional process will be less hierarchical and non-linear. Some of this happened on 7/7 in London as citizen journalism made an impact with people sending in phone images and creating weblogs to relate the day's events. A lot of media organizations learnt lessons about how to harness user-generated content on that day. They learned to share their journalistic space with the public. However, this was still a long way from the kind of proactive Networked Journalism that could have informed the cycle of sensitivity with greater meaning. In a truly connected news media world this would recycle back in a renewed sense of the possibilities of journalism. We will look at this in greater detail in the chapter on Editorial Diversity.

2.5.6 Journalism and the audience

We have already seen how the audience is both deserting mainstream news media and fragmenting. Here are two groups that Dan Gillmor identifies that New Media can help attract back:

> First are the people who have been active, in their own way, even before grass-roots journalism was so available to all. They are the traditional writers of letters to the editor: engaged and active, usually on a local level. Now they can write weblogs, organize meetups, and generally agitate for the issues, political or otherwise, that matter to them . . . The second, and I hope larger, group from the former audience, [are] the ones who take it to the next level. We're seeing the rise of the heavy-duty blogger, website creator, mailing list owner, or SMS gadfly – the medium is less important than the intent and talent – who is becoming a key source of news for others, including professional journalists. In some cases, these people are becoming professional journalists themselves and are finding ways to make a business of their avocation. (Dan Gillmor)[57]

I would add two more groups. These are the people who are not the kind of activists that Gillmor describes. The third group are the Virtually Passive. Many people will still want the old relationship they had with the news media. They will want packaged news delivered to them. I believe that many people will continue to consume most of their journalism in this way. The fourth group are the Social Users who will consume news and take part in what Gillmor calls the "conversation" as part of social networking. They are not activists in the ways that he describes but will still provide content and interaction with the news flow. Some of their social news flow is so local and so personal that it is of no interest to Networked Journalism. But the structures that it creates will be a remarkable resource for wider engagement. This is not just a question of researching a young politician's character by checking out compromising photos on *Facebook* from their youthful hedonistic past. It is about Networked Journalism tracking and initiating conversations on these sites that engages the users with the stories and issues that the news media is communicating.

Of course, these are not mutually exclusive groups – we can all be members of different groups at different times. But journalism has to connect with these groups if it is to thrive. Engaging the "former audience" through Networked Journalism has three benefits:

1   it brings the audience back to the process;
2   it brings content to the process; and
3   it brings moral and political value to the process.

The news media needs the numbers. It needs to travel way down the long tail and in to every niche to sustain its business. It can go some way to do this by clever marketing and research. It can go further by tailoring its product to these difficult-to-reach audiences. But it would be much easier if it made the audience part of the process and allowed them to help shape the news media we expect them to consume. Networked Journalism is a strategic as well as tactical concept. It is about more than focus groups. By incorporating bloggers, for example, mainstream media are creating a network that is effectively self-selecting, which is surely a marketing person's dream. The Networked Audience is offering content in an incredibly efficient way. Most user-generated content (UGC) is not paid for and even where it is the rates are usually low because the public values the participation as much as the pay. Networked Journalism is a social good.[58]

Managing the engagement with the former audience is not always efficient. Transaction costs must be kept under control. That is partly because most media organizations are still operating in a way that separates out "professional" and "amateur" content. It is also because they have not yet developed the techniques to process the volume of UGC or interactivity they sometimes get. Steve Herrmann from BBC Online says they were swamped by UGC on the day of the London Bombings. Now they have a systemized UGC Hub and special software that crunches audience emails, extracts images and puts them up for viewing as thumbnails for BBC journalists. But this can go much further. The BBC hub, for example, still only skims the surface because it continues to separate the public from the publishing process. It also insists on strict verification procedures rather than allow content with caveats.

Networked Journalism brings a moral and political value to the process for the audience because it effectively dilutes or shares the power of the media with the public. It encourages the audience to share responsibility for reporting and promotes greater media literacy. If you are part of a process you will inevitably feel ownership. The news media has to create systems that allow much less mediated interaction with the audience. There has to be much more openness to input, greater facilities for access to flows of information and raw material, and much greater transparency. The media has to show trust to expect it in return.

2.6   The Business of Networked Journalism

> We are the independent observers of the world, who go places our audience can't go, dig where our audiences can't dig, study and interpret what our audiences do not have time to study and interpret, so that our audiences can better understand the world. (Michael Oreskes, *International Herald* Tribune)[59]

Michael Oreskes' description of journalism is still the core component of its business offering for a Web 2.0 or even Web 3.0 world. Networked Journalism is about amateur and professional as complementary and increasingly interchangeable parts of a process. The new dynamics that I outlined above liberate journalism to do things it could not do in the past. Surely that is the very definition of an opportunity? And it is an opportunity for the commercial news media as much as the public sector. As someone who has worked in both public and private news media, I understand the importance of both to each other.

It is vital for the survival of journalism that what people value in mainstream news is taken into online journalism. All the surveys tell us that young people are not getting in to the news habit. However, one interesting study[60, 61] showed that the early adopting, social networking generation still *trust* old media more, they just don't use it. So one of the key tasks is to find ways to bring its values and its product to them, to make it part of their lives again.

In the digital era anyone thinking about sustaining or starting a news media enterprise has to ask themselves some very basic questions:

- What business am I in?
- What do I mean by journalism?
- What content do I have?
- How will I deliver it?
- Who wants it?
- Why do they want it?
- What will they do with it?

These were all questions which were often taken for granted by Old Media, but they are vital for anyone seeking to make progress in the new media landscape. So far, much of new media business has been hit and miss. A thousand flowers have bloomed but very few have taken root. There has been very little analysis of what works and what doesn't, although there are many people who claim to be able to offer expensive advice. The market will help to sort out the wheat and chaff. But I think that media academic Adrian Monck from City University in London is right to identify the problem of "connoisseurship." Too many online entrepreneurs are indulging in the production of journalism that they find delectable rather than giving the public what they want or need. Networked Journalists are producing Pinot Noir when the people prefer Chardonnay.

My "advice" to those seeking to sustain good journalism boils down to three core principles:

1   Concentrate on creating good Networked Journalism. Any product that is created by public investment has to have a future.
2   Think much harder about what is going on in the new media landscape and think conceptually. Ignorance is not bliss, imagination is required.
3   You are here now, well done. But you are not necessarily the person who knows how you will be here tomorrow.

2.6.1   Market freedom, freedom of expression

There are various *models* on offer, but more important are the key *concepts* in play. Some of the business models are familiar, defensive, financially driven tactics such as conglomeration. It makes sense for shareholders in the short term but it is hardly an answer for those who value diversity or growth. Mergers can be healthy in a rapidly growing market where there is a duplication of production methods and a surplus of competitors. In a declining market they can also rescue businesses that are not sustainable independently.

But journalism is different. A single organization, like News International in the UK, has a variety of products, ranging from *Sky News* to *The Sun* to the *Times Literary Supplement*. I see no grave danger in the fact that all these outlets are linked. But there is a danger when one organization goes on to have a substantial market share, especially when it replicates that dominance across other platforms. This applies as much to the BBC as it does to Rupert Murdoch. So far what we are seeing is both taking their market power online.

It is political and economic variety which underlies real editorial diversity. In the marketplace of ideas you need a plethora of people setting out their stalls. But you do have to accept that we are living in an age when media companies will be born and die much more quickly. The early twentieth century saw a brutal decimation of Victorian institutions, replaced by an army of new media companies, including the creation of a public sector. We wait to see the longevity of *Facebook* or even *Google* compared to the century old life of *Reuters*, but no business has an inalienable right to exist.

2.6.2   Market freedom – Net neutrality

As the big Old Media players go online they meet companies like *Google* which exercise such power over the Internet. We are already seeing how *Google* has intervened in news directly through *Google News*. But it will be as important a market driver and influence on journalism through the way it constructs its search facilities.

The idea of Net Neutrality[62–64] is, therefore, vital in preserving a free market in the media – both commercially and in terms of freedom of expression. This is the idea that links should be determined by their popularity and relevance rather than through payments made to the search engines. The counter argument is that search is the only way to make money online and that revenue has to come from somewhere to fund more services and future development of broadband.

In terms of Networked Journalism it is an especially acute dilemma. We value the transparency of Net Neutrality. That will be vital to sustain the process of universal access for the public. It is also essential as a way of guaranteeing trust and accountability. So you either try to retain net neutrality or you embark on the construction of a series of checks, balances, and oversight that looks dangerously like over-regulation of the Internet. Or you allow the big corporations to set a pricing structure that restricts access to markets and denies the public choice and information.

2.6.3   Networked Journalism fills the gap

> For at least 10 years we are going to have to have an act of faith and pump money into digital markets without significant return . . . and we will do it with the expectation that things will change. (Alan Rusbridger, Editor, *The Guardian*)[65]

There are some practical implications of what I have set out. What is hard for converting media organizations is to reprioritize without losing core value. For new media organizations the challenge it is to develop that public or political culture that will give them longer-term value. As Rusbridger points out, that costs. New Media companies are not exempt from the need to change and evolve either. *Google* is going through this process. It has had to realize that it is no longer an "optimism" company, it is now a "realism" business. It has had to acknowledge that it is in the world of politics. And when that means China that means compromise.[66,67] What I am interested in is not just the moral balance of the compromise that was made but where *Google* will take the lessons learned. How relevant are its founding principle of "do no harm" and its guiding idealistic lights? Because, as far as journalism is concerned – and *Google* is now very much part of journalism – this is a moral market about trust, authenticity and, in the case of Networked Journalism, transparency and collaboration.

Networked Journalism can bridge the gaps. Through its transparency and accountability it can rebuild trust. But this means sharing responsibility between the "professional" and the "amateur." This is also a way of reducing the need for external regulation.

Networked Journalism can also bridge the funding gap. For the next five years or so there will be a cash flow crisis as media organizations retool for the digital age. They are investing more in news processes as well as new technology and business experimentation. At the same time many are facing catastrophic collapses in revenue. Blogs or User Generated Content and collaboration help to fill that gap. But more importantly than that for the medium term, it builds the online communities that will feel disposed to invest in a product in which they play a role. Involve the public and they are more likely to buy into the business. That investment may literally be shareholding, but is more likely to be forms of subscription. And that community is a resource that in turn can be monetized as a network rather than as individual purchasers.

2.6.4   Networked Journalism – a different business

Corporate America is scared. Things are changing too fast, consumers are too powerful and marketing is too fragmented. The One Corporate Voice now has to speak with multiple messages for infinite desires stretched across psychographic lines on varied platforms. Marketing today is better because of the ability to have real conversations and relationships with consumers.

It's also a lot easier to find the people you want to reach. But marketing today is also harder. It requires patience, some prescience and lots of participation. It demands new metrics of measurement. And yes, it calls for risk and a long-term view. (Gary Goldhammer, Media Commentator)[68]

Networked Journalism is a way of building that "long-term" view for a business, but it is not a short-cut. When we look at some of the imperatives it offers we must also realize that they are based on what serves the public and thus shareholders, not the other way around. Of course, there is no reason why Networked Journalism enterprises can't be originated from scratch. They don't have to begin with a mainstream media organization that changes and they don't have to start with a New Media blog or online site. Jay Rosen's *NewAssignment.net*[69] is an experimental attempt to create Networked Journalism projects. It will attempt to combine professional and "amateur" input. Rosen wants citizens to come up with story ideas and to make donations to fund stories that they think should be covered. *NewsAssignment.Net's* editors will still act as gatekeepers who will select the correspondents to carry out the assignment, but the citizen journalists will stay involved:

If I can improve it, get the funding, find people who know how to operate in the more open style, NewAssignment.Net would be a case of journalism without the media. That's the beauty part. Reporter + smart mob + editor with a fund get the story the press pack wouldn't, couldn't, or didn't. (Jay Rosen, *NewAssignment Net*)[70]

Rosen does not expect his project to challenge the major media outlets. He says it is a "boutique" attempt to see which forms of crowd-sourcing and alternative fund-raising might work. But however it originates, the following are some of the principles or business models that Networked Journalism will use.

2.6.4.1 *Accept obsolescence*

There is no reason why we *need* so many newspapers or TV strands. There are only so many hours in the day for so many people. Digital platforms bring an explosion of choice, but there will be a reckoning. I have cited many reasons why the demand for journalism will rise but there are good reasons why people find better things to do. The consumer was always King but now they can choose their kingdom, too.

2.6.4.2   Capture the community

Nowhere is safe from Networked Journalism. A short walk from my offices in London, Fleet Street is now devoid of newspapers. They went elsewhere to capitalize on new technology. If I walk five minutes in the other direction to Covent Garden I come upon the genteel offices of *The Lady*, unmoved since its foundation in 1885.[71] It is a relic of a bygone era, with classified ads for nannies sustaining editorial featuring Royal gardeners. It has a readership of high income, older middle aged women in the south-east of England. It is a classic offline demographic that looks like it is about to disappear off the edge of the digital world. Its editor Arline Usden says that the pace of change is slow:

> The magazine's management is conservative in attitude, so we were also probably the last magazine in Britain to use computers for production. When I first joined the magazine as Editor, 16 years ago, the editorial department did not even have a fax machine. The magazine has only recently accepted credit cards for its advertisements. (Arline Usden, Editor, *The Lady*)[72]

But *The Lady* is now online and it even has original video of its last reader's event at the Waldorf Hilton. Despite its conservative approach and old-fashioned culture, it seems to me that *The Lady* is ripe for Networked Journalism. It already brings its readers together for literary lunches and provides a vital nanny-finding service through its classified adverts. It has a community of 40,000 dedicated people who share its values. These are people who spend their life networking and are articulate and literate enough to produce content. After all, today's early adopters are tomorrow's silver surfers.

2.6.4.3   Diversify

Networked Journalism allows media businesses to go into other Internet activities like travel and retail. Trusted media organizations have always done this to a degree, such as the travel clubs at regional papers. I see no reason why online media should not exploit its consumer/contributor base. I see this as analogous to a Department Store. One floor can be selling journalism without having to compromise its core values just because you are selling other products to the same people in other parts of the store. The community that journalism builds seems terribly wasted if it is only given one service.

2.6.4.4 *Specialize*

The long tail does offer hope for minority news businesses. Rick Waghorn[73] is my favorite example of this. The former local sports writer went online when his paper starting laying off journalists. He has created a website dedicated to Norwich City, a second string regional soccer club, but with a fan-base of tens of thousands. With the help of a former advertising salesman from the newspaper, Rick created a business through banner ads. Now he's revamped the website and is franchising the format across the region. He's not a millionaire, but he has created a terrific website, and he is starting to pay his bills. He is an outsider who exploits his online status to beat mainstream media deadlines and to engage with his readers. But he is also a professional who pays for a press pass to the club:

> At this stage in my fledgling online life, I'd hesitate to describe myself as the goose that laid any sort of golden, journalistic egg financially – albeit, month on month, we nudge in the right direction. And it helps that I don't have a print press team, a van driver and a paper boy on the pay-roll. But two definites have emerged. Readers still have a huge appetite for good, well-sourced and trusted comment on any subject that plays on a passion; and a journalist's best pal in a media office is an ad rep. (*Rick Waghorn*)[74]

Waghorn's intimate knowledge of a particular field, his superb website-cum-blog and his committed community makes him a Networked Journalist.

2.6.4.5 *Hyperlocal*

While the Internet may be global in its reach, it can also be "hyperlocal." But experiments in Internet news focused down to a very local level have not been entirely successful. In the US the *Backfence*[75] franchise of local Internet community sites folded despite $3 million investment. There is an obvious problem that if you target a few streets, or even part of a city, then you are restricting yourself to a tiny audience which may not be able to support even a website. But there is also the problem that people may not see themselves as part of an easily defined *geographical* community. As blogger and lecturer Jeff Jarvis suggests:

> After trying one of everything in hyperlocal, I've come to believe that this will happen only by combining those various models – so people can join in however they want to – and by answering the questions: How much news

will members of the community create and share? What do they need to do that? What motivates them? How can local news organizations enable and encourage them? . . . Local is people. Our job is not to deliver content or a product. Our job is to help them make connections with information and each other. (Jeff Jarvis)[76]

One attempt being made in London is *The Southwark News* which combines a paid-for local weekly newspaper and a website. Founder and editor Chris Mullany told me that they are struggling in one of the world's most competitive media markets, but what surprised him was where the competition is coming from:

> We are a local with a 10,000 circulation in one of London's boroughs with a variety of people in different areas, from London Bridge and Borough to Bermondsey, Peckham and Dulwich, and I thought that we were hyperlocal. But you get even more hyper local than that through the community message forums and blogs. These are a real threat and surprise to me. It is in these community message boards and forums that many people like to read about and participate in the news in their community. (Chris Mullany, Editor, *Southwark* News)[77]

That seems to suggest that with all the competition from city free newspapers, the local or hyperlocal market is going to be just as crowded as the national scene. If journalism is going to survive at that level than it needs to be multi-platform and 360 degree connected. It needs to be Networked.

2.6.4.6   Socialize

Advertisers have already realized that they have to insert themselves in to people's online conversations and relationships. It's what Tariq Karim from *Netvibes*[78] calls "attention mining." Viral adverts are far more successful than banners because they engage the consumer in an activity that they can share, and that feels like all the other good stuff online. News has always worked hard to put up invisible barriers between itself and the rest of the media. But that is just not sustainable online because, apart from the mega brands such as the BBC or *New York Times*, they just don't have the presence to attract enough passing traffic. I see no conflict here editorially. Most news media organizations have already expanded into arts, sport, and lifestyle journalism. It is a question of linking the lifestyle to the journalism. All the time there are new Online technologies such as "widgets"[79] which promote this kind of connectivity, allowing journalism to insert itself as a kind of hyper-link in to all sorts of other Internet dialogues. Local newspapers, for example, could offer widgets featuring photos covering neighborhood events. Then if people go to the event and write about it on their blog, *MySpace* page or in *Facebook*, they could feature a collection of photos from the newspaper that simply links back to the paper's site so people can buy hard copies or download files of the pictures.[80] *Facebook* already has a "Causes" team which helps facilitate people running campaigns, so why shouldn't it have a "Journalism" team which facilitates Networked Journalism?

2.7 Networked Journalism and Public Service

> So does the media have a responsibility to inform the electorate in an age of information overload? Of course, just as schools, and unions, and churches and political parties and every other institution in society has such a responsibil-ity . . . just as every citizen has such a responsibility to both himself and his fellow citizens. But the media has a much more immediate and urgent task . . . That task is to reinvent the media business so it can continue to sustain the quality journalism that is so vital to informing the electorate. Everyone has a stake in that task . . . because if we fail at it, any discussion of the media's respons-ibility to inform anyone will be a mere academic debate. (Michael Oreskes, Editor, International Herald Tribune)[81]

We have already seen how public service journalism is threatened by digital developments. Networked Journalism is a way of justifying it in the new era. Oreskes is right to identify the political rationale. Ultimately, people have choices about the way society is run, and they can choose a better news media if they want. Journalism has not been good enough at making that case in the past and must do more to sell its role in society to the public.

But he is also correct to say that the media business has to reinvent itself. There are two types of public service journalism. First there are the straight-forward public subsidy organizations such as the US National Public Radio or the BBC. Second, there are the private organizations, which deliver pub-lic service content. Both need to embrace the networked paradigm if they are to claim the kind of moral responsibility that Oreskes sees as a core func-tion of media in a civilized society.

The BBC is the biggest example of publicly funded journalism in the world and it is the most secure. It has gone online with great aplomb and has achieved even greater global reach for its content. Its news services have a healthy medium-term future thanks to the funding deal with the British government that is the envy of commercial media companies all around the world. It means it has to make efficiency savings but that is a question of management having to prioritize.

The BBC already has one of the most highly developed and successful Networked Journalism operations in the heart of its massive newsroom in West London. Tucked away behind the vast open plan offices and studios that house the main broadcast operation is the User Generated Content (UGC) Hub. Here a team of about 15 journalists process the vast amount of material sent in by the public to the BBC. Most of it is filtered through the BBC *Have Your Say* website. It all started with the Asian Tsunami back in December 2004 with emails and photos being sent in by people who witnessed the disaster. More recently BBC news has used UGC in its bulletins about the Virginia Tech shootings, the Heathrow and Glasgow attempted bombings and recent flooding across much of England. They even teamed up with *Google* to offer an interactive map which allowed readers to click through to photos and videos sent in by flood-struck citizens.

The Hub gathers the information and verifies it through the normal journalistic practice of phoning and fact-checking. This produces witnesses who are sometimes used in the rest of the BBC's coverage. It also turns up new stories. In 2006 in the UK there was a story about faulty petrol which emerged through the UGC hub. Petrol retailers denied any problem, but the UGC hub was able to find enough motorists with misfiring engines to stand the accusations up. The UGC hub allows the BBC to make contact with hard-to-reach groups such as ex-armed forces personnel. An item on former soldiers suffering mental illness was supplemented by some stirring testimony gathered through the *Have Your Say* portal. And the public are taking the initiative, as BBC Interactive Editor Vicky Taylor explains:

> when the terrorist attack happened at Glasgow airport, the pictures from bystanders arrived in the BBC central UGC hub area 30 minutes after it first happened and were on air or on BBC sites shortly afterwards. We receive around 200,000 messages a month and get around 12 million page impressions to the debates monthly. (Vicky Taylor, Editor, BBC Interactive)[82]

This has meant adopting new technology, such as software, which brings all content into one area where thumbnails are displayed and audio video and pictures are separated into two areas. This is then put into folders and tagged for future use. But Assistant Editor at the Hub, Matthew Eltringham, is clear that the BBC is a trusted journalistic brand and that putting UGC on air does not mean they are surrendering editorial control.

> We still have to check everything that we use in the same way that journalists have to verify conventional witnesses or material. We speak to people who contact us and we check out what they say. People come to us because we are the BBC and we are trusted so we are not going to compromise on our standards. (Matthew Eltringham, Assistant Editor, BBC Interactive)[83]

Some Net radicals will criticize them for this desire to retain control, but it is clear that they are opening up vast possibilities for the public to be part of broadcasting and adding great value to the BBC's journalistic operation. Very soon they will have to reconsider whether they do separate the citizen from the journalist.

The BBC News has already embraced interactivity and networked news processes. However, it can go much further to challenge its own culture without losing its values. Historically, the BBC has fostered an institutional Reithianism that reifies public service broadcasting while resisting any attempt to share it. Despite the best efforts of well-intentioned managers, it is still a closed system. Networked Journalism allows the BBC an opportunity to share its resources in a more open way. It should become a facilitator and a commissioner of citizen journalism and of community media. This will mean that it loses some of its power. But there is no reason why it cannot sustain its core functions of filtering, editing, and packaging, while surrendering some managerial oversight over all the activities that it supports. Letting go may also involve BBC funds being devolved to local or specialist communities. The model would be similar to the production of party political broadcasts now, but on a bigger more systematic scale. Another model would be the BBC World Service Trust, which draws upon the corporation's media skills to support media development throughout the world. The BBC provides the technical resource but the producer or client helps determine content. Any price paid in terms of a dilution of editorial control at the margins will be more than compensated for by the long-term value of engagement. The BBC has always been superb at relating to its audience as an audience, but now it must bring them into the newsroom. The BBC is fortunate in that it has vast resources to make this happen. But other public service broadcasters have even more reason to do so, because they do not enjoy the financial backing of a license fee. They have an economic as well as moral motive to retain their social role.

2.7.1   Public service/private sector

In Britain a debate is now raging about the very nature of public service journalism. With the analogue switch off in 2012 the broadcasting regulator Ofcom will have to propose a different way to subsidize the news media. It is a debate that has ramifications across the media world. Ofcom gives three main reasons for considering a revolution in the financing of public service broadcasting:

- The rapid take-up of digital television is reducing the viewing share of the traditional public service broadcasters, and hence the value of the analogue spectrum.
- Viewers – especially younger audiences – are increasingly watching content on Internet and mobile platforms, and are starting to move away from traditional TV.
- Changes in spectrum policy will affect the way in which public service aims need to be financed in the future. (Ofcom PSB Report)[84]

Certainly the first two reasons apply globally. And I would suggest that this debate effects all news media organizations for two reasons. First, with convergence we will all soon be broadcasters of some sort. Second, in the new media landscape the value of public service journalism should be recognized by society throughout the media. In a Web 2.0 world what we read and listen to is just as important as what we watch.

In the UK, Ofcom's answer is a Public Service Provider. It is currently consulting on what form that should take and it promises to be anything but a genteel discussion. Everyone in the private sector from *Discovery* to the *Daily Telegraph* will be able to make the argument that they are contributing to public service broadcasting. If you define public service as diversity and authority in news then surely *Sky News* has a case? If you define it as fostering community arts, then surely the excellent local newspaper website for *Newbury Today*[85] with its video reports on village rock festivals should qualify? Does it have to be news media at all?

Some of the PSP's services would not resemble linear programming at all. For example, the PSP could harness the lessons of gaming to develop models for the successful engagement of audiences – for instance considering issues of health, social welfare, political engagement and economic policy. (Ofcom PSB Report)[86]

I think that in an age of Networked Journalism we have to think this broadly about public service. The fundamental definition was always that public service was what filled in the gaps of market failure. But that is an essentially negative distinction that looks over-simplistic in a digital democracy. The Internet is, in itself, a public service because it is, in principle, a free structure for communication. We have to decide what kind of journalism we want. Most will still be provided by the market. But where it is not, the case to be made for public service must be based on services and not institutions.

2.7.2   Public service, networked democracy

We are beginning to see the potential for a genuine revolution in the delivery of public services through harnessing interactive media. Many government services are migrating online and, in the process, are taking on some of characteristics which would once have been the preserve of public service broadcasting. This applies even more to cultural activities such as the arts, museums and galleries sector which – in many cases – are moving beyond simply providing access to cultural artefacts, into a mode where many institutions are finding that the facilitation of learning, understanding and participation are more central to their missions than ever before. These and others present compelling reasons why we might want to extend the case for public service broadcasting and re-evaluate it in the light of changing circumstances by looking at it in the wider context of public service delivery as a whole and diminishing the special status which we have previously given to mass media. (Anthony Lilley, *Magic Lantern*)[87]

The new public service journalism has to be part of a new democratic compact between state and citizen. This includes recognizing that journalism or the news media is about realizing the potential of greater media literacy. I will deal with that in a later chapter. But as Lilley says, the very nature of public service media is changing. Governance itself is going online. Public culture and education is going online. Much of this is happening at a low level in the media food chain. And it is being driven from the grass-roots upwards. Networked Journalism is by its nature more democratic. It is both a way of measuring and delivering public service where a need is identified. Instead of handing subsidy over to the professionals and the media organizations, society can insist upon the public sharing the process.

There are other benefits from Networked Public Service Journalism:

- It allows the former audience to become participants in the process. They have part ownership so they will take responsibility.
- The public service journalism can be delivered more cheaply. The public will provide content but it will also be easier to target content at specific communities of need.
- It will be more open to funding from other sources such as Foundations, Corporate Social Responsibility Schemes, and local government because there is a direct public involvement.

Public Service Journalism is already migrating away from its traditional homes. Serious long-form journalism is actually expanding, if you take into account the burgeoning market for topical non-fiction books. In the past a serious journalist might spend months researching and writing an article that would fill part of a magazine or a half hour documentary. Now she writes a book. In the past charities spent money on PR. Now Foundations are increasingly looking to fund journalism directly to promote knowledge about a cause or in general. The semi-academic journalism website *Opendemocracy.net* is supported in this way. Its CEO Tony Curzon Prize told me that they are a public service business:

> We have 3 million unique users a year and what they are after is authenticity. One of the most exciting things is that when people give us money they say that "the media is manipulated so we need to give you money." My favorite was when someone who sent $50, said we were "the only free website worth paying for." We have insiders all over the place who have ideas and things to say. And we've got 3 million minds who are interested. The business model is that we broker ideas to minds. Those 3 million people are the equivalent of advertisers and they will pay a premium. 10 "people" cover 90 percent of our costs – they are mainly US foundations. It's a commercial model because it pays my salary and many others. It is extremely commercial; we are selling minds to foundations. (Tony Curzon Prize, CEO, *Opendemocracy.net*)[88]

This is just one way forward for redefining public service media through the model of Networked Journalism. But I would argue that journalism as a whole is a public service. Networked Journalism allows all the news media to make a social claim, even when its product is not overtly solving a market failure. But there is much more that Networked Journalism can do.

We have seen that Networked Journalism is a way of defining the latest historic manifestation of the news media. We have seen how different it is from what has gone before. I have made the case that it can be profitable and that it can produce public value. This is why I think that we can be optimistic and claim that we are on the verge of something like a Super Media. This is why journalism is worth saving. In the next sections of the book I want to look at how journalism can save the world. What can it do for our politics in an age when terror and community are so important? And I also want to explore how our understanding of journalistic diversity and literacy must change to realize the progressive ideal of a more connected, cosmopolitan global journalism.

Chapter Summary

- Networked Journalism is a hybrid of Citizen Journalism and Mainstream "professional" journalism.
- Networked Journalism uses New Media technology alone or in combination with traditional practices.
- It is about a more open, shared process rather than the end product.
- It retains the core journalistic functions of filtering, editing, and packaging and performs the key journalistic roles of reporting, analysis, and comment.
- It replaces hierarchical and linear modes of production and consumption with multi-dimensional interaction.
- It uses multiple areas of communication such as wikis, blogs, and social networking.
- It enables journalism to cross the old limits of time and distance.
- It allows the journalist to engage more fully with both the audience and the subject.
- It increases trust and transparency.
- It allows the free market to develop different ways of doing media business.
- It allows for a new form of public service journalism that is more broadly defined and more widely applied that produces a new compact between society and journalism.

3

"Will Nobody Do Anything to Help?"
Networked Journalism and Politics

3.1 Introduction

> *It used to be thought – and I include myself in this – that help was on the horizon. New forms of communication would provide new outlets to by-pass the increasingly shrill tenor of traditional media. In fact, the new forms can be even more pernicious, less balanced, more intent on the latest conspiracy theory multiplied by five.*
>
> (Tony Blair, MP)[1]

The reporting of politics is the most important function of journalism. It is how societies have a conversation about power. How else can we have a meaningful debate beyond our most local community except through the news media?

In this chapter I am going to explore the way that Networked Journalism is changing the terms of that debate and how it can do so in the future.

There is a deep democratic deficit across much of the world. In the past 30 years we have seen the expansion of representative democratic systems across much of the globe, and yet politics is seen to be in crisis. The legitimacy of politicians and the engagement of citizens are deeply in question. In an age of "mediation politics" in the so-called "global village"[2] the debate about this gulf between ideal and reality is increasingly situated in the news media itself. The expansion of the Internet and digital communications accelerates this tendency. They appear to offer increased opportunities for enhanced democratic discourse. So institutions are looking to invest even more in the political potential of the media. But as we saw in Chapter 1, the new media also provides a route for disengagement and fragmentation of the public sphere.

The response to this has been clumsy. At present much of the policy on public engagement is the wrong way around. There is an assumption that contemporary mainstream politics is important. Policy-makers appear convinced that their way of working can be adapted to engage the public without any profound changes. This is very similar to the way that many in the mainstream media once viewed their consumers. It was felt that if the product was revamped and if new media was exploited to provide new platforms, then surely the audience would return. In the cases of both politics and the media this ignores a much longer-term trend in disengagement from traditional politics and mainstream media coverage. As I suggested in the previous chapter, both politics and political reporting has to move to where the public is going. Indeed, the politicians and media should be leading the way. The news media is learning that lesson very quickly, spurred on by commercial imperatives. Politicians are moving at different speeds on this, but all are behind the public's own attitudinal shifts.

This is not to say that there was a Golden Age of deep engagement, some democratic polis where people, politicians, and the media shared a common space on equal terms. There are various myths about the popular press in the past. These myths exaggerate the power of the media and the degree to which public opinion is able to flow as a direct democratic force. For example, one piece of received wisdom is that the US Network TV News shows somehow turned the course of the Vietnam War. In fact Nixon was re-elected at the height of the media campaign revealing the horrors of the war in south-east Asia. In the UK there is the legend of the intelligent tabloid, such as the *Daily Mirror* in the 1960s and 1970s. According to some like John Pilger[3,4] (who was there and did do some crusading journalism of the highest order), it was uniquely able to combine campaigning left-wing politics with a popular touch. If this Golden Age of intelligent tabloids ever did exist, it was brief and unsustainable. As we discussed in Chapter 1, the periods when high politics and serious journalism were truly part of a common popular culture were always questionable. Indeed, it is arguable that in a progressive open society, journalism, politics, and the public should always be in tension and not reconciled. As soon as the relationship becomes settled then it is already in decay.

In most Western countries at the moment, the reporting of politics has never been more extensive, detailed, and professional. Anybody interested in the proceedings of Congress, or Westminster, or Brussels, or the United Nations is super-served thanks to online information and digital and 24 hour news channels. Official and independent political websites now offer vast amounts of primary data. There are thousands of specialist online and magazine publications that provide research and commentary on all aspects of the world's political machinery. But this is targeted largely at the politically engaged elite and the fear is that the rest of the population is not paying attention.

The wider public has available to it a greater amount of political information than ever before. The media provide instant reportage, analysis, and commentary on the political process as it happens. Yet most of the evidence is that people find it a turn-off. This could be because people are less interested in mainstream politics. After the extraordinary spectacle of the end of the Cold War and the phase of democratic liberalization from 1989 onwards, the drama of politics has become less compelling on its main stages. History is by no means over, but political history is not being made so much by party leaders and governments as by economic, social, religious, and ethnic forces. The political story has become too complex for conventional political journalism. Mainstream politics in many Western states is going through a dull phase where the ideological fault-lines do not seem to go so deep. The 2007 French Presidential elections were notable for the clear contrast in character and policies between the two candidates. Turnout was high. But this was exceptional and differences probably exaggerated. In an age of anxiety about global risks such as terror and climate change, the narrow party political discourse can seem sterile. In a time of greater individual personal freedom and responsibility the mainstream political process seems more remote and less vital to our real lives. This is not necessarily a bad thing in itself. At the same time there is evidence that people are still very concerned about other forms of politics and want to engage with the big issues. There is increasing philanthropy and charitable giving and growing membership of pressure groups and special interest campaigns.[5,6] It is not that people are less "political," but more that mainstream politics does not deal with the right issues in a relevant or trusted way. The problem for the mainstream media is that it is still covering that kind of politics. So the public indifference and distrust of politics applies equally to political journalism. However, the media must also take some of the blame itself.

There are extraordinarily high expectations of the media's role in politics and a widespread disillusion with the part that it actually plays.[7] I am deeply suspicious of research data on trust. I think it is very difficult to measure, let alone over time. I suspect that people voice greater distrust to opinion pollsters than they actually feel. It is fashionable to appear worldly wise and cynical. To a degree it is a kind of intellectual laziness. But, even allowing for that caveat, the figures do not look good. Surveys suggest that in the US and Europe trust in the news media has fallen by about a quarter over the past two decades. *Pew* studies talk of a drop from 80 percent to 59 percent in "newspaper believability." Likewise, TV networks used to enjoy trust about 80 percent, while now the highest score is 66 percent. More specifically, the number of Americans who believe that their media is politically biased has risen from 42 percent to 60 percent.[8] This is a long-term trend but it is not irreversible. Indeed, more Americans approved of the coverage of the 2006 elections (42 percent) then approved in 2004 of the media (33 percent). Trust can go up as well as down. I think that the *Pew Media Report* summary for 2006 of the US situation applies internationally:

> About the best that can be said for the public's view of the press is that the situation is no longer on a steady and general decline.
>
> Americans continue to appreciate the role they expect the press to play, and by some measure that appreciation is even growing.
>
> But when it comes to how the press is fulfilling those responsibilities, the public's confidence continued to slip[9]

Increased skepticism on the part of the public about political media and politics itself is not necessarily a bad thing. A reflex questioning attitude is surely a healthy stance to take to those in power, be they in the media or government. However, it can become destructive and divisive if it turns in to a complacent cynicism that automatically rejects the idea of politics as a rational and vital part of human society. There are physical limits to the public's engagement with politics. This is something that politicians and political journalists often forget. Not everyone wants to be on the school board or canvassing voters. And likewise not everyone wants to spend their time consuming politically edifying journalism. We have lives to lead. But the figures and common experience tells us quite clearly that the kind of political media we have and the politics it attempts to represent does not match public aspirations. So the public want better political journalism, but mainstream media fails to deliver. The gap is partly because of the much wider public drift away from traditional media that we described in Chapter 1. But it is also because much of mainstream political media really *is* biased, partial, and shallow. It *is* obsessed by political process and commercial profit. And it really *is* generally unconscious and regardless of what its audience cares about.

Networked Journalism offers the potential to address this problem. Some would argue that the new technologies and the new social conditions that are changing the news media also offer a chance to change politics. Long-time Democrat campaigner and Internet evangelist Joe Trippi is adamant: "There is only one tool, one platform, one medium that allows the American people to take their government back, and that's the Internet."[10]

In what way can the idea of Networked Journalism shape these developments? We are starting to see the emergence of a complementary culture to the mainstream of political journalism. It is not the same as the media counter-cultures that have deliberately set themselves apart from or in opposition to mainstream politics in the past. This is not analogous to the underground journalism of the 1960s in the US or the Samizdat media in Eastern European Communist countries before 1989. Very often the new forms of alternative media are seeking to impact upon the mainstream rather than offer an altogether separate model. Their content as opposed to their form is not always politically radical. I do not deny that the Internet is spawning genuinely counter-cultural models of journalism. But I am interested here in the majority of independent new media journalism that intersects with mainstream media and politics because that is where Networked Political Journalism is being created.

The Internet is already playing a high-profile role in recent US election campaigns. The US is a resource-rich early adopter of new media, so what happens there is at the same time both pioneering and exceptional. It offers clues rather than prescriptions for the future. Online reporting and campaigning has become a significant factor in the mainstream media and the main party campaigns. It has also allowed the creation of a system of "netroots" activism and alternative political media. But can this be described as Networked Journalism? Just because Hillary Clinton launched her campaign online doesn't mean that the bloggers or *YouTube* now determine political reporting.

There is a contrasting scenario in Westminster where the political bloggers often deny any journalistic or political pretensions. Yet they are intimately involved in the reporting of Parliamentary politics in the UK. Will this form the kernel of a new kind of political journalism in Britain? The authorities are keen to use online platforms as a way of boosting voter participation. Some recent experiments such as the British government's e-petition scheme have had unexpected results. In the UK and across Europe there is a lot of money being poured in to the idea that New Media might revive popular interest in politics. But without an understanding of how the news media must become more genuinely connected with the public, it is difficult to see how it can succeed.

The ultimate test of the new age of mediated politics is whether it can play a part in the development of regions that are not rich in technological resources. Africa is adopting new media but at a pace and in a way that is specific to its needs. There have been huge strides forward in recent decades in democracy in Africa. But there is still a crisis in accountability and governance across much of the continent. The failure to establish a thriving pluralistic press means that the role of the media in African political development is still potential rather than proven. Can the Networked Journalism paradigm fit the African practice? First, let us look at the impact of forms of Networked Journalism in the US.

3.2   Networked Journalism and US Politics

The US has the most and least democratic system of politics in the world. It offers the greatest access to open political choice to anyone prepared to vote and campaign. And yet the professionalization of US politics means it has become so dominated by money that power feels more mediated by fund-raising than policy debates. This is the nation that pioneered most modern techniques of electioneering. Spin doctors, attack adverts, and rebuttal units all emerged first from US campaign teams. In a mediated age, many of those practices are directed squarely at the media. Indeed, through political TV advertising, US political machines have *become* the media. There is no question that New Media is now very much part of this process. But, this is the interesting question: is it changing it? My answer is: "Yes" in process, "Soon" in practice, and "Perhaps" in principle.

The figures are already impressive. The US is an early adopting nation. According to the Pew Trust, in the year of the 2004 presidential elections 42 percent of Americans had broadband,[11] 37 percent of Americans used the Internet for political information[12] and 13 million went online for political acts, such as donations to candidates.[13] Spending on political Internet advertising has risen from $29 million in 2004 to $40 million in the 2006 mid-term elections. But that is still only 2 percent of all political media spend – compare it with $2 billion spent on terrestrial TV ads. The 2008 campaign is already suggesting that those figures are rising rapidly. Internet activists would argue that there are different effects at work here. Most of them will be marginal, but in politics it is the marginal that matters. If there are a few percentage points that can be shifted then a whole campaign can gain or lose momentum. And, as we shall see, it is very often the marginal voter that decides close results.

Internet activists would also argue that the way they impact on politics is quite different to previous campaigns' use of communications. In the past there was a division between straight-forward activist voter campaigning and activist media campaigning. The former involved leafleting, canvassing, letter writing, phone banks and town hall meetings. The latter involved TV adverts, lobbying of journalists, and media appearances. The Internet brings the two categories together. Email, online video, websites and web forums allow activists to get their message out and then engage in a dialogue with the voters. The Internet gives activists an easy opportunity to canvass and converse with the voter without having to use mainstream media at all.

The great example of this is, of course, the internet-based liberal lobby group *MoveOn*, and its campaign to secure for Howard Dean the Democrat nomination for President in 2004. There is no doubt that web forums such as *The Daily Kos* are now part of the fabric of US politics with the ability to generate debate and money for causes they seize upon.

What I am particularly interested in is not the fund-raising email traffic but the more blog-related Internet activism. It is very difficult to separate them out. Indeed, one of the interesting aspects of New Media and politics is the way that policy communication, fund-raising, discussion, and simple mud-slinging can all be combined through the connectivity of new media communications. For example, an activist will post a compromising video on *YouTube* and then link to it in email fund-raising messages. Then all you have to do is stand back and wait for mainstream media to pick up on the story.

3.2.1   A decade of blog power

This is not entirely new. The US already has a decade-old history of Internet sites and bloggers impacting on political journalism. In January 1998 the *Drudge Report* broke the story about Clinton's affair with Monica Lewinsky. Although, of course, Drudge was actually publishing a story that mainstream media had uncovered but not revealed, as the original Drudge posting makes clear:

> The DRUDGE REPORT has learned that reporter Michael Isikoff developed the story of his career, only to have it spiked by top NEWSWEEK suits hours before publication. A young woman, 23, sexually involved with the love of her life, the President of the United States, since she was a 21-year-old intern at the White House. She was a frequent visitor to a small study just off the Oval Office where she claims to have indulged the president's sexual preference. (Matt Drudge, *Drudge Report*)[14]

In 2002 Senator Trent Lott resigned after comments he made implying support for racial segregation. The actual remarks were made at an event covered by *C-SPAN*, the cable politics channel. But the mainstream media did not follow it up. Instead it was left to bloggers like *Atrios* to express their rage and to do the historical fact-checking and contextualization.[15] The bloggers unearthed previous occasions when Lott had made similar remarks. This turned a one-off indiscretion in to a behavioral pattern. At that point the political correspondents returned to the fray and Lott was forced to retract and resign as Majority Leader. The blogs did not "get" Lott on their own, but they forced the mainstream media to do its job.[16]

Bloggers have also turned on the journalists themselves. In September 2004 Dan Rather, the famous CBS News anchor, resigned after blogs appeared to show that a news story on *60 Minutes* was based upon forged unsubstantiated evidence that has become known as the "Killian Documents." The post on the *Free Republic* web forum is worth reading in full. Its author, "Buckhead," demonstrates perfectly how the Internet allows the activist to tap in to the expert knowledge of the "amateur":

> Every single one of these memos to file is in a proportionally spaced font, probably Palatino or Times New Roman.
>
> In 1972 people used typewriters for this sort of thing, and typewriters used monospaced fonts.
>
> The use of proportionally spaced fonts did not come into common use for office memos until the introduction of laser printers, word processing software, and personal computers. They were not widespread until the mid to late 90s . . . I am saying these documents are forgeries, run through a copier for 15 generations to make them look old.
>
> This should be pursued aggressively. ("Buckhead" on *freerepublic.com*)[17]

Dan Rather is still contesting his removal from CBS and the facts of this case. But it certainly demonstrates the effort and skills that bloggers can deploy in their critique of conventional media. In February 2005 CNN's chief news executive, Eason Jordan, had to resign after an Internet campaign prompted by his claim that US soldiers "targeted" journalists in Iraq. It was an isolated comment made during a private World Economic Forum panel discussion. Ironically, the story first broke through a posting by an attendee of the meeting on the WEF's own blog. The officially sanctioned blogger was Rony Abovitz, a Florida-based "technology pioneer." It was rapidly picked up by right-wing commentators and bloggers and created a blog-storm of patriotic outrage.[18] The meeting was on "Chatham House rules" which means that you can not quote directly from participants. It also meant that the WEF never released the tape of what Eason said. Eason's resignation statement said that "my comments on this subject in a World Economic Forum panel discussion were not as clear as they should have been." Like many people who have spoken out of turn on mainstream media and found their careers ruined, Eason discovered that the Internet is an equally testing medium that can reach into places old media never strayed.

The liberals had their revenge in February 2005 when the left-leaning website *Media Matters for America* uncovered Jeff Gannon. Gannon, real-name Duckert, was supposedly a news wire journalist in the Washington Press Corp. But liberal bloggers revealed him as a Republican activist plant used to ask "soft-ball" questions at otherwise difficult White House press briefings. Oddly, liberal bloggers found themselves exposing someone for being gay and a blogger.[19] But it was clear he was not the "official" mainstream journalist he claimed. Such are the ironies of the Internet age.

3.2.2   Lieberman and Lamont: the Internet wins and loses and wins

In the summer of 2006 Senator Joseph Lieberman, a three-term US Senator and former presidential and vice-presidential nominee, lost the Connecticut Democratic senate primaries to a relatively unknown candidate, Ned Lamont. A net-roots campaign by highly-motivated Democrat activists who opposed Lieberman's pro-Iraq war, pro-Bush, pro-Israel stances galvanized a highly effective and often vicious Internet-led campaign against the incumbent. Ned Lamont enjoyed local and national support from the liberal political blogosphere, both in terms of financial donations and political publicity. Much of this was straightforward campaigning but done online instead of by phone or by leaflet. But the Internet was also used as a channel of communication – it opened up a new forum for argument that helped frame the nature of the campaign. The battleground was the Internet as much as the doorstep. Doctored photos, smearing videos, and polemic were widespread.

Just one day before Democratic voters in Connecticut went to the polls, Senator Lieberman's campaign website crashed. Allegations were thrown around from both sides, some saying it was hacked by the Lamont campaign, others saying that Lieberman forgot to pay his bills. Lieberman's Wikipedia site became another place for political skirmishing as rival posters attempted to re-edit the Senator's online biography. At one point the *Daily Kos* website posted juxtaposed images from a Lieberman TV advert. The script said it showed a sunrise, but his assiduous Internet opponents sourced the photograph and showed that it actually depicted a sunset. It was a symbolic victory, but one that added weight to the implication that not only was Lieberman too right-wing, but that he was not honest.

The Lamont victory in the primary showed that netroot activism has the power to mount dangerous challenges to incumbents who would have previously considered themselves safe. The bloggers were acting like attack journalists. They were reporting on Lieberman in a highly partial manner but it was putting him under real scrutiny in a way that the mainstream media would never have tried. These activists were conducting a form of journalism. They were reporting what Lieberman had done – including the famous "kiss" of George Bush, an image that lived on in perpetuity and exponential multiplication thanks to the Internet.[20] The activists were also creating analytical journalism, albeit highly partisan, trying to explain why their opponents were doing what they were doing and saying what they were saying.

In a sense this is a trend that has developed alongside the Internet. Other politically partial media organizations such as *Fox News* have found a ready audience for more ideologically driven coverage. US politics has always been adept at creating and dealing with interested parties. Now the Internet and digital technology is allowing the news media to join that plurality of pressure groups. Making concessions to the traditional interest groups has long been a necessary strategy for US politicians if they want to survive. This is for a very simple reason: it is the interest groups who have the wealth and influence to support potential replacements. What the Lieberman–Lamont campaign has shown, however, is that netroot activism has acquired those powers as well. The power that the netroot activists hold is multi-faceted. Traditional interest groups have the financial clout of a collection of wealthy individuals, yet netroot activists can generate a similar power via their sheer numbers. Ned Lamont's campaigns got the majority of its funding from blog-based donations. The traditional interest groups are able to supply their chosen candidate with the necessary funds to deal with the PR and media tasks. But the netroot activists have taken the power of new media into their own hands. They create the videos, write the reports, make the allegations and publicize it all through their own networks. With the mainstream media flocking round blogs, this user-generated content is becoming increasingly influential.

Blogs now have a role in setting the parameters of the debate. Bloggers were determined that Lieberman's pro-war position needed challenging, so the parameters of the primary were set in terms of pro and anti-Iraq War.

Lieberman had no real choice as to which side he was going to be aligned with. Yet the debate itself remains in the hands of the politicians. Policies are not created by polemical ranting on a blog. But to be able to create those policies, US politicians will increasingly need to operate within the bounds being set by netroots activists.

Of course, Joe Lieberman has now won Connecticut as an "Independent," beating Ned Lamont. It shows that the netroots activists and bloggers are by no means all-powerful. There was an element of the netroots story becoming a factor in its own right. When the election went out to the public as a whole – as opposed to the much more connected community of Democrats eligible to vote in primaries – the influence of the Internet was diluted. It is not being ignored, though. All the evidence from the Democrat Presidential Primaries is that the blogosphere is a growing factor. At the same time it is becoming professionalized, with Hillary Clinton putting on faux amateur films on to *YouTube*.[21] The net-roots are the new roots and they are here to stay.

3.2.3   *YouTube* political reporting

Blogging was once primarily about text. But increasingly it is about online video. Anyone can write, but for a television culture, the power of the moving image is what has the most direct impact. The crucial thing about these videos is they do not go away. In the past, the effect of an aggressive comment towards an annoying activist in a car park would last only as long as the media networks aired the footage. Now those clips are copied onto hard disks across the world and are viewed by thousands of users, over and over again. There is nothing that the campaign effort can do to remove them; they simply have to fight fire with fire and hope that their opponent is victim to a greater number of videos tipping the balance in their favor. In this sense the 2006 mid-term elections were another online turning point. *YouTube* didn't even exist in the 2004 election but now it have may have helped decide the Senate and so create a lame-duck President.

Senator George Allen's race in Virginia hinged on just a few thousand votes. How many people downloaded the *YouTube* video of his infamous "macaca" gaffe – where he used racist language to an opposition volunteer who was filming Allen's rally speech? Nearly 400,000.[22] Another video which showed his campaign security staff manhandling a liberal blogger was watched by 180,000. They can not all have been Democrat partisans or people from out of state. Many must have been potential supporters who were persuaded not to vote for him by what they saw. And, of course, the people who downloaded it talked about it and forwarded it in emails, so the effect rippled outwards and Allen's chances were sunk.

The 2006 election in Missouri was another marginal, settled by about 20,000 swing voters. Michael J. Fox, who suffers from Parkinson's disease, made a TV advert in support of the Democrat candidate Claire McCaskill, a supporter of stem cell research. That didn't get much attention. What did was a video of right-wing "shock jock" Rush Limbaugh's attack on Fox in which he implied the former actor was exaggerating the effects of his condition. More than 1.1 million people downloaded that video. Surely Limbaugh's comments and Fox's dignified rebuttal can only have helped secure victory for Republican Jim Talent's opponent.[23] McCaskill's Internet-aided victory meant the Republicans lost control of the Senate.

It is one thing to post clips on to a website – be it user-generated, such as the Allen "macaca" incident, or clipped from mainstream media, such as the Limbaugh footage. But what we are witnessing in the latest presidential campaign is also an explosion of "creativity" in online political video. How much of this is truly citizen media as opposed to sly viral confections by campaign teams is going to be difficult to judge. Is the "Obama Girl" video a positive or negative for Senator Barack Obama?[24] It certainly casts him in a good light and adds a sense of humor to his image.

This culminated in the *CNN/YouTube* Presidential candidate debates of July 2007 (see Figure 3.1). More than 3,000 people posted their video questions, but only 39 were selected by CNN for the two-hour show. It was a strange mixture of mainstream and new media which kept editorial control in CNN's hands. But it also allowed slightly edgier topics to creep in to the debate and it certainly posed them in a different way. There were questions about health from two brothers spoon-feeding dinner to a father suffering from Alzheimer's; about Darfur from an American in a refugee camp; and about gun laws from a man cradling a rifle which he described as his "baby." John Edwards' campaigner Joe Trippi thought the debate was a "freewheeling" success. Obama's strategist David Axelrod said his man "relished it. He thinks the American people have been cut out of Washington politics." But blogger Jeff Jarvis felt that an opportunity had been missed:

> [The questions] CNN chose . . . were insipid, sophomoric, pointless, and silly: someone held up a coin and asked the candidates to define the words there – "In God we trust." A snowman sock puppet asked about global warming . . . The two media did not mix well. CNN displayed the *YouTube* videos in

Figure 3.1   CNN/YouTube debate – Candidates stand at their respective podiums during the CNN/YouTube Democratic Presidential Candidates Debate July 23, 2007 at the Citadel Military College in Charleston, South Carolina (Photo © Stan Honda/AFP/Getty Images)

small squares on a big screen shot by a big camera – reduced, finally, to postage stamps on our screens. It seemed the network was ashamed to show the videos full-screen because they would not look like real TV. But, of course, that's just the point. They weren't real TV. They were bits of conversation. (Jeff Jarvis, Media Commentator)[25]

I think Jeff Jarvis is being a bit harsh and possibly a little puritanical. Perhaps the *CNN/YouTube* debate's main achievement was that it managed to bring the Democrat contest to a wider and younger online audience. Perhaps it has set them to thinking harder about how they will project their political views in the future. At the moment most overtly party political videos on *YouTube* are simply clips from mainstream media coverage or campaign adverts. In future the politicians will have to be more creative if they are to join that wider conversation happening online.

The bloggers in the US think 2008 is their year. Mainstream media remains dull and uninspiring with the exception of *Fox News* or *Jon Stewart's Daily Show*. In the face of falling ratings the political corps is sticking resolutely to the tried and tested formulae. This is why the self-appointed Queen of liberal political blogging, Adriana Huffington, has put together a project with the academic prince of Internet discourse, Jay Rosen. They are going to create a blog network of citizen journalists to report on the campaign. It has a bold manifesto:

> Our volunteer reporters will aim to provide an authentic counter-narrative to the lockstep consensus we often get from the mainstream media, and will take inspiration from bottom up efforts . . . given the right circumstances, large groups of people are smarter than an elite few. (*Huffingtonpost.com*)[26]

It is a brave and interesting attempt to aggregate and focus the efforts of citizen journalism to have a real impact on the way that a campaign is reported. This is quite different to the self-determined blogging storms that I cited above. It is an attempt to cohere, if not corporatize, the blogosphere. At this point it becomes Networked Journalism.

The candidates certainly agree that blogging is important. All the campaigns now have interactive or Internet campaign directors. And all of the Democrat hopefuls turned up for the political blogfest that is the *Daily Kos* annual convention. But while the bloggers and politicos conduct their love-in it is possible that the audience/voter is shifting elsewhere. Political pages on social networking sites such as *MySpace* and *Facebook* are getting much more traffic from regular voters than the hard-core political blogs. They may not be setting the political agenda, but they are certainly where the bulk of personal conversation takes place. The Presidential candidates know this and have all set up personal spaces. The comments on these spaces are a breath of fresh air. Inevitably there are disruptive postings and the candidates obviously do not have a lot of time to respond. So, in that sense, they are not quite entering in to the spirit of the genre. However, anyone reading the interaction on the three main Democrat candidate sites[27–29] cannot but be impressed at the diversity of the people, the range of opinions and the originality of what they have to say. It is chat rather than deep debate, but it suggests a connectedness that only the Internet can offer. In that sense I think Jeff Jarvis is right with his general view that the Internet is "opening up a dialogue between candidate and constituent that was not possible before the Internet".

In his book, *The Argument*, Matt Bai questions the success of the Internet in changing actual policies. But he has no doubt that it has changed politics:

> It hardly mattered whether the progressive blogs were reaching 500,000 readers or 5 million. However many people came to blogs like *Daily Kos* they were the people who cared most about politics, and thus, they were the most likely to evangelise everyone they knew. The advent of the broadband Internet had made viral marketing the single most efficient way of getting an idea across to select consumers, and the political blogs were about as viral as Bird Flu. (Matt Bai, *The Argument*)[30]

Email, online video, websites and web forums allow activists to get their message out and then engage in a dialogue with the voters and the news media. The Internet allows journalists to do the same in their political coverage. This is Networked Journalism. Whether this will lead to a more Networked politics and whether that politics will produce different policies and governance is the big question. No doubt the 2008 Presidential race will give us some clues. But fundamental shifts in power will take longer to show than the short history of the Internet and politics in the US allows.

3.2.4   Networked Journalism and British politics

> They must tell the plain, simple truth that this generation has the capacity to destroy the human race. Because of technology and the advance of science, it also has the capacity to save it. The information we get about that choice is integral to the role of a journalist and crucial to our survival. (Tony Benn)[31]

British politicians are rarely tempted to indulge in high-minded rhetoric about New Media. So it is interesting that Tony Benn, a veteran socialist, has seized upon the political importance of the Internet:

> It is quite clear that the Internet poses a serious threat to the privileges of the rich and powerful. All the emphasis on crime and drugs and pornography used to justify the suppression of the Internet is really aimed at suppressing knowledge of the radical political alternatives that are now available. (Tony Benn)[32]

Mr. Benn was in power the last time a British Prime Minister, Harold Wilson, got excited about "The White Heat of Technology." That ended in the White Elephant of the supersonic jet Concorde. But this time Mr. Benn thinks that technological innovation will bring political benefits as well as economic gains. There are other politicians now in high places in Government, such as the current British Foreign Secretary David Miliband, who have dabbled in blogging and seem conscious of the new information age. The former Prime Minister Tony Blair famously admitted that he barely knew how to use a PC when he became Labour leader, let along surf the net. But he and his administration rapidly came to understand the importance of the digital dividend:

> There is no new economy. There is one economy all of it being transformed by information technology. What is happening is no dot.com fad that will come and go – it is a profound economic revolution. (Tony Blair, MP)[33]

He put all Government services online and invested in persuading the education system and business to prioritize digital investment and training. However, I do not believe that he ever really considered the impact of the Internet on the way that politics itself would be reported. As he left power in 2007 he seemed as disappointed with New Media and politics as he was disturbed by the news media overall. He even went so far as to advocate increased regulation of online journalism:

> As the technology blurs the distinction between papers and television, it becomes increasingly irrational to have different systems of accountability based on technology that no longer can be differentiated in the old way. (Tony Blair, MP)[34]

Which Tony is right? In a mature and, some would say, sclerotic democracy like Britain's, there is a sense that politics and journalism are locked in a dying embrace. The waltz of spin and distortion has become a *danse macabre*. The public is increasingly disaffected by conventional politics and mainstream media coverage. Does the Internet offer the potential to inject some life back into the relationship? This matters. For all the talk of e-democracy and direct digital governance the majority of political discourse is still conducted through the media. As the media become more complex and increasingly connected with other forms of communication a new dynamic is evolving. Let us have a look at one case study of this new relationship.

3.2.5 "Three Jags" and the bloggers

> The narrative currently is that a conspiracy of politically motivated bloggers are doing down Prescott. The reality is that the truth is doing down Prescott . . . The truth is that our political system is rotten and the politicians are allowed

to get away with it by enfeebled lobby journalists who would rather keep their relationships sweet than their readers fully informed. (Paul Staines aka "Guido Fawkes")[35]

This is the story of the former British Deputy Prime Minister John Prescott, his secretary Tracey, a US billionaire and a blog named after a seventeenth-century terrorist. It is the story of some cowboy boots, an office affair and the Millennium Dome. It is also the moment when the blogosphere staked its claim for a walk-on part in political journalism in Britain. Some would argue that bloggers were only a minor factor, but I would suggest that, combined with other digital forces, they are opening up the potential for a more Networked form of political journalism. This was a very British affair. Westminster politics is a peculiarly parochial and centralized business. The UK national media is unusual in that it is centered exclusively in the capital city. And the political media is based at the heart of the ancient quarter of Westminster. But I think that this story and the way it was treated does suggest how political reporting is going to change with respect to all parliamentary democracies as the information exchange goes online, and the debate leaves the corridors of power to the co-axial cables of the Internet.

The actual details of this case study are complex and much is still lost in the mists of denial and innuendo. Those readers who are not familiar with either this story or British politics should not worry. Sit back and enjoy a narrative that is on a par with a comedic version of *The Da Vinci Code*. Put briefly, the John Prescott/Tracey Temple/Philip Anschutz story was in fact two stories that intertwined for a couple of months in 2006. It began with a conventional sex scandal exposed in the newspapers in classic kiss and tell fashion. First the aggrieved truck-driver husband and then the woman herself told their tale of a Whitehall sexual farce. The British Deputy Prime Minister John Prescott's affair with his secretary Tracey Temple gained greater journalistic traction because many of the liaisons took place during working time and on official business and so he may have broken ministerial codes. Bad election results in local elections combined with a row over Mr. Prescott's "grace and favour" country mansion added to the pressure upon this redoubtable politician, who was a favorite with the Labour party grass-roots and key ally of Tony Blair. But what did it for Mr. Prescott was not the sex or the photos of this working-class hero playing croquet in between high level meetings. What fatally wounded Mr. Prescott was a podcast.

David Hencke is an experienced award-winning political correspondent at the *Guardian* newspaper who has covered Westminster for decades. On

June 29, 2006 the *Guardian* posted a podcast of "Westminster gossip" by their "investigative ferret" Hencke. What Hencke said on the podcast is worth quoting, as it shows Networked Journalism in action as a newspaper journalist lets down his hair and shares the newsgathering process with the audience:

> Imagine my surprise when I received a rather surprising telephone call with some rather juicy gossip about John Prescott, this came when Mr. Prescott was facing rather a lot of criticism, my source who had contacts in the US, had the rather extraordinary story that Mr. Prescott had paid a secret visit to the ranch home of Philip Anschutz the man who runs the Millennium Dome – furthermore, no-one knew about this, and he'd been entertained there by the man who is a prominent Republican. My source, who believe it or not, had got the information from an over-heard conversation among British diplomats at a restaurant in Los Angeles thought this was red-hot stuff. We put this to Mr. Prescott. Had he had a free trip not declared while he was there? Sadly for us but good for Mr. Prescott he had done this but he had not broken any rules. Sources thought that because this had never been declared Mr. Prescott might be in a bit of trouble. In fact Mr. Prescott had disclosed this to his Permanent Secretary [a senior civil servant] and while accepting the entertainment on this rather posh ranch home of Mr. Anschutz, had made a donation to the British Red Cross rather quietly so that he would not be seen to be taking money from the Americans. So while Mr. Prescott might appear to have got in to a lot of trouble for his croquet games and his mistresses, the story this time was of Honest John the man who made sure he did not break the anti-sleaze laws. (David Hencke, *The Guardian*)[36]

Hencke's belief that the story stopped there was odd, and it is strange that this story, which was at least embarrassing for Prescott, even if not illicit, wasn't followed up by the *Guardian*'s print version. But two days later, on the Saturday, *The Times* broke the whole story of "The Dome, the US billionaire and John Prescott's night on the ranch" as its lead. On the Monday, the right-wing blogger "Guido Fawkes" – real name Paul Staines – weighed in with this attack on John "Prezza" Prescott:

> Prezza's story is falling apart – he stayed the weekend on "a private visit" the cost of which was donated to charity, except it turns out it was paid for by the taxpayer. He had no involvement in the decision making process awarding the billionaire ranch owner the Dome contract, yet we have been told for months he is a hands-on DPM. His story is bollocks. You can tell it is a big story because Nick Robinson [The BBC's political editor] is ignoring it – the Beeb knows this could be fatal for Prezza. Particularly if it is true that the *Daily*

Mail has bought up the eagerly awaited story from an official government driver about Three Shags' backseat fumblings with Rosie Winterton* et al.

*So sue. Rosie threatened to sue *The Sun* if they named her as Prescott's other mistress. Caligula made his horse a senator, making Rosie Winterton a Privy Counsellor is just taking the piss out of the public. (Paul Staines aka *"Guido Fawkes"*)[37]

This is a colorful and frenetic outburst of allegations with no real new information on the Anschutz story. But he has introduced a whole new sexual allegation. That alone was enough to keep up the momentum among the media pack which had by now scented blood. But what is as significant is the attack on the BBC political editor Nick Robinson. There is an assumption even by the blogger that until the main broadcaster carries the story, it has little impact. Staines' conspiracy theory that Robinson is somehow protecting Prescott may have been groundless, but it had an effect.

The following day the story started to go in to a cycle of cross-referencing between mainstream and New Media. The newspapers started to report "rumours on the Internet" although they do not go as far as the blog.

Two web diaries linked to Tory supporters named a Labour MP as Mr. Prescott's mistress, an allegation he and the woman deny . . . One website is run by a Rightwing Tory activist in his late thirties. A Tory spokesman said: "He has no connection whatsoever with the Conservative party. It is categorically untrue that we have been involved in spreading these rumours." The allegations were repeated on another website run by a former Conservative parliamentary candidate. (*Evening Standard*, July 4, 2006)[38]

At this point the online coverage also turned into a spat between the professional blogger, Nick Robinson and the amateurs. In his blog for July 5 the BBC's political editor launched an attack upon the blogs and another Conservative blogger, Iain Dale, in particular:

This is another example of some blogs trying to make the political weather. First, they demand to know why the mainstream media – and, in particular, the BBC – are not covering an alleged "scandal". Then they report unsubstantiated allegations which have been denied by those involved, which some newspapers then report as second hand news.

Let's be clear. This isn't because they are better journalists, free from censorship. They often have a political agenda. (Nick Robinson, Political Editor, BBC)[39]

This is a fascinating moment. Paul "Guido Fawkes" Staines had never pretended to be anything but politically-biased. The strap-line for Staines' site professes that "tittle-tattle, gossip, rumours and wit are what this blog aims to provide."[40] Robinson is entirely right, if a little defensive. The blogs did have an effect and they did drive the story forward, or "make the weather." Guido's next riposte to Robinson delights in the fact that he has riled the BBC's political editor, and he celebrates the power of the unaccountable blog. Guido claims that he has no complaint against Robinson personally, but against the BBC:

> Nick's comment does . . . come over as a tad arrogant, does the BBC have a monopoly on political/weather reporting? Nick is a great reporter, but his hands are tied in an emasculated post-Hutton BBC constantly worried about future funding. If the rest of the media want to follow Guido's reports that is up to them. (Paul Staines aka "Guido Fawkes")[41]

By now the mainstream media was feasting royally off the blogs. When John Prescott finally took to the airwaves to defend himself, he found that the Internet allegations were being thrown at him by the mainstream media journalists. He appeared on the BBC's Radio 4's *Today Programme*, the UK's flagship political morning radio program, to be grilled by the BBC's most ferocious inquisitor, John Humphreys. The BBC journalist demanded: "There are now reports, and they're circulating on the Internet, as you know, that you have had other affairs – is that true?"[42]

This was the moment when blogs had officially arrived in British political journalism. It was a moment which, of course, Guido then reported in turn on his blog:

> John Humphrys did what he is paid to do this morning. Three times he asked Prescott: have there been any other affairs? Three times he blustered without answering the question. Because of course there have been many other affairs, not just "one mistake" as he disingenuously repeated over and over again. (Paul Staines aka "Guido Fawkes")[43]

As is the way with British politics, this all ended up in an internal parliamentary inquiry that found that Mr. Prescott had breached ministerial codes. However, the Commons Standards Committee said no action should be taken against the Deputy Prime Minister because he had subsequently registered the visit. They had no powers to examine the wider issues about conflicts of interest and so Mr. Prescott ended up with a slap on the wrist. But his political career was effectively over. So was this a triumph for the British blogosphere? And what implications does it have for Networked Journalism?

Other political bloggers joined Paul "Guido Fawkes" Staines in celebrating their newfound influence. Conservative blogger Iain Dale[44] does not claim to be a journalist, but he does claim to have moved stories that the mainstream media had left alone. He says that journalists leak to him information that they cannot publish themselves. His complaint is that the professionals use the bloggers' material without attribution:

> On any given day, you will find on *Ephraim Hardcastle* [The *Daily Mail* gossip column], the *Londoner's Diary* and other diary columns two or three stories that they will have got – totally lifted – from me or Guido. No attribution or anything. At least bloggers link back to wherever they first read a story. (Iain Dale, blogger)[45]

The professional journalists who covered this story have insisted to me that the blogs were not decisive in uncovering the facts of this story. But one mainstream political broadcaster did say that the political blogs are now required reading for the hard-pressed modern journalist. She pointed out that they don't have time to spend hanging around in the Westminster bars anymore because they are on air or filing all the time, so the blogs are their way of getting the gossip. Indeed, professional journalists have always used gossip magazines, such as *Private Eye*, as a source for marginal stories and as a place to test out unsubstantiated rumors. However, the blogosphere now makes that an interactive, 24/7, networked phenomenon. That worried some political correspondents:

> My view is what they are doing is completely indefensible. They are hindering, not helping the story. There are serious issues being discussed but they see it as a cheap publicity stunt to get their names in the media. I talk to bloggers and I use them but they print stuff they've got no evidence for. That can't be right.[46]

It is true that bloggers are protected. It is difficult to sue if the site is hosted outside of the UK. Individuals are less liable to litigation and they are not subject to the corporate pressures that a mainstream media brand might feel in trying to protect its reputation for trust-worthiness. The BBC's Nick Robinson's blog is subtly different to his broadcast work. It is more speculative in tone and each item is less "balanced" in the formal sense required

on air. But it is still a long way from the "dangers" he perceives that independent blogs pose:

> Bloggers say something is not being reported because we're wimps.
> Nonsense. It's not being reported because there are no facts. We've got to be
> careful we don't use blogs as an excuse to bypass our own standards, rules
> and ethics of journalism. There is a risk people can use blogs as a way to get
> things on air or into print they wouldn't have conventionally done themselves.
> (Nick Robinson, Political Editor, BBC)[47]

The truth is that political journalists are much more limited in what they
can say than the bloggers. A professional journalist who wants information
from politicians sometimes has to allow themselves to be "used" by politicians. Political journalists should learn to love the blogs. This is partly
because they themselves are increasingly bloggers. Remember, the whole
Prescott saga started with David Hencke's salacious sounding pod-cast.
But it is also because the independent online media does represent a vital
injection of new perspectives and fresh information. It offers an alternative
conduit for political discourse that has its own claim on veracity and per-
spicacity. As "Guido" puts it:

> The days of media conglomerates determining the news in a top-down
> Fordist fashion are over. The news is no longer what Paxman and Robinson
> say it is. Big Media is going to be disintermediated because technology has
> drastically reduced the cost of dissemination. And don't think I'm some out-
> sider blogging in his pyjamas – every broadsheet diarist has taken stories from
> my blog. My sources are the thousands of political junkies who come to the
> blog for gossip. Younger, more savvy journalists whose stories get spiked are
> probably my best sources. (Paul Staines aka "Guido Fawkes")[48]

Tension between journalists, let alone between journalists and those in power,
is one of the defining characteristics of the British political media scene. It does
create an often rancorous climate that can lead to poor quality or partial journalism. That will happen online as well as in the mainstream platforms. It is
also arguable that this competitiveness is what enables the British media to
avoid the cozy, separate culture of the White House or Elysée press corps.
Bloggers will contribute to that competitiveness, but if mainstream journalists
retain their professional quality then surely they have nothing to fear, and
everything to gain, from a more connected relationship? It may not always
be pretty to watch, but Networked Political Journalism is happening at

Westminster. Instead of retreating to old positions, it should be used as a way to open up political journalism and put pressure on government to do the same.

3.2.6   Beyond the blogs: civic engagement

Networked Journalism is not just about blogging or interactivity. Networked Political Journalism goes further than a symbiotic relationship between mainstream media and bloggers. There is a much bigger role for political journalism than simply dealing with the institutions of representative democracy. Civic engagement is becoming more dispersed and some fear it is disappearing. As we have seen, social networking sites are now a forum for political messaging, so they are already evolving a new kind of journalism, too. How the news media inserts itself into that kind of discourse remains to be seen. But if Networked Journalists want to join in that political conversation in these new spaces then it will have to adapt itself.

Networked Political Journalism will also have to look to the new channels of political communication opened up by e-democracy initiatives. All authorities, and increasingly businesses and social organizations, are creating networks with the public. These combine the functionality of the organization's online activities with a desire to communicate in a meaningful way with the consumer or citizen. For example, a local authority website for paying for parking permits can also be used as a way of consulting residents. Those kinds of spaces are where Networked Political Journalism needs to be, in the same way that local journalists used to attend Town Hall meetings. Again, when the Networked Political Journalism "goes" to these new spaces it is on different terms. Now the public will be part of the process helping to set the agenda and control the flow of information. Networked Political Journalism will be the facilitator of that process, not just the reporter.

Too often governments see e-democracy as a way of cutting out the media and establishing a direct relationship between government and the governed. The fact is that a Networked Media is a vital way to make that relationship work in a practical and representative way. The public does not want to have to mediate all the political information flows by itself. Networked Journalism is there to do it with them. Take the UK government's attempt to set up an e-petition system whereby individuals could set up a petition on the 10 Downing Street website. Hundreds were set up, many of them trivial, some serious. The most popular one was a petition against Government proposals for road pricing. More than a million people signed up.[49] There was no way that the Labour Government would accept its demands. It was seen as a dramatic slap in the face for the Prime Minister. And his rejection of the petition demands was seen as evidence that e-democracy is a sham. But the problem was not that the petition was galvanized by lobby groups. Nor that it went counter to government policy. The problem was that it was seen as a policy-influencing exercise rather than a form of communication. And as a form of communication it was crude and very much a one-way street. Tony Blair promised to reply by email to all those who had signed, but a million replica emails is not a deeply meaningful political debate. A Networked Media would have allowed for a much more nuanced representation of those opinions and a healthier conversation with more realistic expectations. A wiki, for example, might have allowed a forum for interaction and a series of blogs would have allowed people to express more worked-out points of views and comment. If nothing else, though, it reminded Government of the public appetite to express itself online and the need for greater humility and openness on the part of those in power.

The ultimate goal of Networked Political Journalism is to address the loss of public trust in the media and politics. I don't want the public to love journalists or politicians. I don't want journalists to love politicians or even the public. But networked news practices offer journalists the potential to get more things right by being connected to and corrected by the public. By sharing the setting of the agenda, it gives a chance to make the news more relevant. It is then up to Government to open up the policy agenda. In the end people can only take so much politics or political reporting. Ultimately, it is about the real actions, not the representations. So I am very suspicious of claims that New Media is automatically more democratic than mainstream media. Many of the new platforms lack accountability and institutional regulation, for example. There are other dangers to political journalism in current trends. There is the fragmentation of the news process in which multiple outlets reduce the sense of a shared conversation. There is the potential for digital fraud which could contribute to a loss of trust in the media. And there is the potential for de-skilling of journalists through the economic pressures towards multi-tasking. Networked Journalists need more time, not less, for thinking through their work. Ultimately, though, these dangers are far less worrying than the current failure of "Old Media and Old Politics" to serve the public well. The way that new media technologies as well as Internet competition can add variety and competitiveness means we should get a better relationship between the public and the politicians. There is nowhere that needs a better relationship between Government and the governed than

Africa. Let us now look at the potential for new forms of journalism to impact on the politics of the media there.

3.3   Africa: Networked Journalism, Governance and Development

> Free speech and a free press not only make abuses of governmental power less likely, they also enhance the likelihood that people's basic social needs will be met. (Joseph Stiglitz)[50]

It is one thing to make claims for Networked Journalism in the hugely wealthy and technologically advanced media markets in the US and Europe. It is also possible to see that it is having an impact in the rapidly growing economies of states such as China and India. It would be fascinating to investigate and explain how Networked Journalism may have a future in places like South Korea or Russia as well. It is important that we do not just see it as a process suited only to the US and the UK, the two markets which have dominated this book. But I want to consider a tougher challenge for the future of journalism and that is Africa.

It is impossible to generalize about such as diverse continent but I will attempt to outline a conceptual approach to Networked Journalism and its relationship to ideas of political governance and economic and social development. The media in Africa is at a very interesting moment historically. There are a series of major global initiatives[51-54] happening as part of a global effort to pump more money into the continent's development, to reduce debt, and to promote political progress. There is a renewed interest in the role of the media in Africa for three main reasons:

1   The media is seen as a useful way of carrying development messages. Radio, newspapers, TV, and other forms of communications are very efficient ways of reaching people with information about health, for example, especially in low-literacy societies with poor governmental infrastructure and education.

2   It is an industry worth developing in its own right that helps promote other forms of economic and social development. The media creates jobs and fosters related industries such as advertising and production. Better communication through business journalism, advertising, and general news helps spread the word about products and services.

3   It is a way of holding governments to account and increasing the transparency of aid. A healthy and independent media puts more information into the public domain to allow people to know what is going on. Good political journalism helps politicians to communicate with the voters, but also allows the voters to judge the record of those in power, from parking attendants to presidents.

But while aid agencies and donor countries recognize that a vibrant news media is a good thing, there is less agreement about how to promote it.

We are right to think before we blindly back media for development. At the very moment that the world has agreed to put more money in to Africa there is a rash of analysis – often written by journalists – that speaks of the failure of western donations in the past.[55] Historically, aid can be shown to have failed. By any reasonable cost–benefit analysis, the amount of money poured in to Africa has not delivered substantive, sustainable benefits. Despite hundreds of billions of dollars in aid, it stubbornly refuses to stop being a basket-case. There have been reforms across the continent: the end of apartheid, peaceful changes of power in places like Mozambique, and widespread media liberalization. There have been major developmental successes such as the growth in literacy. Yet despite all this Africa remains hugely underdeveloped. India and Asia in general, are booming. Latin America is pulling further ahead. So why not Africa?

The western media's story of Africa is one of war, famine, and disaster. It's not entirely untrue. There have been far more wars in Africa since the growth in independence after the Second World War. According to the 2006 Amnesty Report:

> At least a dozen countries in Africa were affected by armed conflict. Marginalization of certain communities, small arms proliferation and struggles for geo-political power and control of natural resources were some of the underlying causes of the conflicts. (Amnesty International)[56]

Africa has about half the per capita income of Latin America and is still falling behind, despite rich natural resources that are now attracting the attention of the Chinese, hungry for raw materials and largely careless of African development. According to UNAIDS,[57] the virus caused 2.1 million deaths in 2006 and 2.8 million people were newly infected, bringing to 24.7 million the total number of people living with HIV/AIDS on the continent, but still various leaders such as South Africa's Thabo Mbeki are in denial as to its causes. Public and private sector corruption is still endemic throughout Africa, silting up the economic channels and dissuading legitimate business investment and siphoning off aid funds. Again, according to the Amnesty 2006 Report:

> Overall, widespread and massive corruption in Africa continued to contribute to a vicious cycle of extreme poverty, manifesting itself in violations of internationally recognized human rights, especially economic and social rights, weak institutions and leadership, and marginalization of the most vulnerable sectors of the population, including women and children.[58]

So perhaps it is not surprising or inaccurate that this is the image of Africa portrayed by the Western media. But if that image implies a passive population and a static political context then it is not true. If it suggests that failure is somehow Africa's "natural" condition then it is a lie. Africa has a political problem and while it may be more intractable than most, it is not insoluble. But the first step to solving a political problem is to accept that it exists. What is African media doing to make the connections between failure and politics? Unfortunately, the media is very much part of the problem. Any map of media freedom shows Africa to be on a par with China and the former Soviet states. This repression is one very big reason why African mainstream media have so far failed. However, there is nothing innately wrong with African journalism, as anyone who works with African journalists or attends events like the CNN African Journalism Awards[59] will testify.

This all suggests that media for development, like much other development in Africa, has failed to shift the basic facts of life. Of course, some would say that it hasn't yet been properly tried. Let's leave the historical argument to one side and consider what might work. I am not making the case that this will solve all of Africa's problems. However, all developed liberal democracies accept that a healthy, pluralistic media is part of their success. Why should Africa settle for less? This is the case for media for development and a media that fosters networked journalism. But first we need to understand what we mean by the term. There are two types of African news media – media about Africa and African produced media. Media for development is interested in both.

3.3.1   Western media for development

How the rest of the world depicts Africa has a big impact on how governments make decisions about aid. Clearly, campaigns such as the Live Aid ("The

Day That Music Changed The World")[60] and Live8 ("Make The Promises Happen")[61] helped put public pressure on politicians. They used the media in a very overt way that even enlisted major broadcasters such as the BBC to produce complementary material. Charities are highly conscious of how they can use the media to make their points.

At one level this is a very good thing. Surely, no one could be against having people know more about Africa and to care about its problems. However, there is a danger in framing the African plight as something that we can do something about through rock concerts. The problems that Africa faces and the way that aid deals with them are rarely treated as subjects fit for discussion and dispute. Africa is seen as a given by Western journalists. So the Western news media relates a political narrative that speaks of noble campaigners seeking to persuade reluctant politicians to come to Africa's aid. Charity activists are given a privileged space within TV news reports and much of the written press where they are allowed to criticize governments for not doing what the pressure groups want. The spokespeople are a useful way for journalists to add drama to what is otherwise a pretty complicated and often boring story. Phrases like "but Oxfam denounced the initiative as too little too late," allow the reporter to imply some deep divide, some dramatic debate without having to go in to details, let alone analysis or argument, about the facts on the ground. It's rare to hear anyone mention that the NGOs are also fundraising, unelected sloganeers who simplify their messages to raise profile as much as to raise arguments. Behind the scenes they are often working hand-in-glove with the same governments they criticize in public. It is unusual for journalists to ask the NGOs why aid has failed in the past, or whether the market might be a better way to deliver results. And yet journalists feel a kind of moral certitude in giving the NGOs an easy ride, because who can be against giving poor Africa more money? In a way I think that this kind of treatment can be as simplistic as the "Africa disaster" coverage of Africa which portrays the whole continent as a passive population enduring appalling "natural" or self-inflicted catastrophe. The archetypal image of this kind of journalism is the pot-bellied infant on a mud hut floor dying with flies swarming over hollow eyes. It does seem that the campaigners have succeeded in persuading the politicians and that more aid will flow in to Africa. I can think of worse things to spend the money on. But I hope that this time journalism provides a more complex picture of the politics that will surround that aid in the future. Indeed, I hope that some of the money will be spent on African journalism itself.

3.3.2   African media for development

There are three sectors of African media. All have a role in development.

First *Community media* are non-profit, small-scale private enterprises and some state-owned community-based radio stations. Community media sees itself as having a special role in advancing development objectives and giving a voice to communities. They are often supported directly by international charities and carry social development messages. These can either be simple publicity material or more sophisticated consciousness-raising tactics such as soap-operas.

Second *State-owned media*, especially the broadcasting services, have the widest reach and potentially the greatest influence. Alternatively, shortages of resources and trained personnel can result in poor-quality programming, pro-government bias and an over-concentration on urban issues. The financial insecurity caused by lack of stable government financing results in a need to seek resources from advertising, thus depressing the opportunity for private stations. In addition to broadcasting, most governments in Africa own or control newspapers and news agencies, and most of them operate with a pro-government bias.

Finally *Private media* are seen as injecting an independent element, able to act as a watchdog of government and able to help hold government to account. Some private media are considered to be driven solely by profit and too compliant with business interests, to the detriment of good quality programming serving a wide audience. Critics suggest they are over-reliant on cheap foreign imports, or "dumbing down" of content. Private print media are increasingly contributing to the diversity of the media landscape.

All three sectors have a role to play in media for development. There are two types of media for development.

Social media for development focuses on communicating information that has direct social effects – usually in educational, health, and economic areas. This is almost entirely carried out by NGOs who use a variety of platforms including radio, theatre, poetry, advertising, and public relations to convey social messages. These are usually focused very closely to specific policy programs such as vaccinations, contraception, and literacy.

They try to engage the external news media through guided trips, advertising, reports, and events such as rock concerts. In effect, it is public relations with a purpose. Likewise, it tries to engage the internal African media, although the evidence seems to be that it spends more time on using direct communication.

Journalism Development focuses on supporting the development of the African news media itself. It seeks to build the capacity for journalism within Africa by training or supporting journalists and the structures, such as regulation, that sustain a news media sector. It supports the news media in its role as a tool for accountability and transparency and as a forum for debate. This is a mix of private and public provision. Organizations such as the BBC World Service Trust support training and the development of regulatory frameworks.

3.3.3 The African context

All media are local media, so we need to pay attention to the special circumstances of African journalism. There is an argument that African media markets are different because of the historical and contemporary political position of African societies. These arguments are useful in that they are helpful in differentiating between the different contexts for media development. However, we should be rigorously critical of this "exceptionalism" as it can easily become an excuse for failure and repression.

There are four main conditions that describe the context for the development of journalism in Africa, although any country can be subject to more than one. They are:

1 Fragile states;
2 Liberation states;
3 Complex states; and
4 Poor states.

"Fragile states" are countries like Somalia, Sierra Leone, and Sudan which have barely functioning public structures. Institutions such as schools, hospitals, and communications are virtually autonomous of the state. Emerging governments in fragile states claim that they cannot be subject to the same scrutiny that a free press performs elsewhere. Indeed, they go further and insist that the media must be restricted, so that the emerging authorities can curtail the kind of journalism that might provoke more conflict. In effect, they say the "watchdog" role of the media has to be suspended. If the government is under physical attack it needs support, not criticism. And if the media views are so powerful that they are causing the conflict as happened in Rwanda, then surely the media must be restricted.[62]

"Liberation states" often demand the compromise of media freedom in the name of achieving and sustaining political power. This is a more assertive version of the fragile states argument, and it is by no means unique to Africa. The argument goes like this: "We have just achieved our independence from the colonial power or the dictator. We should all show patriotic discipline in the face of our troubles and pull together for the common good." When I visited India recently this was still in evidence. There was a sense that the media should be backing India in its bid to become a global power. This is also the case in Venezuela where journalists are asked to ignore the increasing restrictions on press freedom for the greater good of the struggle against the US.

"Exceptional states" make the case for limiting media freedom on the basis that their historical or social make-up means that a free, liberal, pluralistic media is undesirable. Since he took power more than 20 years ago, President Museveni of Uganda has allowed greater press freedom and there are now a number of independent and even critical media voices. But he says that as a country with more than 40 different language groups who have competing political claims, Uganda cannot afford to have a totally free press. Central government has to be allowed to exercise control. That is why Uganda is still effectively a one-party state. Museveni recently closed down a new independent TV station and arrested outspoken journalists under the pretext that too much dissent will reopen the divisions in Ugandan society that allowed the misrule of Obote and Amin.[63]

"Poor states": The final argument is that Africa simply does not have the resources to enjoy the kind of pluralistic, reliable media that can be trusted to play a role in holding governments to account. The journalists are too poorly educated and trained, they don't have proper information and they don't understand the issues. They are badly paid and so they become corrupt. Journalists who acquire education or skills leave the media to go and work for international organizations or the government. More widely, it is argued, there isn't the wealth to support the advertising or subscription that can sustain an independent media.

All these arguments have validity. They should all be borne in mind when planning media for development strategies of any kind. To fail to recognize them would be to go against the grain of media for development. But at their worst these arguments are simply excuses. The key to moving beyond these restrictions on the debate is to address the question of political "ownership."

3.3.4   African ownership of media for development

In the past there was a conflict between the colonialist and independence model of the media's role in Africa. This goes beyond the actual economic ownership of the industry itself. The African Media academic Fackson Banda has argued that establishing political ownership for Africans' exercise is vital in determining the success of media as a force for governance and development.[64] He says there are four ways of looking at this political ownership of the media: ideological; conceptual; procedural; and contextual ownership.

The argument about ideological ownership is over whether media for development is an extension of ideas based on liberal democracy? Or is it an extension of Western imperialism? Should the ideological framework be a communitarian approach or a more US-style free-market model?

There is also a debate about conceptual ownership. Who determines the meaning of the concepts surrounding media development? What are the competing "developments" and "journalisms" being envisaged? Should Africans accept the current trend towards "developmental journalism" at the very moment when many in the "West" consider it a neo-Marxist hangover?

Who will control and take part in this media for development? In other words, who has procedural ownership? Should it be media or government led? How do you involve political actors at both national and pan-African levels, incorporating political elites as well as the public?

And finally there is the debate around contextual ownership. This is partly about how to ensure that ownership of media for development is localized to account for the many "African realities" that we described above, when we looked at the four main contexts for African media development.

These conceptual debates can become positive frameworks for diversity rather than obstacles to progress. It can be done by concentrating on the journalism development model and by adopting the framework of Networked Journalism. This does not imply the exclusion of other media for development approaches, but it does mean concentrating on building markets, capacity, and media literacy.

The only way that Networked Journalism can sustain itself is through creating wealth both as an industry but also as a way of increasing the efficiency of other markets through advertising and the exchange of information. This increases the potential for independent and competing centers of production. Media and communications must be seen as a sector where any private investment in any kind of media is to be preferred to solutions that insist on replicating public service models from the West. In this sense the Nigerian *Sun* newspaper – whose editor Shola Oshunkeye won CNN African journalist of the year[65] is *more* valuable than a niche quality magazine because it is building a mass readership base, an advertising market and a career structure for journalists. It also happens to produce award-winning investigative journalism that people get to read alongside the celebrity and sport news.

The journalists who staff those enterprises need to be trained and equipped. But it would be wrong to think that if you supply enough journalists then you will get enough journalism. Too many journalists leave the media, once they are skilled, to find better jobs. Capacity building works best when it is part of media business-building. Capacity building such as journalism training programs should be run in conjunction with media literacy initiatives so that Networked Journalists can create enterprises integrated in to their communities.

Promoting media literacy in the African context means providing the legal frameworks, regulations, and associations that sustain journalism. Journalism should be part of primary and higher education to foster practical engagement and participation in the media. But there also needs to be more support for the broader civic understanding of the political role that journalism can play in society. As one African media development commentator explains, Africans are already turning to citizen journalism:

> Citizen movements against government incompetence and corruption arise from political mobilization of the grassroots – and in turn ignite media aggressiveness. New media tools, such as text messaging, also highlights the way in which ordinary people – rather than professional journalists – can more effectively counter the propaganda of rogue governments. Professional journalists remain too vulnerable to official intimidation because they operate in the open. Citizens, on the other hand, are harder to identify and have many more communication tools available than they had even 5 years ago, what with the spread of cell phones, the Internet and radio in recent years. (G. Pascal Zachary)[66]

The same dynamic can apply across the whole range of political and developmental journalism in Africa. Citizen input does not just contribute to the volume of political journalism. It changes its very nature. It makes it stronger and more connected. It is cheaper and more flexible. And because it is working with local communities, it is more reflective of particular circumstances. But it is not a free for all. It can be sensitive to the needs of fragile states or exceptional circumstances because it is still mediated through journalists. It will spring from the initiative of African citizens who want to be part of their media, just as citizens have jumped at the chance in the West. But that does not mean that media for development can not help the process along.

3.3.5   African Networked Journalism coming alive: mobile phones

There is no doubt that Africa is suffering from a form of digital divide. Some areas of the continent still do not have access to the so-called World Wide Web. Many places do not have the regular electricity supplies required for any meaningfully connected environment. And yet the explosion in mobile phone use should give us a model for how African Networked Journalism can take off. Usage of mobile phones is growing at an annual rate that is twice the rest of the world:

> Between 2000 and 2005 there was little growth in access to fixed-line telephones, with seven countries experiencing negative growth. Mobile telephony, on the other hand, experienced tremendous growth across all sub-Saharan countries surveyed, with 10 countries having compound annual growth rates of 85% or higher. (AMDI report)[67]

More Africans now have privately provided and privately owned mobile phones than unreliable land-lines which depend on state provision. Kiosks selling blocks of pre-paid mobile phone use are now a regular sight by African roads and at markets. Farmers and traders use phones to make deals and check prices. Banks are beginning to allow customers to cut out corrupt middle men by paying directly for goods and services by mobile. This technology which is now running in Kenya is actually in advance of Western use of mobile phones. Text messaging has now become part of election campaigns. In the 2007 Nigerian elections, monitors used texting to pool instant information on ballot fraud. *Voices of Africa*,[68] a media for development organizations, is planning to set up a network of journalists armed with GPRS mobile phones. Complete news packages, video footage, and stills captured by the reporters on their mobiles will then be sold on to agencies, television stations, and newspapers to help finance the scheme. They are setting up a special version of the project to report on the 2007 Kenyan elections.

Kenya sums up the contradictions of the news media in Africa. Its highly paid politicians have passed another Media Bill restricting journalist freedoms. At the same time, Kenya's highly developed media is getting ready to employ user-generated content such as mobile phone photos on websites such as that of the *Kenyan Standard*. This evolving network of alternative digital channels of communication offers a unique opportunity for media development to sidestep the usual problems of supporting journalism in Africa. The priority should be to develop the capacity of citizens to communicate and of journalists to exploit that technology. That would create a politically independent resource with huge potential for widespread grassroots impact on media and politics. The old development adage was "give a man a fish and he eats for one day. Give him a net and he finds food for ever." The new one should be "give a journalist training and he knows what to do. Give him a mobile phone network and the public does it for him."

3.3.6   African Networked Journalism coming alive: bloggers

I have already suggested that it is wrong to see blogging as the limit or even the primary form of Networked Political Journalism. But it is a vital part of the Networked Political Journalism world. Figures are difficult to gather, but the Kenyan *Blogs Webring*[69,70] which aggregates blogs, began in 2004 with just 10 sites – now it has more than 430. Africa has seen some dramatic use made of Internet communication. Thanks to email and websites, journalists in Zimbabwe are still able to carry out proper reporting. Although they cannot publish openly within Zimbabwe they are able to convey information to expatriate sites such as *The Zimbabwean*.[71]

These allow people outside Zimbabwe to text payment for fuel vouchers to beleaguered friends and family in a country where petrol shortages and raging inflation are making their lives a misery. It also allows the news to reach the million or so Zimbabweans in exile. And, of course, those people in Zimbabwe itself with Internet access can consume an unfettered version of what is happening in their own country. While there is not widespread access in rural areas there is good Internet availability in Harare and the other main towns. The proof of the power of this process is the fact the Robert Mugabe is desperate to stop it. He has now passed a law enabling security forces to intercept and monitor all email and Internet traffic.

Even the most remote and difficult stories are being covered by the bloggers. As Africa correspondent Steve Bloomfield acknowledges[72] much of the best on-the-ground reporting from Darfur has been done by bloggers, rather than professional journalists.[73] During a 12-month stint in Darfur as part of the African Union Mission in Sudan (AMIS), Werner Klokow, a South African infantry major, blogged regularly on the problems AMIS was facing in the region. This extraordinary blog has a series of photos that provide a stunning visual accompaniment to his terse, fact-filled accounts of what it was like in Darfur. In another blog, entitled *Sleepless in Sudan*, an anonymous Western aid worker recounted the daily struggles of delivering humanitarian assistance in Darfur. It provides unique insights in to the reality of the refugee camps, both reportage and comment:

> The local government authorities hate Kalma camp (they're not so keen on a huge crowd of angry armed men so close to a state capital and major airport) – as far as they're concerned, everyone would be much better off if the people of Kalma camp would just go back home. In this spirit, they have done a pretty impressive job in making people's lives even more miserable than they already are through the economic blockade of the camp, attempted relocations and more recently a stubborn refusal to carry out headcounts that would allow those who are still not registered to finally receive ration cards. ("Sleepless in Sudan" blog)[74]

These are invaluable sources of Networked Journalism. But they are still voices from outside of those African countries. The best blogs report on the quotidian facts of life as lived by civilians. One of the most popular networked journalists in the Democratic Republic of Congo, Cedric Kalonji, wrote: "I admit I give more coverage to things that aren't going well in my country, but on this blog, I only speak of what I see personally from day-to-day." He too combines stunning photos and text (in French) to create testimony to the everyday life of an African from political campaigns to the return of traffic lights to Kinshasa.[75] The blog may be about ordinary life, but even my poor French tells me that the comments he gets show that he is sparking off real and open debate in one of the most volatile and politically abject nations in Africa. Take these reader reactions to his simple photo[76] of slum children in Kinshasa:

> What upsets me is to see these children without shoes, without schoolbags . . . perhaps without a school. Cedric, this photo is timely. My God. It's time to do something.
>
> (Moi ce qui me fait mal, c'est de voir ces enfants sans chaussures, sans cartable . . . Sans école peut être. Cédric cette photo tomba à pic. Mon Dieu. Il est temps de faire quelque chose.)
>
> What scares me is that one of them walks like a soldier, doing a military salute . . . Is this what he dreams of? Or is it just an impersonation?

(Petit rajout: ce qui me fait peur, il y en a un des deux qui marche comme un soldat et qui fait un salut militaire . . . C'est peut être son rêve ? Ou juste une imitation?)[76]

The *"bankele"* blog in Kenya is far more directly political:

> This week our members of parliament gave us another bile-inducing moment with yet another attempt to raise their salaries. These are people who live in an economic matrix where they believe that ordinary laws do not apply to them. They raise their own salaries (which other job can claim that?), pay a pittance in taxes, and are able to propose and play with myriad bills – that all concern other peoples money. (*"bankele"* blog)[77]

Likewise, this angry personal posting from Titilayo Obisesan on the state of public infrastructure in the oil-rich delta region of Nigeria:

> I felt very ashamed and disgraced at the state of Port Harcourt. As if my grief and disappointment was not enough, two days later I had the unfortunate privilege to travel by road from Port Harcourt . . . to Lagos. This journey proved to be nothing less than a most nightmarish experience. Saying the roads are very BAD is an understatement. From the very little my eyes have seen of . . . the oil-rich region of the country . . . the only way I can describe the state of the Niger Delta region is what I have termed the RAPE of the NIGER DELTA. (Titilayo Soremi, blogger)[78]

Those kinds of voices give the lie to the idea that Africans are not angry about what is wrong in their countries, and that they do not want more from their politicians. The Internet also allows a space for pan-African debate, as this ironic posting by Obed Sarpong of Accra in Ghana shows. He is responding to South Africa's decision to impose stricter border controls:

> What would have happened if Zimbabwe and the rest of Africa (including my Ghana) closed their borders on South Africa when they were struggling under the barbaric white apartheid regime, ha? . . . South Africans owe pan-Africa a moral obligation and in every way must pay the restitution when they could – to any African. Just kidding. I know South Africans fear for their jobs. That may be genuine; but didn't we all when we helped them? (Obed Sarpong, blogger)[79]

If blogging is about being cynical on a global scale then Obed Sarpong is proof that it has truly come of age in Africa:

If my instinct is anything worth to go by, I'd accuse Western powers, Americans governments (I've nothing against their innocent citizenry), Russia; and some Mid-East crooks like Iran, Syria and Saudi-Arabia of murder and frown on them for orchestrating sufferance on the world's populace.

I don't know why I should be thinking this way on a cold-windy-dusty-cloudy day, fractioned with occasional dashing of sunlight to my home in Osu – here in Accra. So don't ask me about those things I've just scribbled on some people sitting in their various countries. I shall tell you, anyway. (Obed Sarpong, blogger)[80]

This is poignant political blogging at its most personal. It is the authentic sound of one person in one particular place speaking to the world. It is giving Africans a voice that is creating online communities both locally and across borders. This rapidly developing use of the mobile phone and Internet shows remarkable innovation and flexibility. It demonstrates a huge demand for Networked Journalism and suggests there are vast resources of citizen creativity waiting to be exploited. But at present there is an understandable reluctance on the part of traditional media for development organizations to take up the challenge. They have their reasons. They argue that new media is a tiny minority of the news media and that it serves an articulate elite. Why divert funds from the urgent task of basic journalist training or lobbying for freedom of expression? I would argue that Networked Journalism does not argue that you should abandon mainstream media. Quite the opposite. As a recent report on the future of African media concluded, it offers a way forward for both:

The flowering of new media platforms presents an opportunity to guide media initiatives through new channels and secure support of a pan-African approach to media development. Such an effort will need to allow for shared and coordinated projects and learnings, to create more sustainable models of media development, to open up space for advocacy, to invite more integrated funding and to respect the need for tailored content for local audiences. This type of initiative would reduce some of the challenges faced [by African media], and we welcome the opportunity in the future to survey what will be a media landscape with not just local, national or regional, but global consequences. (African Media Development Report)[81]

Networked Journalism is a fresh chance for media for development in Africa. It offers ways of overcoming the barriers that have blocked media development in the past. Western donors and African governments, media organizations and investors should realize that this is a chance to forge a new paradigm. It will be different from what has gone before and almost certainly be different to what is happening in the West. Its greatest task is to help in the renovation of African politics. Development will be much more likely with improved governance. Better reporting of African politics is an essential pre-condition for that to happen. But as I outlined in the previous chapter, Networked Journalism needs investment and commitment. There is pitifully little being done to address this need at present and it is time for those who value the role of the media to seize this opportunity.

3.4   Conclusion: Networked Journalism and Politics

A pragmatic optimism about political news media can be grounded upon our experience so far of Networked Journalism. I acknowledge the reservations. There are limits to democracy. There are always groups who seek to retain power by restricting transparency. There is a limit to political literacy and a need for efficiency. A representative democracy can only function if at some point in the process the representatives are allowed to get on with the job. It is always difficult to measure media effects. And there is a long debate to be had about what exactly *is* political, in a post-industrial world. Likewise, how do we separate out journalism from general political communication? These include public relations, propaganda, and public information, which must be aligned with the news media frame.

Conventionally, studies of political communication site the media between political actors and the public.[82] Increasingly, this view will become simplistic. Politicians will be able to use new media technology to communicate directly with voters and vice versa. I share Joe Trippi's hope that this will reform the structures of politics itself:

> As people reconnect, politics will change globally. It is only a matter of time. As the process is given back to the people, as networks are empowered, self-government will reawaken. Joe Trippi[83]

I am less confident than Trippi of the timing and the extent to which this will happen. I am skeptical that this will result in new policy outcomes or a deep power transfer from political actors to voters. That has to come from social and political actions, not just messages. But Networked Political

Journalism has already demonstrated that it is shifting power around. It is re-ordering the conventional political processes. It is reflecting a deep-felt urge among contemporary citizens for a more direct and open form of political communication. It is time now to see how journalism and society can prepare for that possibility.

Chapter Summary

- For many reasons including some factors beyond politics or journalism there is a democratic deficit globally as the public express a communications disconnect between power and the people.
- The News Media provide more political reporting than ever before but are not trusted.
- In the US blogs and netroot activism are changing the framework of political communications.
- Traditional mainstream media and political campaigning is still dominant.
- New forms of online communication and journalism offer the potential for a genuinely novel political dialogue, but it may remain marginal.
- In Britain independent New Media journalism has a much more local effect, usually in a symbiotic relationship with mainstream news media.
- Efforts to inculcate e-democracy will only be effective if they incorporate Networked Journalism.
- Africa has a different media market with special problems and opportunities to exploit the political value of new media.
- The creativity of African use of mobile phones and blogging suggests significant potential for the development of political journalism in a Networked paradigm.
- New media technology will only secure a reconnection of public and power if it is mediated by a more Networked Journalism.

4

Fighting Evil
Terror, Community, and Networked Journalism

If "SuperMedia" is to come to the rescue, we need to make sure it has the tools for the job. New challenges require new powers. There is no greater challenge to the ability of journalism than terrorism. The incidents and issues around public security and community conflict are among the most difficult to mediate for journalists. They are complex and they are vital. The news media is very much part of these narratives. If the news media get it wrong, we will all pay the price. But there are lessons that we can learn from looking at the extreme issues that terror and community raise. Grappling with the task of getting it right is a good way to understand how Networked Journalism must be different in its composition, its practice, and its relationship with society. This chapter will look at the role of a more networked journalism in community issues in Britain and then the international context of the global debate over faith and politics.

4.1 Terror, Public Security, and Community Cohesion

> I'm sure by now the media has painted a suitable picture of me, this predictable propaganda machine will naturally try to put a spin on it to suit the Government and to scare the masses into conforming to their power and wealth obsessed agendas. (Mohammad Sidique Khan, London bomber)[1]

The videotaped message by British suicide bomber Mohammad Sidique Khan was an extraordinary example of a terrorist using the media. His actions were a challenge to the media in more ways than perhaps he realized. By "terror,"

I mean a range of interrelated issues. To understand acts, such as the bombings of 9/11 in New York or 7/7 in London, we have to know much more than whom the perpetrators were and what motivated them. That is difficult enough. But we also need to understand a lot of other things. We need to analyze the relationship between various international conflicts in places like the Middle East and the way immigrant groups behave in host societies. We need to interpret the various political dynamics within modern Islam and their relationship to other ideologies, faiths, and to new social conditions. Journalism has to be able to investigate the power struggles within factions of Western governments, local community groups, and national or regional forces around the world. The media has to give a voice to those hurt by terror and those driven to use it. It must allow a dialogue to take place, but it must not become a propaganda tool. This is to ask a lot of conventional journalism. But some would say we should ask even more.

Journalism is no more immune to moral demands than any other section of society. Certainly, journalism should strive for objectivity, impartiality, and a rigorous professional code. Like the police, politicians, educators, or any other socially influential group, journalism should, at least, avoid harm and, ideally, act as a progressive force. In other words, journalism does bear responsibilities. However, the real question is how those are best insisted upon and exercised. In the context of reporting terror that is all the more important and difficult.

Terror is an especially mediated form of politics and violence. It is deliberately created as a spectacle, and it is most immediately understood as a compelling object for media consumption. The attack on the Twin Towers was not intended to bring the US to its knees economically or militarily. It was a gesture of power, an image of defiance and a token of threat that was intended to frighten, humiliate, and provoke. Jihadi websites are created for a reason. Their job is to communicate information for the terrorist groups and their supporters and to recruit and fund-raise for the cause. They exploit new media's global reach and unaccountability. Likewise, Al Qaeda has become adept at releasing audio and video through online and other outlets to maintain its presence. As Britain struggled to understand how home-grown terrorists could commit the atrocities perpetrated on 7/7, it was the terror group itself that supplied the answer. A long video by former teaching assistant and suicide bomber, Mohammad Sidique Kahn, explained in great detail his political and religious motivations. It was expertly choreographed with the requisite Al Qaeda combat gear. It even included some pre-rebuttal in the form of a tirade against the media, quoted at the beginning of this chapter. It was a morally distorted form of Networked Journalism, proof that Networked is not always noble.

The creation of this terror and any solution to it is grounded in community. One of the tragedies of the phrase "The War On Terror" is the implication that it can be defeated militarily. No significant terror group has ever been policed out of existence. All "victories" over terror have been achieved ultimately by political and social processes. That does not mean that governments should not prosecute the campaign against the terrorist, but it does mean that we should pay more attention to the conditions that sustain it. By understanding the communities that "host" terrorism, we can begin the process of eroding their support. This is true on a local and on a national scale. If communities, such as Muslims in Britain, are going to be part of the struggle against terror and not part of the problem, the media has to help convey another set of messages. It must, for example, promote the debate between Muslims themselves about how they will respond. It must also mediate a conversation between Muslims and the wider community that seeks to reduce the threat while preserving community values and identity.

This needs to happen on an international scale as well. This is a version of the rather crude "draining the swamp" metaphor. Achieving peace in Palestine and reducing poverty in Muslim countries will not be enough for Al Qaeda. They have all sorts of global and specific aims that go far beyond that. Their motivations are often psycho-political as well as materially driven. But we are not seeking to appease or satisfy the terrorists, we are seeking to dilute their support and their impact to such a degree that they become irrelevant. There needs to be much greater understanding of these issues on the part of different populations. But there also needs to be much better knowledge and more robust and open debate among Muslims in different countries about the reality of politics in places like the Middle East. Young Muslims in Britain, for example, regularly cite the treatment of Muslims in the Middle East and especially the Palestinian Territories as a cause of their anger against the British government. And yet they seem unaware of the way that Palestinians have been abandoned and mistreated by many fellow Muslim countries in the region. Their information flows are highly selective and inadequate and the wider media is not doing enough to correct that state of affairs. The news media is critical to this process, because how else can the public form their views of otherwise inaccessible people?

At present we do not get a full and rich picture of our fellow human beings through the conventional media. We need this more intelligent and more "human" understanding in order to reach beyond the stereotypes. Only through a more sophisticated media process can we learn how to move forward into a future in which support for terrorism is diminished because people feel a sense of justice and solidarity with one another. This is partly about maintaining a critical understanding of how Governments and other authorities mediate the fear of terrorism as a way of retaining political power and ideological control over certain debates.

There are three demands being put upon journalism under these circumstances. First, to consider carefully its role as part of the terror process, and second, to understand its role in portraying the communities involved. There is a third demand being put on journalism directly by the terror threat. Terror groups like Al Qaeda have an ideology which is antithetical to all the values of a liberal, free media. The way that this form of terrorism is constructed and expresses itself presents a specific challenge to the positive role of journalism in a multi-cultural liberal society that we enjoy in post-Enlightenment, free market societies. This is why the more extremist demonstrators against the Danish Cartoons carried banners denouncing freedom of speech. Journalism must respond to the terror threat by upholding freedom of speech in a responsible fashion that acts as a model for liberal values that others will wish to embrace.

Those are the challenges, but how much does journalism have to change to respond to these demands? I believe that the news machine is not built for this task. *The Times* newspaper Deputy Editor, Ben Preston, rightly points out that we tend to exaggerate the power of the mainstream traditional media to control agendas. He believes that the news cycle is always a crude process whereby professional journalists are always catching up with events and their implications:

> In the case of the sudden media interest in Muslim culture in Britain I think it was the politicians who opened up a whole area of debate which hitherto people hadn't been that interested in going into or some people had been nervous about going into. It then became the subject of heated discussion. And I think the media will follow where people take them, to a degree. I think you can probably see more recently how some of the heat has gone out of that debate and how people have come to more settled and informed opinions. That's a positive outcome from having had a national conversation about it. (Ben Preston, Deputy Editor, *The Times*)[2]

As British commentator Simon Jenkins said, "The unshackled and irresponsible press sometimes gets it wrong. But I still prefer it, warts and all, to a shackled and responsible one."[3] And that is the conflict here. We want a news media that is independent, virile, and critical. We don't want journalists to be social workers or diplomats. Indeed, it is possible to argue that through a combination of ignorance and over-sensitivity, much of mainstream journalism failed to identify the threat of extremist Islam until it was bloodily effective and already entrenched. But we also want a media that does not leave a trail of anger and distrust in its wake. I believe that Networked Journalism offers a way through this dilemma that allows journalism to retain and enhance its core critical function while allowing a fuller and more positive engagement with its role in the problematics of terror and community.

4.1.1   Bias and ignorance

There is a problem with overtly or subconsciously racist news outlets which are too eager to pander to prejudice. They are easy to identify but harder to deal with. There is nothing unique or unprecedented about Islamaphobic journalists. The media has always shared society's bigotries. The history of the past century is manifest evidence of the appalling results when those attitudes are allowed to develop unchecked. But the evidence is also that those prejudices are often left behind on a rising tide of integration and understanding. The racism routinely displayed in British or US popular culture during the 1960s simply would not be tolerated today. We should not assume that will always be the case. But we should not simply concentrate on the worst cases. So, I want to focus not on the proudly racist but on the blithely ignorant. An example of this was the case of Molly Campbell, or Misbah Rana, in the British media in 2006.

Misbah Rana was the 12 year-old daughter of the marriage of Pakistani Sajad Ahmed Rana and Scot Louise Campbell. On August 25, 2006, she got on a plane with her sister Tahmina and went from their home in Stornaway – the main town of Lewis in the Western Isles of Scotland – to Glasgow and then met up with their father to travel on to Lahore in Pakistan. This was one year after the London bombings. Initially after the bombings, the UK media had focused in on the actual bombers and their background. Even the popular press was highly conscious of its responsibilities and made overt calls for tolerance and understanding. This restraint loosened as the attention subsequently shifted to a much broader examination of the wider culture and ideology of British Islam. So the Misbah Rana story broke at the height of this media fascination with all things Muslim. It was also during the traditional summer "silly" season for the UK media when Parliament doesn't sit and when generally the news flow is pretty slow.

The immediate reaction by *all* the media was to label this a child-abduction case. She was described as Scottish girl Molly Campbell. The police held a press conference where they did not use the word "abduction," but a grandmother of the child implied that she had been taken against her will. The UK media accepted this cue with little pause for thought. The BBC and all other broadcasters led their bulletins with lengthy features explaining the problem of "child abduction" and "arranged marriages" in South Asia. *The Times* went further and linked it to a campaign they were running on international abductions and arranged marriages of children. They were all spectacularly wrong. It was, in truth, a good old-fashioned custody battle. The girl had gone voluntarily with her father, who had split from the mother. But using its instinctive news judgments, the British media could not conceive how anyone could possibly prefer a Pakistani father in Lahore to the delights of Stornaway.[4]

Now was this Islamophobia on the part of the press? Well, underlying it, yes. But it was also incompetence and bad journalism. They didn't check their story properly, they didn't question the background of the relationship of the child with her mother, and they didn't try to get a quote from Pakistan. Within 24 hours the real story was emerging and both *The Times* and the BBC went into reverse gear. They started calling Molly by her chosen name, Misbah, corrected their reporting and apologized for their mistake. But by then the damage had been done, and another negative assumption about Muslims had been deepened. It was by no means the most wicked thing said about Muslims, nor the most ignorant, but because of that I think it does show how the news media is not self-aware and self-critical enough about these issues. This is not about political correctness, or treating Muslims with special reverence, it is simply about getting the story right. It is about having enough people with knowledge of these issues – in this case, Muslim communities, to help stop the herd from stampeding off in the wrong direction.

Samira Ahmed is a presenter/reporter for *Channel 4 News*, a program with a reputation for a liberal approach to stories with an ethnic element. And yet she found they too were in danger of going down the same unquestioning path on the Misbah Rana story.

> I remember just turning across news bulletins that day and they all had a top package with the facts about the story and then they had a second package about the evils of forced marriage. And I just remember bursting out laughing because I thought this probably isn't about forced marriage. For me it reminded me just how deep the ignorance goes and this rather shocking assumption that

why would any girl possibly choose to live in Pakistan over Stornaway and that's when you realise what kind of people actually make editorial decisions in most newsrooms. (Samira Ahmed, reporter/presenter, *Channel 4 News*)[5]

Samira Ahmed believes that better informed journalism is a prerequisite for tougher, more responsible journalism. She warns that journalists may lack the tools and confidence to investigate stories properly:

I'm concerned that there's still so much ignorance about the basics of Islam – not because one should be understanding for the sake of it, but just as a journalist you want to know these things so you know what you're covering. I sometimes find there's this real fear among journalists of tackling sensitive topics in a robust way because they're a bit ignorant. (Samira Ahmed)[6]

Networked Journalists are not frightened of opening their minds *before* they start writing the story. They have permanent networks that allow a great diversity of influences upon their work. This need not compromise their journalistic independence. An example is Nick Carter, editor of *The Leicester Mercury*, a daily evening newspaper in a British midlands city with a majority of its population now from immigrant backgrounds. A few years ago Carter realized that his paper was out of touch with its readership. It was missing stories, losing readers and failing to attract the advertising it could from Leicester's ethnic communities. It was also reinforcing a lot of negative feelings about issues that touched on ethnicity by treating them in the same formulaic manner. Over the past few years, Carter has done two things that have made the *Mercury* more networked. He is now on the city's Community Liaison committee, which means that the newspaper is at the heart of the multi-cultural communication process. He hears direct the concerns and aspirations of the many different people in Leicester. He also hears how the various authorities are trying to deal with the issues. This allows him to put the individual news stories in to a strategic perspective.

This leads to the second difference. He has encouraged an editorial policy which he described as looking to start stories about ethnic "problems" on what he calls the "second paragraph." Take a story about a primary school which suddenly finds itself swamped by a sudden influx of Somali families and which can't cope with the drastic increase in the demands on its resources. Traditionally, the article would start on the frightening top line of pupils suffering because immigrants are making excessive demands upon a school. Carter wants the newspaper to reflect its wider understanding of the issues. He wants his reporter to start the story on the second paragraph, which is about how the council and the school and local communities are mobilizing resources to cope with the emergency. All the same facts are in the story and the problem is recognized as serious. But the Networked Journalism solution is to accept a wider input from the public in to the editorial framework of the way the problem is mediated. Carter believes this is all part of a recognition that journalism is part of a connected community:

> The responsibilities the *Leicester Mercury* now accepts as a consequence of sitting round the [Community Liaison Committee] table mean we work harder to look for the positives in our communities particularly where they demonstrate that people from different cultures are living and working together. We are more aware of those small groups of extremists who want to divide our communities and spread fear and suspicion. And we are better able to provide a platform for all the communities in which we seek to sell. Inevitably this puts more pressure on us to make those right decisions and it does mean we have to spend more time thinking about the consequences of everything we do. (Nick Carter, Editor, *Leicester Mercury*)[7]

I would argue that, far from surrendering editorial authority, the *Mercury* now speaks with more integrity and additional kudos. It will probably sell more copies and advertising as well. Indeed, some would say that the Mercury is only changing tack for business reasons. I am not sure that matters too much. But what has that school story got to do with terror? I would argue that a media that can represent people fairly as well as thoroughly, and that takes its social responsibilities seriously, is more likely to mediate other divisive issues in a way that opens up possibilities of reconciliation or at least of understanding. I do not think that people become bombers because of simple social or economic factors. But they are surely far less likely to do so in a society that acknowledges the significance of the background context for conflict. There is a continuum between the global clashes and local disaffections. The media must mediate both. When it is networked it does so better.

4.1.2   Diversity and fragmentation

We have already pointed out how there is more fragmentation in the new media landscape. [Chapter 1, 4.3 and 4.4]. While there is a threat to the diversity of the mainstream media, there has been an explosion of choice for ethnic audiences, especially diaspora populations. The fear is that people will not share their news consumption, and that we will exist in journalistic bubbles of specialist media. The implication is that this will reinforce differences and even prejudices. This is partly about the ease with which more marginal or extreme voices access global audiences. Conspiracy websites such as *9/11 Truth*[8] or Jihadist websites, such as the now defunct *Global Islamic Media* website[9] are only the click of the mouse away. But it is also about perfectly respectable ethnic media. It's not just what people are consuming; it is the separateness of the act itself.

> The fragmentation of the media is taking place within the context of a public that is becoming more diverse itself. But, as personal choice and control increases we should be concerned if communities of interest replace responsibility, that the ego drives out the egalitarian and the Daily We becomes the Daily Me. An increasingly competitive marketplace could see comment and opinion replace fact and argument as people seek out information that stokes the harsh fires of prejudice. So the need for the news media to act as a civic forum, a channel of communication and public debate has never been more pressing. (David Lammy MP, British Minister for Culture)[10]

Muslims in places like Paris, Chicago, or in Britain's larger cities use new media, digital broadcasting and other methods, such as the distribution of cassettes by imams and mosques, to create a rich and complex media. This reflects the diversity of their own backgrounds. Muslims still consume mainstream media in great numbers. They do not want to abandon it – but they feel that it does not do enough to speak for them or speak fairly about them.[11]

Media organizations have made efforts on both fronts. They have put in place policies which seek to increase ethnic representation within their ranks. This kind of technique can produce superficial results, but what has tended to happen is that well-educated middle-class Asians take the best jobs, leaving the more disaffected groups, such as working class urban Muslim males, untouched. In Britain the BBC has also created the Asian Network and other ethnic digital stations which provide a more tailored service that is still recognizably part of the BBC. But the challenge is how those services provide integration, rather than fragmentation, and how much they inform the wider media coverage. There needs to be more networking between the journalism in the specialist and mainstream newsrooms. An interesting attempt to do just this has been started at the British commercial TV news service ITV. ITV News (made by ITN) has launched a partnership with a regional Asian newspaper, *Awaaz*, that covers the north of England. ITV will consult *Awaaz* on stories relating to Asian communities and will also draw upon the newspapers' specialist editorial resources. ITV News' Deputy Editor, Jonathan Munro, believes that it is more than just a newsgathering exercise:

> We approached *Awaaz* in the run-up to the 7/7 anniversary to help us establish a better understanding of the Muslim community and enable us to cover certain stories more comprehensively. Coverage of the Misbah Ranah story has shown that news organizations don't always get it right and we need a better grasp of the issues affecting our Muslim and Asian viewers. (Jonathan Munro, ITV News)[12]

In the context of terror, journalism must be considered as a network of consumption and of production. If communities consume in a diverse way then that is a positive enrichment provided by the new media landscape. In the modern world we increasingly have multiple identities and it is surely a good thing if journalism reflects that state of affairs. But how much better if the journalism itself is more networked and can make the links of common interest or dialogue? This is of paramount importance in the global context.

4.1.3   Networked Journalism and global politics

One of the most bizarre stories I have seen recently was a *Fox News* item on the Palestinian children's TV show *Tomorrow's Pioneers* on *Al-Aqsa TV*. In this episode of the weekly series, a child presenter is being incited by a man dressed up in a Mickey Mouse suit to wage ideological and real war against the Jews (see Figure 4.1). The presenter of the show, 11-year-old Saraa Barhoun, is quoted in the London *Observer* as saying, "We love life, but we are happy to be martyrs."[13] For once, one could share fully in *Fox News*' sense of outrage.[14] Although I was bemused to see they were as angry about the implied copyright violation for *Disney* as they were about the rampant anti-Semitic sentiments being expressed on the publicly funded Palestinian equivalent of *Sesame Street*. Sadly, *Fox News* chose not to bring together Palestinians with others to discuss how a society can be so dysfunctional that it creates this kind of media culture. No-one appeared to explain or justify. Prejudices were left unchallenged on both sides. Much of the mainstream media completely ignored the story. Partly, I suspect they did so because the more liberal media were nervous of suggesting that the program symbolized something more widespread in Palestinian culture, rather than just being an extreme example of Hamas propaganda. We need more broadcasters who, like *Fox* in this case, take an interest in international affairs and the ideological differences that exist. But we also need a more Networked Journalism that tries to open up debate between the world's publics. This is partly about better journalism that puts difficult issues like the *Al-Aqsa TV* program up for debate. Even considered, thorough, and balanced treatment is not enough. The global networked media needs to open up the channels to the people.

One example of this is the effect of Aljazeera upon both the Middle Eastern and wider Muslim publics and on other news organizations. The Doha-based network has been a catalyst for media reform over the past decade. Its very existence has had a Networked Journalism effect upon the global media. It is watched in every international news organization, as it gives the "non-Western" view on world affairs. It also produces any number of scoops because of its access to Arab and Muslim organizations or contacts. It is now generally admired by journalists around the world. It clearly does have an institutional bias that reflects its roots in the Middle East, but this is not significantly different to the way that CNN or the BBC is conditioned by its origins, paymasters, and cultural make-up. Aljazeera has also proved that there is a market for relatively independent and trustworthy journalism in the Middle East and

Figure 4.1 Palestinian children's TV gets political: Tomorrow's Pioneers on Al-Aqsa TV (Photo © AP/PA Photos)

beyond that is not commanded from London, Atlanta, or New York. As well as *Aljazeera English* we now have a variety of 24 hour news channels throughout the Middle East. Aljazeera has also created a different audience with new expectations. As their former Chief Correspondent, Yosri Fouda, explained in a speech to POLIS, the simple act of a phone-in changes cultures:

> We would get a couple of guests in a studio and chat together with open tele-phones live. It was historical. When the public rang up they couldn't believe it was really live, they kept asking who would monitor the calls – they couldn't believe they were able to talk direct on air. It's empowering people because information and facts and that sort of journalism can only empower people. And when you empower people who are not meant to be empowered, that's what really pisses [off] the government. And if a government feels that it is pissed off, then there must be something wrong with it. (Yosri Fouda, *Aljazeera* crrespondent)[15]

So, on the one hand, *Aljazeera* was a way of giving voice to people, and on the other, Yosri Fouda was also a conduit for Osama Bin Laden. He was "Osama's Postman," as George Bush's White House saw it. Fouda insists that any journalist would have wanted to broadcast that material:

> Every single source would like to use you, and the mechanism works exactly the same whether it's a head of state or a terrorist organization for this matter. It's down to you, as a journalist, your judgments on a certain situa-tion. And I was lucky, Al Qaeda invited me for some kind of exclusive and I ended up interviewing the two main 9/11 masterminds. But, I was not there to argue with them, to debate certain things. I came back with information, with facts, that even the CIA did not have. (Yosri Fouda)[16]

In a bizarre way, *Aljazeera* was bringing together Osama Bin Laden, the US administration, and the Arab public (see Figure 4.2). It was one of the first Middle-Eastern broadcasters to allow Israelis regular airtime. *Aljazeera* has a bias; it is not sympathetic to US or Israeli foreign policy, but then neither is the BBC. But it is a major step forward for a more networked global journalism. By its very existence, *Aljazeera* has added to the diversity of world journalism. The fact that it is comprised of many former BBC and other Western journalists emphasizes how linked it is to the rest of the global journ-alism culture. With the addition of other channels, such as *France 24*, and African versions, we are seeing the creation of a diverse and interconnected broadcast news world. If that system can begin to exploit the potential of its

Figure 4.2 *Aljazeera*: the typical newsroom design of a modern global broadcaster but with its own editorial take on the news agenda (Photo © Karim Jaafar/AFP/ Getty Images)

online operations in the way that Reuters has done, then there is a vast potential for interaction between the blogosphere, citizen journalism, and these vast global platforms. Setting up a 24-hour news channel that pumps out the same agency footage and has beautifully coiffeured presenters reading out the same headlines is relatively easy. The trick will be for those channels to draw upon their core audience communities and the wider public to create a genuine communications network.

4.1.4   The Cartoon challenge to Networked Journalism

Networked Journalism has to deal with novel cultural issues that raise whole new ethical dilemmas. The Danish Cartoon saga of 2005/2006 was a manufactured controversy from start to finish. But while it is exceptional as a media event, it represents many of the challenges of a diverse but un-networked media world. On September 17, 2005, the Danish newspaper *Politiken* ran an article under the headline "Profound fear of criticism of Islam." The article discussed the difficulty encountered by the writer Kare Bluitgen, who was initially unable to find an illustrator prepared to work with him on a children's book about *The Quran and the Life of the Prophet Muhammad*. Three artists declined Bluitgen's proposal before one agreed to assist anonymously. (According to Bluitgen, one artist declined because of the murder of the film director Theo van Gogh in Amsterdam.) Then followed a series of deliberately provocative actions, all of which were stage-managed to provoke a reaction, which in turn became the story.

As a gesture in support of freedom of expression, a Danish newspaper ran a competition to publish satirical cartoons of the Prophet. Danish imams took offence and began legal proceedings. They toured the Middle East showing the cartoons to religious and political leaders, whipping up offence and calling for boycotts. Six months later they started to get some results. A series of incidents occurred, many stage-managed by groups with local axes to grind across the Middle East. Islamic radicals seized the chance to parade their outrage – often directing it against local authorities as much as the Danes.

At this point it became worldwide news and the debate about whether to *re*publish the cartoons became as important as whether they should have been published in the first place.

At the time this was happening, I was the program editor at *Channel 4 News* – a serious one hour live nightly news and analysis program made by ITN for Channel 4 in the UK. On the previous day's planning shift, I had noticed on a Reuters agency picture feed a small item about protests in Syria against the Danish cartoons. The story had barely figured in UK newspapers but I thought that it might make an interesting down-bulletin feature which raised a classic "free speech versus minority sensibility" debate. My assumption had been that we would show the cartoons in full in some way. However, on the morning of the day we transmitted the story the issue had taken off and was hitting the headlines for the first time in the UK. The editorial management team realized that we were in a far more problematical place.

With an hour to go before we went on air, my editor and presenter and I had an interesting ethical debate. I wanted to show them clearly because I felt that it would be bizarre not to broadcast images of something at the heart of the story. But we decided not to. Partly because there was a sense that this was getting out of hand and violence might be provoked in the UK by their transmission – did we really think that was worth it? It was partly because other broadcast outlets were not showing the cartoons – and no newspapers ever printed them in full in the UK either. Finally the calculation was made (and this is much easier for a one-off program) that the onscreen value of showing the cartoons was not worth the obvious offence that would be caused.

By a slim margin I think that we made a sensible but weak decision. We ended up broadcasting 13 seconds of the cartoons filmed by a news agency being held by a Muslim who was campaigning for a boycott in the Middle East. You could see the cartoons and you could hear the man describing why he found them offensive. It was part of an explanatory three minute film that was followed by a discussion between a Muslim organization representative and a former British newspaper editor. Not showing them did not really deprive anyone of vital life-saving information and the cartoons were easily available on the web. In this case the cartoons were made to provoke; the offence was not incidental. By publishing them we would have been repeating the provocative gesture in itself. So with hindsight I think that it was a very close call and an understandable decision. But my instinct is that we could have made a riskier decision that found a way to show the cartoons in greater detail, perhaps with health warnings. The BBC decided to show a similar version to *Channel 4 News*, but much shorter in duration – just three seconds. It really wasn't enough to give any idea as to how offensive the images were in themselves. The great dividing line for the BBC was that it did not wish to be seen to be "publishing" the cartoons. A rumor that the BBC program *Newsnight* was going to do just that was enough to provoke demonstrations outside the Corporation's main news studios in West London. It was those demonstrations and similar ones outside the Danish embassy in London that made me wonder if the British mainstream news media had been editorially weak. The protestors were denouncing the very idea of freedom of speech. Of course, they were utterly unrepresentative of Muslims as a whole. But it did feel that we had made a compromise to a group who had raised a particular cultural objection to *anyone* seeing these cartoons – not just a measured request for restraint. This is the deeper challenge the cartoon controversy represents.

The cartoon debate is representative of a global argument among Muslims about how they send messages to the world via the media. There are the 'extremists' who welcome difference and conflict and reject liberal ideas of the media as a conduit for cohesion. They are happy to use the mainstream media and to create their own highly networked communications. But they see that as serving their political goals which preach purity and separation. Then there are the 'moderates' who are also divided among themselves as to how they want the media to treat these issues. In the case of the Cartoons, the moderates could claim victory in the light of the high degree of restraint on the part of the British media. However, the extremists could also claim to have got what they wanted because the cartoons were not fully published in the UK mainstream media. The extreme Muslims succeeded in defining the story as one of Muslims versus Free Speech. By not showing the cartoons the mainstream media acceded in practice to their demand that offence came before free speech.

In fact, the Cartoons saga may have preserved rather than damaged the media's right to give offence – even to a vulnerable minority. By acting responsibly in this case, I hope that it will allow the news media to defend better examples of where artistic or political freedom demands that people say or show things that a minority find offensive. The issue was, in a sense, repeated, when various Muslim groups issued *fatwahs* when the British government gave a knighthood to Salman Rushdie, author of *The Satanic Verses*, in 2007. This time the media and the government stood firm in what was clearly a case of defending legitimate artistic expression.

Networked Journalism could have done much more to mediate the Cartoon Controversy. There was an explosion of comment in the blogosphere around these issues. This occasionally surfaced in the online mainstream media in the form of angry disputes in forum posts and comments. It revealed a deep and widespread level of confusion and fear about the cultural issues it raised. It showed that there was a desperate public desire to communicate and debate and a general lack of places to have that conversation. Mainstream media failed to connect with that public discourse. It was limited in a sense by its own difficulties in covering the story. While I was pondering in effect how not to show the cartoons, my audience had already seen them and moved on to the consequences. Networked Journalism could have made that debate a reality by connecting the different levels of discourse. It could have linked the different groups and involved them in a more interrelated debate about both the issues and the media treatment of them.

The lesson of the Cartoons and the other issues I have raised in this chapter is that journalism can not pretend to operate in a vacuum. If news journalists are not conscious of their audiences then other people will be. If we do not find a way of connecting people then other people will. As we have seen, the extremists are expert in exploiting new communications technologies. It is not the job of journalists to counter this or to seek to mobilize political sentiment. But it would be bad journalism and a market failure if journalism did not seek better connectivity with the various publics. In the context of community and terror, I believe there is a moral imperative as well.

4.1.5   Misunderstanding Muslims

If the media are at times failing to understand and communicate Muslim community and terrorist issues, at the root of this, some argue, is the "failure" of Muslims to explain and express themselves. This is not the same as "blaming the victim." There needs to be a more concerted effort on the part of society and Muslim communities themselves to communicate to the wider public the kind of debates – about growing up, being British, doing well at school – that Muslims have every day. This is important because, when terror incidents happen, it is the normalcy of most Muslim lives that should be in the back of people's minds.

But is it the fault of the media that all Muslims get tarred with the same brush, that the anti-terrorist Muslims don't get a voice? Muslims don't organized themselves along the same clear hierarchical lines as Christians or other social groups might do. Often the media is looking for representatives or typical examples where they don't exist and so they end up asking the wrong people the wrong questions. There are vast differences within "the Muslim community," with more than 60 different national and linguistic backgrounds, even among London's Muslims. According to the highly respected British Muslim thinker, Yahyah Birt, it is "the ethical responsibility of journalists" not to look for a single representative Muslim voice, but instead to convey a "constellation of voices."[17] I would suggest that, putting ethics aside, it is certainly good journalism (and probably Networked Journalism) to do so.

Despite the high levels of media interest in creating stories about "normal" Muslims, there has been a lack of response from Muslims themselves. There has been defensive defensiveness and a deliberate withdrawal from debate. This may be down to fear within the Muslim community, and particularly the cautious culture among imams, who have been less willing to speak out against jihadist interpretations of the Qu'ran. And should the media include radicals in the debate? How useful is the recent trend of giving a platform to former extremists such as Ed Husain, author of The Islamist?[18] Some Muslims describe them as "charlatans," and say that their exposure promotes dangerous ideas, giving the impression that all political Muslims are on this conveyer belt towards extremism. But it is important to bring the information they have into the open about the motives and organization of radical Muslim groupings. It is only when that has happened that we can move the debate on. Muslims need to be more connected to the potential for communication that the news media offers. This is partly about initiatives, such as media training for imams. But it is also about the evolution of a more Networked Journalism that engages the public in the process of reporting their communities and that allows people to access different viewpoints.

4.1.6   Networked Journalism: Global is local

Globally the media has to come to terms with the issues around terror and community. It has to be better informed about the technical detail and the complexities of the arguments. This requires a greater sophistication in the treatment of Muslims as a community and as a factor in international affairs. It is a sophistication that will also allow a greater skepticism about claims made on their behalf. We are now in a new phase of Muslim–Media relations. Increasingly, journalists are finding ways of asking the right questions, but the relationship is still characterized by mutual hostility and a lack of capacity for understanding on both sides. Only through Networked Journalism and a greater degree of editorial diversity and media literacy can the relationship and the outcomes be improved.

There is already evidence that this is happening. The recent growth of a multiplicity of international rolling news channels, for example, allows competing perspectives of global affairs. *France 24, Aljazeera English, Al-Arabiya,* and *Russia Today* have all launched in the past few years. We are promised a pan-African news channel, *A24.* As with any journalistic market that competition can produce difference and diversity. It can also inform the different news products with a more complex view of stories. Simply having *Aljazeera* turned on in a Western newsroom means it has a cross-fertilizing influence. That is a form of connectivity. But with their restricted budgets and limited formats there is a question mark over how effective these channels are at truly connecting with their audiences. When they deal with the big issues of terror and community that we have raised in this chapter, there is every chance that they will deal with them in the same way that the media always has. That is, as a top-down reflection of the agenda of those in power, both the authorities and the terrorists.

Only when journalists share the responsibility of reporting on community and politics will we get journalism that avoids amplifying the act and its effects through the actual coverage. In the wake of terrorist acts the journalist owes allegiance to no-one but the public. Networked Journalism makes that manifest. By connecting with the citizen the Networked Journalist facilitates a debate that can be some sort of beginning for civic engagement even when that social cohesion is under the most strain.

Chapter Summary

- Terror is a highly mediated form of extremist politics and violence.
- Terror is grounded in local and global communities.
- Networked Journalism tries to understand and connect the issues of terror and community.
- Networked Journalism uses networks to make itself better informed.
- Networked Journalism can counter the shift from the diversification of media toward the fragmentation of society by connecting different media and public groups.
- Networked Journalism can make connections on a global scale.
- Networked Journalism must retain its core journalistic principles, such as the primacy of freedom of expression.
- Networked Journalism is more reflective about the process of mediating terror and community.
- Networked Journalism works to bring separate communities into the discourse about terror and security.

5

We Can All be Super Heroes

Networked Journalism in Action: Editorial Diversity and Media Literacy

The challenge of terror has made it painfully clear that we need more journalism, not less, and that it needs to be better. I have argued that this journalism needs to be much more connected. As each journalist can do more, each will provide more. Welcome to the era of SuperMedia and the hero of the age, the "Networked Journalist." They will still have recognizable core tasks and skills. We want someone to filter the vast information flows and to do it quickly. We have untrammeled access to a great slew of facts, opinions, and imagery. We need editors. We need someone to make choices, to prioritize the data and commentary by judging its significance. And it has to be packaged. We need people who can process the information in a way that we will find accessible. And it has to be done fast. Journalism can be even more useful in giving us topical reportage that monitors what changes in our increasingly fast-moving world. To have validity as journalism, rather than simple testimony, news communication has to attain a degree of authority. People have to trust it as a version of reality that aspires to objectivity, fairness, accuracy, and thoroughness. It might be valuable without that quality, but it is not journalism. You can bring those skills to bear through a specialist agency, in other words, a journalist. Or the participants can take those roles upon themselves. Either way, you get Networked Journalism. In this final chapter I will try to set out how we can save journalism. By that I mean how we should change journalism. To do that we need to invest in Editorial Diversity and Media Literacy. I will end by suggesting what this could then offer in political terms.

Networked Journalists need to be better journalists than ever, because they are working with people who think they know better – the public. And very often they do Information is everywhere and easily accessed, so Networked Journalists have to add extra editorial value. In this age of "information overload" there will be even more demand for journalists as editors and for trusted brands which can be relied on to filter out rubbish and to package what is useful in an authoritative way. In a world of ever-increasing media manipulation by government and business, it is even more important for investigative journalists to use technology and connectivity to reveal hidden truths. Networked journalists are open, interactive, and share the process. Instead of gatekeepers, they are facilitators: the public become co-producers. Networked Journalists "are 'medium agnostic' and 'story-centric.'"[1] The process is faster and the information sticks around longer, spinning out endlessly. Of course, the Networked Journalist must know how the technology works and how to use it: blogs, aggregator feeds, tags, links, and all the rest of the jargon. They must be able to put video or audio online, to podcast, and to text alert. They can crowd-source and they can set up wikis. It is not all new or high tech. Journalism in a networked age is also pouring into old forms. Some tried and tested "platforms" are being rediscovered for journalism. There has been a growth in serious topical non-fiction books, such as *Fast Food Nation*,[2] and feature-length documentaries, like *Farenheit 9/11*,[3] to give just two examples. These are classic formats finding renewed and enhanced value in an age when the fast and the furious, the glib and the superficial, were expected to triumph. Instead, people like Michael Moore, Morgan Spurlock, and Eric Schlosser are finding a new audience hungry for long-form work. But they are also exploiting new technology to promote their films and books and to extend the impact of their work online. Networked Journalists must not only be clever enough to embrace the current set of changes but also flexible enough to exploit the next set of opportunities to arise.

The other part of the connectivity equation is public media literacy. We do not need to turn every citizen in to a journalist. But in an information economy and polity every person has a right to access. In a more connected environment people need a sophisticated set of skills to exercise that right in a meaningful and practical way. So we need to provide the learning experiences and participatory opportunities that will allow the public to be networked to journalism. At one level this is a relatively straightforward question of adjusting curricula through the education system and beyond. But at a deeper level it is also a challenge to the idea of an "informed public".

For journalism to be genuinely transparent and effective in the new media environment I have set out, society needs to understand and support a different relationship between audience and producer of news media. That means that all institutions, from government to public relations to charities will have to re-orientate their approach to the public and the media. They will have to become more media literate and more supportive of media literacy among their voters, clients, and supporters. It starts by enabling citizens to be a part of the news production process. But this is a new media world where concepts such as Creative Commons mean that media literacy is also about an intellectual and even ideological literacy as well as a set of practical skills. For this all to be the case we must invest as societies in Networked Journalism. I would argue that this is money well spent. Media literacy is a social good. It is not as vital a public service as Defense or Health, for example. But it is an important pre-condition for all the other social goods to be delivered in an efficient and democratic manner. It promotes transparency and governance through civic engagement. It is at that point that Networked Journalism gets political. So what is to be done? First, I will look at the evolving concept of media literacy from the professional journalists' point of view and then from the perspective of the citizen.

5.1 Editorial Diversity

Networked Journalists need to realize that they are competing with a vast array of alternative attractions. They must understand the diversity of their audience. By this I don't just mean the public's ethnic or political make-up. I mean the fact that increasingly we will all have multiple identities facilitated by new media technologies. We can veer from being personal to professional, mix business with pleasure, blend learning with entertainment and do our information gathering while interacting socially. News must do more than reflect this diversity of communications practice. It must be part of it. The composition of newsrooms must reflect their audiences in terms of their identity but also in terms of the journalists' behavior. Diversity should be seen as a resource, not a moral requirement. Networked Journalism makes this easier as the production process allows greater input from the public. But what skills and qualities will the Networked Journalist need to create a SuperMedia?

One problem is that there is a lack of editorial diversity at a time when we will need it most. Take the actual social make-up of the news media. You might think that factors such as the global expansion of Further Education and the ease with which we can all access Internet journalism should mean that the news media would be more varied in its composition than before. Instead, mainstream media threatens to become narrower and fragmented, rather than pluralistic and rich. It is still dominated by relatively small social groups who create quite exclusive cultures. These vary according to the society and news media involved. But the concentration of media practitioners from restricted groups is common in most media markets. In the UK, for example, there has not been a widespread increase in black or Muslim journalists or journalists from outside of a middle-class metropolitan caste. This is despite a concerted effort, by broadcasters in particular, to encourage recruitment from ethnic minorities. These initiatives have been partly offset by other trends such as the growth in journalism studies in Higher Education. The professionalization of journalism tends to exclude non-elite social groups. I have no objection to media studies or journalism training courses as a way of preparing for a news media career. Quite the opposite. But these courses are hugely popular and entry is very competitive and so the problem is that they are likely to discriminate in favor of the best-prepared and socially advantaged. It may also be that it is only middle-class offspring that can afford the initial low wages offered in the entry-level jobs that give access to much of the commercial news media. Their parents will subsidize them while they work for free to gain that vital first experience and contacts. This trend has combined with a growing feeling among young people in minority groups that mainstream media is not for them as a consumer, let along as a practitioner. It is important that media colleges work even harder to attract a more diverse intake if they are to provide the news media with the diversity of human resources that it needs. However, as always with the news media, it is the industry itself that creates the demand.

Networked Journalism is not the only solution but it offers a way to replace fragmentation with diversification. It offers a chance to replace professional exclusivity with a participatory inclusiveness that might lead to a greater variety among the people who can enter and even run the news media. Networked Journalism can bring the production skills and communication techniques of mainstream news media to online participatory journalism. It is in the self-interest of the news media to employ a variety of people who will connect with the various audiences. In addition, the public's expertise manifested in citizen journalism can help build new creativity and skills in mainstream journalism. With Networked Journalism we can all learn together on the job.

What we should learn is how to enhance the increasingly formulaic, unreflective, and uncreative state of contemporary mainstream journalism. As the pace of news accelerates and as editorial budgets tighten, the way news is produced becomes more predictable and less nuanced. Networked Journalism offers greater diversity of content if it is thought through properly and imaginatively. It can provide greater range, depth, and context. What we are striving for here is what I call "Editorial Diversity." Essentially, this is an openness to engage with new sources, perspectives, and narratives and an ability to use them to create networked journalism. Here is an example that Tom Armitage gave in an article about "Next Media":

> When riots erupted in the French banlieues last autumn, the Swiss newspaper *l'Hebdo* (www.hebdo.ch) sent journalists to blog from the epicentre of the disturbances, working out of a microbureau in the town of Bondy. In doing so, they discovered that what makes a blog successful isn't the technology that powers it, or any aspiration to journalism, but the voices that write it.
>
> As a result, *l'Hebdo* changed tactics. It took seven Bondy residents back to Switzerland, gave them a crash course in journalism and blogging and then handed the blog over to them. The resulting *Bondy Blog* (previon.typepad.com) continues to be a great success, and is still of relevance in the current French political climate. It would not exist without a fusion of old media skills with new media technology and attitude.[4]

This is a good example of a partnership project, there are plenty of others,[5] but the point of Networked Journalism is that this should become increasingly routine. This will sometimes be counter-intuitive for the journalism. As Jeff Jarvis explains, sometimes they must do less to do more:

> Try this on as a new rule for newspapers: Cover what you do best. Link to the rest. That's not how newspapers work now. They try to cover everything because they used to have to be all things to all people in their markets. They took wire-service copy and reedited it so they could give their audiences the world. But in the age of the link, this is clearly inefficient and unnecessary. You can link to the stories that someone else did and to the rest of the world. And if you do that, it allows you to reallocate your dwindling resources to what matters. (Jeff Jarvis, *Buzzmachine*)[6]

As Jarvis points out, in an online video age this can also apply to TV news. Applying this principle should allow journalists to do more. To do, as Jarvis says, "what matters."

To do more, journalists will have to be better equipped. To provide the kind of value-added analysis or reportage, they will have to "speak" to more sources, not fewer. They will have to be more trustworthy and authoritative in the face of the subjectivity available freely in the Blogosphere. As one historian of journalism has pointed out, this can be seen as a return to the core values of journalism. But now we need to combine good old-fashioned editorial skills with new Networked aptitudes and competences:

> Burned-out reporters can be forgiven for dreaming that the coming of this analyzing and appraising [instead of basic fact gathering] will lead to a life of leisurely speculation. But, alas, more industrious reporting, not less, will be required . . . Getting at the meaning of events will demand looking beyond press conferences, escaping the pack, tracking down more knowledgeable sources, spending more time with those who have been affected . . . More and more diverse sources should improve story ideas and stories, and help reporters know more when they say what they know. (Mitchell Stephens, *Columbia Journalism Review*)[7]

This newly liberated editorial resource may be directed towards more local or more specialized coverage. It may also be used to pursue what many mainstream journalists have always claimed as the ultimate in news media endeavor – investigation. When Networked Journalists invest in digging deeper, they can make that go further by sharing the results rather than following their former instincts and try to protect their results. When the British *Guardian* newspaper broke a series of exclusive stories about the UK government's relationship with the Saudis over a BAE weapons contract, it decided to put the vast amount of data it had acquired online. *The BAE Files* website[8] that it set up goes further than just putting all their published articles and some background features online. It has very clever interactive graphics that allow you to follow this highly complex story. It has wonderful video clips of interviews with key participants. But perhaps most importantly, it also puts a vast amount of links and primary documentation online that will allow other journalists to pursue this story further internationally. It has the potential to reform the whole way investigative journalism works. As the reporter who led the investigation, David Leigh, says, that is important because stories are now global:

> We're trying to think our way towards a new kind of journalism. Everybody says the Internet is a new world with citizen journalism, a global audience and everybody having their say, and we tried to do it that way and say "this is a

new kind of journalism and we will put everything in front of everybody."
The thing is all the criminals are global now, the police forces are gradually
starting to go global and now the journalists are global as well. We need to
catch up. (David Leigh, *The Guardian*)[9]

In the old days Leigh would have written a book about this investigation and
it would have gathered dust on library shelves. Instead, the *Guardian* has
created a fascinating website which should attract custom. There is no sub-
stitute for giving investigative journalists more time and having faith in their
ability to get results from digging deeper and researching more widely. But
the Internet and other new technology can help. Websites with the crowd-
sourcing potential of *The BAE Files* can push the story along by encouraging
other journalists or the public to feed back information into their newsroom
about this or other similar stories of global corruption.

5.1.1   The Wiki principle

Let us have a look in more detail at one famous example of how people have
tried to use a New Media device to re-invent journalism. The wiki is clearly
very different from "Old media" or mainstream news gathering. It offers
facilities for communication that are different in quality and scale to liner
media. But as we shall see, new technologies bring problems as well as opportunities in practice.

The wiki principle is most famously enacted in the online encyclopedia
of the same name.[10] The idea is that a consensus is reached by open interaction. Normally, an encyclopaedia would commission an expert to write
an entry, in much the same way that an Old Media journalist would be
expected to report upon an event or fact. That way you get one, usually authoritative, version of reality. The wiki principle takes advantage of software to
allow a collective version of reality to be produced. In practice this means
that the Wikipedia is unstable because it is constantly being added to and
checked. But because enough people are checking and amending, it tends
towards a detailed and consensual version. Anyone who posts an extreme
view or an inaccurate item is more at risk of having it removed. Tests have
indicated that, overall and over time, Wikipedia is not much less accurate
than Encyclopaedia Britannica.[11,12] Both make mistakes, but at least Wikipedia's
are quickly correctable. And in return we have this extraordinary online resource
for free that has put a colossal amount of information into the public realm

in an easily accessed format. I always treat Wikipedia information with caution, but I am very grateful it is there.

Could this work for journalism? Well, it has already been tried, with at least one unhappy result. Back in June 2005, *The LA Times* famously allowed readers to intervene on the wiki principle with a wiki editorial about the Iraq War. This is how technology correspondent Dan Glaister described what happened next:

> By early morning, readers were inserting a tone that was more shrill than the high-minded balance of the original: "The Bush administration should be publicly charged and tried for war crimes and crimes against humanity." At 9am, the editorial was erased by a reader and substituted with another. Bizarrely, the new version echoed the position of the original. By mid-morning, the editorial had been replaced by the more reductive "Fuck USA." By lunchtime, the founder of Wikipedia got in on the act, "forking" the editorial into two pieces, representing opposing viewpoints. "I'm proposing this page as an alternative to what is otherwise inevitable, which is extensive editing of the original to make it neutral . . . which would be fine for Wikipedia, but would not be an editorial," wrote Jimbo Wales, who advised the paper on its experiment. At 4am the paper's managing editor got a call from the office. Explicit images known as "goatses" had appeared on the wikitorial page. The experiment was terminated. (Dan Glaister, *The Guardian*)[13]

There is also a *Wikinews*[14] website which attempts to enact the *Wikipedia* principle for journalism. At the time of writing it was one of the dullest, least topical, and uninformative news websites I have seen. The Africa section hadn't seen a new story for more than a week. These sites seem to be most useful when there is a very major story such as Hurricane Katrina which generates enough disparate sources of information to make a wiki interesting. It seems to me, though, that both *Wikinews* and the *LA Times* experiment misunderstand how networking can work with the journalism. The *LA Times* attempt made the mistake that using the wisdom of the reader is a one-off exercise. They also assumed that the newspaper should surrender control. Inevitably, both the news organization and the readers themselves will get more proficient, but why try to construct an Op Ed article out of a mass of different voices? In that example, the wiki did not, in itself, contribute to news reporting or analysis. In Networked Journalism it does not matter if the core journalistic functions of reporting, analysis, and commentary are carried out by the "amateur" or the "professional" journalist,

Figure 5.1   Virginia Tech – mainstream media makes its presence felt while the inside story was being told on the Internet (Photo © Chip Somodevilla/ Getty Images)

but one or more has to be fulfilled. The *LA Times* experiment was perfectly valid as an art work or an online chat room but it was not successful Networked Journalism.

I can imagine that a wiki would work well as an attempt to create a community's version of an event. In the case of the Virginia Tech shootings (see Figure 5.1) there is some evidence that this happened to a degree in a spontaneous manner.[15,16] By tapping in to the whole Virginia Tech community it might have been possible to construct a fuller picture of what happened in terms of how each person at the University experienced that day's events. As Dan Gillmor wrote in the wake of the Virginia Tech shootings:

> We used to say that journalists write the first draft of history. Not so, not any longer. The people on the ground at these events write the first draft. This is not a worrisome change, not if we are appropriately skeptical and to find sources we trust. We will need to retool media literacy for the new age, too. (Dan Gillmor)[17]

And a wiki could have informed us with an analytical approach to the incident with Virginia Tech students, officials and academics combining to offer their collective understanding of the cause of the killings and of other associated issues such as gun control. Finally, a wiki for Virginia Tech surely would surely have given us moving and involved commentary by those affected. However, this would only have been journalism if it had been through some sort of Networked Journalism phase or function. As Academic Paul Bradshaw says on his wiki about wikis:

> Like blogs, wikis will only flourish if as much time and care is invested in them as are invested in editing articles. Weaknesses identified, such as vandalism and inaccuracy can be addressed if web-literate editorial staff are assigned to monitor and facilitate the wiki – to prevent legal issues, to attract A-List contributors and build genuine online communities. (Paul Bradshaw, City University Birmingham)[18]

This should apply to all Networked Journalism. New media can provide shortcuts and new resources but there is no magical way to replace editorial investment. I suspect that wikis are too clumsy and require too much oversight for them to work effectively as vehicles for effective news gathering or dissemination. When an event is topical (*Wikinews*), as opposed to historical (*Wikipedia*), the wiki principle becomes less useful as journalism. But there are other New Media formats apart from wikis which may offer more to journalism.

5.1.2   Editorial diversity skills

It is clear that alongside traditional editorial strengths, it will take a whole new skill-set to exploit these new practices. Here's one New Media expert's suggestion of a list of the new competencies that he would expect the next generation of journalists to bring to a job interview:

> I'd be looking for one of the trinity: multimedia, interactivity, data.
>
> - Can you code a Flash stage for chaptered Soundslides?
> - Can you edit audio, photos, and video into a compelling multimedia presentation?
> - Can you manage a community of users?
> - Can you moderate comments and forums and reader-contributed stories and photos and video?
> - Can you build a maps mashup that feeds itself with data scraped from public records?
> - Can you design interactive graphics in Flash?
>
> If the answer to any one of those questions is "Yes," things are looking up, but just *knowing* that you should be able to answer "Yes" to some of these can get you hired these days. (Ryan Sholin, *Invisible Inklings*)[19]

Sholin is enough of a journalist to admit that no-one will have all those skills. He stresses that the core ability will still be story-telling. But he is right to characterize these as a mind-set as much as a skill-set. Journalism schools and companies will have to prepare their people for this new working world.

This should make for a kind of journalism that is much better grounded in the real experience of a wide range of opinion. This does not mean that the journalist has to surrender their critical faculties to the "wisdom of the crowd."[20] One of the key aptitudes that the Networked Journalist will need, akin to that of a social scientist, is how to analyze the data collected. But it will also require the editorial judgment to differentiate between the merely popular and the truly perceptive insights. Good journalism has always been about this. Too often in the past mainstream journalism has acted upon the principle of the lowest common denominator without even bothering to check what that means. In the future, as the easy journalism will be more readily available, the premium will be on the journalism that either adds value or differentiates itself from basic information. As with all good journalism there will be special value accorded to the ability to look in the opposite direction to which the herd is travelling.[21]

One key skill will be adaptability and an open mind. Things will not settle. While journalism struggles to adapt to the opportunities offered by new technologies, visionaries are trying to realize a new way of communicating that supersedes the very binary logic of the current Internet. At present, the Internet works so well because it can micro-process so much data so quickly. It sifts and it links but it does not think intelligently about what you are trying to find out. When we communicate with each other on the Net we do it largely on a telephonic model. What if there was a new public infrastructure that could intuit search or initiate dialogue on your behalf? And what if that function was utilized by journalists?[22,23] Imagine a form of journalistic research that could communicate interactively in an intelligent way with the audience. Imagine if you could ask them for their experiences of an issue and interrogate them about their responses to build up a complex picture of public opinion. It would be like having a million reporters asking questions. As the technology changes so rapidly, the danger is that we don't all have the knowledge and skills to understand how to use it. That is why we need much greater media literacy.

5.2 Media Literacy

The ability to access, understand and create communications in a variety of contexts. (Ofcom, the British broadcasting regulator)[24]

That deceptively basic definition of media literacy is just a starting point for the people who regulate broadcasting in Britain. Indeed, they are the people many think will be involved with regulating the Internet, too. They broaden the definition themselves to include this description:

Media literacy has parallels with traditional literacy; the ability to read and write text. Media literacy is the ability to "read" and "write" audiovisual information rather than text. At its simplest level media literacy is the ability to use a range of media and be able to understand the information received. At a more advanced level it moves from recognising and comprehending information to the higher order critical thinking skills such as questioning, analysing and evaluating that information. This aspect of media literacy is sometimes referred to as "critical viewing" or "critical analysis."[25]

For Networked Journalists the definition has to be even broader. This is why: Journalism will need more editorial creativity as described above. Much of this will come through the initiative and applied inspiration that has always made for good journalism. This is the magic formula: Competition plus imagination plus investment equals SuperMedia. The global media industry has already made a huge investment in New Media. It needs to do something similar again with Networked Journalism. I hope that the shareholders and stakeholders will see the value of investing in this process. It is a logical progression of the first phase of the move online (see Chapter 1). We can already see that the public is prepared to invest its efforts in Networked Journalism. Citizens have produced vast amounts of journalism for virtually no financial reward. That will continue. But to underpin this there needs to be a deeper change in the way that society as a whole supports Networked Journalism. This is best understood as an investment in media literacy. It is about a lot more than just understanding how the media works. It should also be for everyone, not just media students or mainstream journalists. This has implications for general education as well as specific media studies or professional training.

Media or Journalism Studies should be renamed Media Literacy. Journalism Colleges have to recognize that they are providing the professionals for the

Next Media instead of teaching what was known decades ago. This is about more than setting up an online college newspaper. Journalism training should still include writing courses, for example. But in an age of much more informal and conversational communication, journalists should be taught that there are more styles than the often-bizarre formulae of newspaper or TV presenter speak. Entrepreneurship must be part of the process because every journalist will have to be more "business creative." This is partly because the monetization of content will become more complex. With more diverse or fragmented audiences, the producer will have to spend more time finding or connecting with their consumer. This will become an editorial process as much as a commercial one. Journalism and Business Schools should work more closely together as information becomes more important to the economy and as the economics of the media itself becomes more complex and more connected to other industries.

Media Literacy courses will have to teach about the citizen journalist and how to work with them. They have to teach the principles and practice of Editorial Diversity. Many of the ideas in the previous section require training and preparation. Some of this will be practical, but it will also be ethical. In the past journalists have been reluctant to codify their work too strictly. I think this is a sensible instinct because journalism is about the specific and the challenging. It does not work well under the sort of regulations and guidelines that are required for doctors or teachers. However, there should be much more debate and reflection within the industry. This should be available as part of the editorial diversity training process for all journalists, not just for top managers attending international conferences. And it should be a process of self-criticism that must always include the public, rather than the exclusive gatherings that often characterize the media's self-meditations. It should not stop when the media student enters the newsroom. In a rapidly changing media environment journalists will have to become more like architects and lawyers and seek regular career enhancement training. They should also be teaching the citizen journalist. If the citizen is going to work as a journalist then it would be useful for them to understand core principles such as accuracy, thoroughness, fairness, transparency, and skepticism.

I have kept repeating throughout this book that, for the Networked Journalist, many of the core journalism skills and values will become more, not less, important. But there will need to be educational attention paid to preparing Networked Journalists for at least three interesting differences when operating online:

1   Creative Commons;
2   Freedom of speech; and
3   Net neutrality / copyright

5.2.1   Creative Commons

The idea of Creative Commons is also a campaign.[26,27] It is the idea that conventional copyright online is a barrier to the very diffusive genius that the Internet brings to communications. Networked Journalists should support this idea and be trained in how to get the most out of the sharing principle. This goes against the grain of mainstream journalists, who depend upon the idea of exclusivity. In practice, though, I do not see that as an issue except with image rights. Networked Journalists will have to become adept at managing limited exclusivity combined with maximum exposure. Journalism is not like most creative industries that need to protect their intellectual property to maximize income. Journalism profits by linking to multiple platforms, as most news organizations have found when being "cannibalized" by news aggregators such as Google News. It does mean that those media organizations which simply replicate facts will suffer. The audience discounts the value of basic information, but it puts a significant premium on the speed, accuracy, and packaging of the delivery.

Some media will remain at one remove. As we discussed in Chapter 1, some news organizations will still charge for access. But even this minority should still seek to be networked in the sense that they will seek to exploit the value of their consumer community. This should go further than the traditional reader survey. *The Financial Times* for example has a fantastic wealth of economic knowledge among its readers that could provide invaluable insight for its journalists. It is in the interest of all media organizations to make their consumers more media literate so they can participate in that process.

5.2.2   Freedom of expression

Freedom of expression is another principle that the Internet has claimed for itself and which presents a challenge to mainstream journalism. Part of media literacy will be learning how to deal with the rights and responsibilities that come with the greater opportunities for freedom of speech afforded by new technology. Mainstream journalists have found themselves rather shocked at close up and personal contact with the public. The *Guardian* newspaper was one of the first to go big on blogs by its own journalists. Its *Comment Is Free* website has created a global online forum where Guardian staffers and guest bloggers provide a daily diet of opinion. Perhaps because of its minority liberal views (even in the UK the *Guardian* is a small sales broadsheet) it attracts often vituperative responses which journalists find rude and pointless. Veteran political journalist Jackie Ashley's reaction was not untypical:

> I've received dozens of emails which say nothing more than, in effect, "you stupid cow, what a lot of rubbish." I really can't see the point of sending abuse, under the cloak of anonymity. It's about as grown up as kids sending each other anonymous notes in class saying "you're fat" or "nobody likes you". What I will say in defence of professional columnists is that most of us have years of experience covering say politics, social policy or international affairs . . . There will always be those who know much more about a subject than a columnist. And equally there will always be those who think they know much more. I'm delighted to hear from both: just so long as you make proper arguments and don't call me a fucking stupid cow. (Jackie Ashley, *The Guardian*)[28]

Even those journalists who run this kind of forum feel disillusioned:

> There is a sense that blogging gives us an access that was not there in the past, but some of us are feeling disillusioned in the blogosphere. There can be a sense of Us against Them. A number of bloggers feel their job is to hold Mainstream media to account or to try to undermine our authority. That's a worthy aim as there is a lot of arrogance in journalism. But we were hoping they would give us more insights into subjects we don't know enough about. (Ros Taylor, *Guardian Unlimited*)[29]

This is a universal problem which has led to people like Internet pioneer Tim O'Reilly trying to work out a code of conduct. The man who invented the phrase Web 2.0 is now trying to draw up a blog etiquette.[30] Part of media literacy is surely learning how to conduct oneself in a conversation without resorting to lies and insult. For the Networked Journalist, media literacy is about giving outspoken views a space, without crowding out other shades of opinion. This monitoring and moderating role is something that journalists should be good at. But doing that online requires a calibration of control that preserves open access and vitality, but prevents anarchy.

5.2.3 Net neutrality

Net neutrality is a truly Internet-specific concept. It argues that the World Wide Web is intrinsically egalitarian. Information shared on the Internet should not be corralled by a pricing or access system. Part of media literacy for Networked Journalism is in understanding the value and limits of this ideal. Connectivity thrives in the public sphere of news media when there are the optimum circumstances for communication. Any barrier, tariff, and exclusion of information that happens at a primary level is counter to the free flow of material. In a pragmatic sense, it distorts the market in ideas. In a moral sense, it is politically negative if certain groups of people do not have the same ability to benefit from the Internet as others. However, journalists and the public have to understand that the online world is not unmediated even now. There are already different costs to access the Internet and broadband as well as specific areas or sites. The search function is not neutral, and linking is done in different ways with varying connectivity. For example, if someone links to my blog on an RSS feed, they see my posts, but they may not see the comments. Media literacy is about understanding how to make the maximum connectivity with the minimum bias. Where there are distortions they should be made clear. Networked Journalism has to have the media and Internet literacy to deal with threats to net neutrality, which should be at least the goal, if not the absolute reality, of online news.

5.3 Media Literacy in Education

It is clear that the Internet and other digital technologies bring a whole new set of complexities to the nature and processes of journalism. Both public and professionals need to be better equipped. We have already seen how media organizations have to respond. There is also a need for more general media literacy. That can only be achieved in the longer-term through education. It is generally accepted by most governments that modern societies need higher levels of education to cope with the demands of information economies. My argument is that we are still not attending to the vital role of the news media at the heart of those systems. Despite the rapid growth in specialized media studies courses and journalism colleges we are not doing enough to enable the wider population with a broader understanding and skills needed in a networked world.

I have made it clear throughout this book that "the Journalist" can be a citizen. Some will be effectively full-time journalists although many won't give up the day job. But with Networked Journalism we all benefit from greater public media literacy, even if the interaction is marginal or occasional. Public education has to prioritize media literacy so that the people formerly known as the audience are given the skills to understand this Networked Media and to be able to use the range of platforms and structures and processes that it offers. At one level this is about basic literacy. The highly text-based new media technologies depend upon good literacy on the part of the consumer. Anyone who has incorrectly typed an Internet search inquiry realizes that. But beyond that elementary competence, they have a right to be equipped to take part in the news media, either for themselves, their communities, or in networks with journalists. This goes way beyond simply putting PCs in to classrooms. This is a serious transfer of emphasis from a defensive to a positive role. It is a move from teaching media literacy as an understanding of the media to teaching it as a way of participating in the news media. It is also a shift from analytical to ethical. The public should be taught the political and social value of media activity. This should be part of everything from Civics lessons at school to professional enhancement training.

There is a historical problem with improving media literacy through education. The people who should do the teaching are themselves from a pre-Web 2.0 world. There needs to be a radical review of teacher training, not just for media studies but for all communications-related teaching. It is not just technical knowledge that is needed. Teachers need to understand that the way that people learn greater media literacy is very much a personal exploration guided and inspired by the communities involved. In other words, people learn media literacy by doing it. They begin by using the Internet to order their shopping and end up organizing a neighborhood meeting. They begin by uploading their holiday photos and end up posting their own video reports of the School Concert. So the teaching experience has to build on that intuitive applied approach rather than the traditional pedagogical structure of theory, principles, and rules.

One of the more enterprising education authorities is in the "Silicon Glens" of Scotland. The National Advisor on Learning and Technology Futures is Ewan McIntosh. He has created a network for digital educators in Scotland which shares best practice and encourages innovation.[31] McIntosh describes many of those in education as "twenty-first-century illiterates." He worries that schools can spend more time blocking pupil access to the Internet then they do on promoting digital literacy. Some teacher unions have

even called for a ban on websites such as *YouTube*. Not only is this a dispro-
portionate reaction, but it also fails to appreciate that social networking is
the key to improving digital literacy, not a distraction.

This is not the place for a detailed exposition of the future of media
literacy education, but some principles have emerged. Just as the public will
in future create more of its own journalism, so the public must create its
own media literacy. As McIntosh puts it, the role of the educator changes so
that "The teacher is no longer the sage on the stage, but the guide on the
side".[32] There are no rules but he insists that teachers should use the same
range of digital media that people have access to in their personal lives:

- Use Blogs – teachers and students have to communicate with the digital
  media when they are learning how to understand and use it.
- Use Games – they impart vital technical skills and ways of thinking
  digitally.
- Use Social Networking – it creates networks that are accessible and
  disseminates the learning.
- Participate – teachers have to do the same stuff as the students to understand it.
- Accept information flux: you are teaching "how to" not "what is."[33]

These thoughts are not necessarily contradictory to mainstream educational
methods. But digital media literacy is still often seen as a separate special-
ism or a low priority. In fact it is almost as important as basic literacy. It should
be part of all learning and underpin everyone's educational resources.
People do show a remarkable ability to create their own digital lifestyles. But
if everyone is to benefit from the full economic, social, and political benefits
of the new media environment then we should invest in creating a more networked education for a networked world.

5.4 Media Literacy in Governance

To create a more widely media-literate society requires a commitment to use
Networked Journalism at the heart of good governance and development.
This will not be easy.

> From a policy point of view, if these and other new forms of boundary
> crossing are to grow, funding will have to shift from support for traditional

journalism to promoting media literacy. Only in this way can the public become the drivers of the news and their stories. Policy support for this might not be very strong because networked journalism goes against the grain of governments. When openness conflicts with traditional modes of operation, governments become uneasy. Few political systems are predicated upon the need for an informed, let alone, networked, public. (Professor Robin Mansell, Speech to the United Nations General Assembly)[34]

As Professor Mansell says, politicians are not usually eager to encourage a stronger news media. There is a growing desire to promote "e-democracy." I suspect that this is partly about politicians attempting to cut out the media from their communications with the public. Putting aside that cynicism though, it is true that the public sphere can be strengthened with the resources of new technology. But you cannot have a real increase in participatory politics without more open government. Unless those in authority are prepared to share access to their processes and devolve power then the citizen remains an observer to the machine of governance. For example, there is no point allowing residents of a housing project to set up a website if the views expressed on it have no impact. Real engagement would allow the residents to use their digital connectivity to make their own choices about how to spend a real budget. In that case, the role of the administration is to make sure those choices are well-informed. It has to be open about the relevant data and policy contexts. It is the role of the politicians to act as supporters of the digital debate. And it is the job of the news media to be part of that net-worked conversation. With Networked Journalism the residents of that housing estate become the citizen journalists that produce a community media that reports, monitors, and debates their digital democracy. The Networked Journalist's role is to enable and to enhance that discourse, not to replace it. All this takes effort and it takes a real will to educate the citizenry for that networked opportunity. Setting up the technological paraphernalia such as the blogs, the online video, and the facilities for deliberative democratic inter-action is the easy part. The real challenge is promoting the media literacy and then not resisting the shift in the political architecture. The journalistic functions remain vital to making that happen.

Any form of participatory project that seeks to build democratic inter-activity through digital communications without addressing the role of the (Networked) news media is missing a vital element in building the new public sphere. Policies that encourage the free flow of information and interaction with the public are policies that create an environment in which

Networked Journalism can flourish. Networked Journalism can be a part of an enhanced public discourse that can contribute to meeting the complex challenges we face. This challenges the classic framework of a media that passes messages from the government to the governed. And so, in a sense, it can seek to address the problems inherent in Lippman and Dewey's debate about an "Informed Society."[35] Previously, there have been two camps. One suggested that the public can make better political decisions if only they were given proper information. The other says that politics is too complicated and that there are limits to the ability of the general public to become significantly involved in running things. Likewise, the two camps disagree about the media. One suggests that if only the media were more intelligent, sensible and responsible then we would have a better informed populace. The other stresses the innate limits of a topical news media with its commercial imperatives and its structural lack of time for reflection, deliberation, and consideration.

The Internet and New Media appeared to some people to offer a way of smashing through this debate. Some Internet evangelicals thought that it might give the people the power to take over the media and government. All politics would be digitally disintermediated. But as we also saw, there is nothing innately democratic about new technology. The Internet can facilitate greater connectivity, but it can also produce more atomization. It can afford greater access to information that the voter needs to make political choices, but it can also fragment the public sphere and make it a less cohesive space for debate. Networked Journalism demands a different role for media literacy that offers a more circumspect, but still progressive hope. It avoids the mechanistic fallacies of the e-democracy activists who are prey to the idea that by putting everything online or by giving everyone a website you inevitably increase political participation. Networked Journalism offers more moderate and complex benefits but they are potentially more significant in the long term. They can only be realized through an investment in media literacy that links a better understanding of communications to an insight in to power.

5.4.1   The politics of Networked Journalism

It is at this point that Networked Journalism should be seen as political. I am not insisting that Networked Journalism inevitably has a particular political effect. On the contrary, it is very much what people make of it. But I believe that it has within its dynamics an impulse towards a more connected, understanding, and secure world. A more academic way of looking at it is to say that Networked Journalism offers the chance to put flesh upon the rather complex concept of a "Cosmopolitan" media:

> The idea and ideal of cosmopolitanism captures precisely this ethical dimension of mediation as enabling or constraining a particular type of reflexive connectivity towards other people who we are different from but share the same world with. Cosmopolitanism, an ancient old concept first celebrated by the Stoics, is here used to reflect on the performative role of Western media in constituting "our" public space in contra-distinction to "others," at the moment when they claim to simply represent it. (Professor Lilie Chouliaraki, London School of Economics)[36]

In other words Networked Journalism offers the possibilities of "closing" the distance between people, even on a global scale. It does this not just through the technology of communications, but by a more contextualized reporting that gives voice to the subject. Instead of simply reporting upon "the other" we are able to report "with" people who are separated from us by geography, class, or other social factors. This does not mean that divisions are healed, but at least they can be crossed:

> When it comes to portraying distant others, the traditional media often fail us badly. They often do not grant those at a distance their own humanity – they either push them away so that we do not see their humanness, or they bring them so close that we cannot see their distinctiveness. But distant others have to be recognised as – others with humanity. Traditional media are often asymmetrical, dysfunctional and flawed in this respect. Networked journalism provides a basis for optimism that public dialogue may become more hospitable, caring and a just space for all. (Professor Robin Mansell, speech to UN General Assembly)[37]

As Professor Mansell rightly stated in her address to the United Nations, any new media technology is two-faced. It can present negative as well as positive potentialities. But Networked Journalism does at least bring decentralized decision-making, non-heirarchical structures and a greater diversity to bear upon media practice. It puts humanity back at the heart of news communications. This brings with it a greater demand for media. It will be expected to play a bigger role in our social interactions. As it becomes a larger part of people's lives it will acquire greater power. And with that power come responsibility. "Responsibility" is a word I have generally shied away from in this book because I think there are good justifications for Networked Journalism, apart from any moral plea or injunction. Now is the time to consider the ethics.

In the past, journalists have tended to see the politics of their work as a proxy for non-media politics. Partisan journalists like John Pilger[38,39] or P.J. O'Rourke[40,41] have tended to concentrate on their journalism as a form of persuasion or revelation that serves political ends. This is an admirable form of mainstream media that adds ideological richness to the flow of news mediation. However, it does not, in itself, change the relationship of the consumer or the subject with the mediator. Networked Journalism can do that. Unlike past versions of the "journalism of attachment"[42] or "committed" journalism, Networked Journalism does not place the moral compass solely in the hand of the journalist. But it does ask the journalist to consider the ethical context of what they do and the way they do it. This is not some soul-searching plea for moral virtue, self-sacrifice or altruism. It is instead an insistence that the politics of connectivity should inform the journalistic framing of an event or issue. This process subtly shifts the nature of journalism from being essentially a representation of a spectacle to a process of connectivity. Good journalism has always sought to be more than "artificial eyes" as it seeks to explain and empathize. But should it be in the business of advocating or even providing "artificial hands"? Networked Journalism has the ability to communicate human problems in a way that offers possibilities beyond reportage and analysis. Networked Journalism stresses empathy and implies political actions, but as the starting point, not the by-product, of reportage. By placing the consumer or co-producer within the process, instead of at the end of it, you bring the viewer into connectivity. By enabling the subject to be part of the process through interactivity and media literacy you likewise bring them in to connectivity. For me this is the best moral potential of journalism. With Networked Journalism that ethical outcome is a product of the way it works. Any more is pure politics.

5.5   Conclusion

This is how SuperMedia can save the world. It does not have the answer to a problem like Climate Change. But it will address the issue in a way that offers a networked understanding and the possibility of engagement. The public needs to understand but also to be involved. If the world is to deal with global warming then solutions will only be found both by international consensus and by a popular acceptance that individual lifestyles must change. Barring some technological feat of magic, we as citizens will need to have more knowledge and more power to reduce carbon emissions. For any policy to work, it must engage individuals to act in a coherent manner. For example, people will have to be motivated by empathy with those who suffer from the consequences of global warming. They also have to be empowered to influence those with the means to change policy. I am not arguing that the news media has to act as a propaganda machine for the Green movement. If anything, the record of environmentalists in the past for exploiting the media actually suggests we should be as skeptical of their claims as that of business or government. But a Networked Media offers the public a chance to be more than simply informed. By increasing the dialogue between public and power it can facilitate change. In the end, it is about turning media literacy into political literacy. This is what Professor Roger Silverstone meant by his idea of a "Mediapolis."[43] The "Mediapolis" is not a utopian place or project but instead a very realistic attempt to conceive of and practice journalism. It insists on the possibility of media as part of change. To be able to do this Networked Journalism must strengthen virtual or digital relationships. It can allow us to:

> understand connectivity in an increasingly networked age, and what the moral and ethical consequences of this particular but core dimension of mediation are. (Professor Roger Silverstone)[44]

Media literacy, in the deeper sense that I have tried to outline here is about helping to build that connectivity. That is why I repeat that Networked Journalism will not emerge without a real understanding of its implications and potential. It is not just another label for New Media. It will require investment, imagination, and innovation.

At present, Networked Journalism is still a novel concept, which may explain the pressing need for much more research and support for innovation. The state of the industry; the training and education of the professionals; the social possibilities; the political potential of this new kind of journalism; all these are barely being monitored, let alone investigated and researched with serious institutional backing. It will require a coalition of the media business, the public media sector, education, and government to address this deficit. POLIS,[45] the think-tank I lead, is an attempt to galvanize this sort of activity by bringing international journalism and society together to research and debate the possibilities of journalism.

I do not want to overstate the deterministic case for Networked Journalism. Even if we are able to achieve the kind of news media I desire, there are no guarantees that it will secure us a happier, safer, or richer world. I am also asking quite a lot of society in terms of investment and effort to create Networked Journalism without a certain reward. But I do believe that the business case, the public policy case, and the social case for Networked Journalism are irresistible. In themselves these arguments are good enough reasons to want to make Networked Media Literacy a reality.

The future will be different again. Any forecast beyond five years is of very limited value, which is why I have not made one. Networked Journalism is not a one-off solution or a prediction. It is a new way of sustaining journalism and its public role in a way that combines old virtues with new potentialities. As we move forward, the landscape will continue to change beneath our feet. Already many of the advantages of new media technology are taken for granted by the present younger generation. That is good, because it means we can move beyond the utopian/dystopian dialogue to a more pragmatic but bold agenda. We can be less starry-eyed about the gadgets and more earnest and ambitious about the practice. We can learn that the pace of change will move at different speeds. It seems that mobile TV is being taken up far less quickly than was thought less than a year ago. Online video is proving hugely popular but in a much less sophisticated way than many providers thought. Convergence is increasingly possible and yet the move from PC to TV or even TV to PC has not happened yet. Interestingly, the conventional blog is now seen as something for older people rather than the revolutionary format that it styled itself just a decade ago. The possibility of a "Semantic" web that has intelligent search functions promises to open up another dimension to online communication and connectivity. Yet whatever platform it takes, Networked Journalism must retain a sense of its principles.

This book has attempted to describe what Networked Journalism should be, but I am more interested in the dynamics than the details. I am more excited by the potential than prescriptions. My hope is to achieve what the late Professor Roger Silverstone wanted from a forum for the research and debate into journalism and society:

> There has to be a way to consider the issues: to till the ground perhaps, so that it becomes more fertile and so that the seeds of political action and professional judgement have greater likelihood of germinating. (Professor Roger Silverstone)[46]

I have outlined the threats to journalism. But I want to end on a sense of the possibilities. This is the most wonderful time to be a journalist. It is also the most opportune time for a citizen who thinks that the news media should be a positive part of their world. No more a mirror, we the media are now a SuperMedia network.

Chapter Summary

- We need more journalism but it must add social and editorial value.
- Networked Journalists should reflect the diversity of the make-up and behavior of their audience.
- Networked Journalists need to use more diverse and creative editorial techniques to build connectivity.
- The public will add extra diversity and editorial value.
- Media studies must become a Networked Journalism thought leadership program.
- Media Studies must include business studies and the public.
- Media Studies must address core issues such as Creative Commons, Freedom of Expression and Net Neutrality.
- Media Studies in education must become a positive empowerment program.
- Media Studies in governance must become part of all democratization projects.
- Higher Education and social research funders need to take research into the news media and Networked Journalism much more seriously.
- Networked Journalism is a way of creating a more cosmopolitan mediapolis.

Notes

Introduction

1   Committee to Protect Journalists, 2005, International Press Freedom Awards, viewed July 27, 2007 <http://www.cpj.org/awards05/galima.html>.
2   Silverstone, R., 2006, *Media and morality: On the rise of the mediapolis*, Cambridge: Polity Press.
3   Tumber, H., 1999, *News: A reader*, Oxford: Oxford University Press.
4   Armitage, T., 2006, 2007 and the "next" big media thing, *New Statesman*, July 31, viewed August 30, 2007, <http://www.newstatesman.com/200607310067>.

Chapter 1: The New Media Landscape

1   Goldhammer, G., 2007, Newspapers parting with experience – and with journalism, *Below the Fold*, June 2, viewed September 11, 2007, <http://belowthefold. typepad.com/my_weblog/2007/06/newspapers_part.html>.
2   Polis, 2007, London School of Economics, viewed September 11, 2007, <http://www.lse.ac.uk/collections/polis/>.
3   Waghorn, R., 2007, Norwich City, MyFootballWriter.com, viewed August 2, 2007, <http://norwichcity.myfootballwriter.com/index.asp>.
4   Terazono, E., 2006, Sales of "lads' mags" in decline, *Financial Times*, 28 August, p. 16, viewed July 27, 2007, Lexis Nexis.
5   Greenslade, R., 2006, Lads turn their backs on monthly magazines, *Guardian zUnlimited*, September 29, viewed July 27, 2007, <http://blogs.guardian.co.uk/greenslade/2006/09/lads_turn_their_backs_on_month.html>.
6   Brook, S., 2007, Bottom falls out of lads' mags market, *The Guardian*, February 19, viewed July 27, <http://media.guardian.co.uk/mediaguardian/story/0,,2015936,00.html>.

7   Kerr, G. pers. comm., May 10, 2007.

8   Wikipedia, 2007, Blog, The Wikimedia Foundation, St. Petersburg, FL, USA, viewed July 27, 2007, <http://en.wikipedia.org/wiki/Blog#_note-0>.

9   Blogpulse, 2007, Nielson BuzzMetrics, New York, NY, USA, viewed July 27, 2007, <http://www.blogpulse.com/>.

10   Technorati, 2007, Technorati, San Francisco, CA, USA, viewed July 27, 2007, <http://upport.technorati.com/support/siteguide>.

11   *Blogging is bringing new voices to the online world*, 2006, PEW Internet and American Life Project, PEW Research Center, Washington, DC, viewed July 29, 2007, <http://www.pewinternet.org/PPF/r/130/press_release.asp>.

12   Ibid.

13   Wray, R., 2007, Broadband spreads across globe, *Guardian Unlimited*, June 13, viewed July 29, 2007, <http://business.guardian.co.uk/story/0,,2102304,00.html#article_continue>.

14   Orgad, S., 2006, *This box was made for walking*. London: Nokia and London School of Economics, viewed July 30, 2007, <http://www.lse.ac.uk/collections/media@lse/pdf/Mobile_TV_Report_Orgad.pdf>.

15   18 Doughty Street, 2007, Doughty Media Limited, London, viewed July 29, 2007, <http://www.18doughtystreet.com/talk_tv>.

16   Thickett, J., 2007, Can quality survive in a market that's changing rapidly?, *The Guardian*, May 21, viewed July 29, 2007, <http://media.guardian.co.uk/mediaguardian/story/0,,2084082,00.html>.

17   *opendemocracy.net*, 2007, opendemocracy, London, viewed September 11, 2007, <http://www.opendemocracy.net/>.

18   Slate.com, 2007, Slate, New York, viewed September 11, 2007, <http://www.slate.com/>.

19   Current TV, 2007, Current, San Francisco, viewed September 11, 2007, <http://uk.current.com/>.

20   Digg, 2007, Digg, San Francisco, viewed September 11, 2007, <http://www.digg.com/>.

21   Preston, P., 2007, If the net is killing newspapers, why are they doing so well?, *The Observer*, June 10, viewed July 29, 2007, <http://media.guardian.co.uk/columnists/story/0,,2099477,00.html>.

22   Ramesh, R., Pilkington, E., Tuckman, J., Watts, J., Tremlett, G., Traynor, I., McGreal, C., Lawson, M., and Henley, J., 2007, The world is watching, *Guardian Unlimited*, June 16, viewed July 29, 2007, <http://www.guardian.co.uk/weekend/story/0,,2102856,00.html>.

23   *The state of the news media: An annual report on American journalism*, 2007, Project for Excellence in Journalism, Washington, DC, viewed July 29, 2007, <http://www.stateofthemedia.org/2007/chartland.asp?id=370&ct=col&dir=&sort=&col1_box=1&col2_box=1&col3_box=1&col4_box=1>.

24 *The state of the news media: An annual report on American journalism*, 2007, Project for Excellence in Journalism, Washington, DC, viewed July 29, 2007, <http://www.stateofthenewsmedia.com/2007/narrative_overview_audience.asp?cat=3&media=1>.

25 The news consumers' conundrum, 2007, Project for Excellence in Journalism, Washington, DC, viewed July 29, 2007, <http://www.journalism.org/node/2327>.

26 Briggs, A. and Burke, P., 2002, *A social history of the media: From Gutenberg to the Internet*. Cambridge: Polity Press, p. 306.

27 Fewell, M., 2006, POLIS Future of News seminar, November, 29. London School of Economics.

28 FactCheck, 2007, Channel 4 News, London, viewed September 11, 2007, <http://www.channel4.com/news/factcheck>.

29 Kiss, J., 2006, Channel 4 News: a future of interactivity and integration, Project for Excellence in Journalism, April 21, viewed July 29, 2007, <http://www.journalism.co.uk/news/story1816.shtml>.

30 Fewell, M., 2007, POLIS Future of News seminar, 24 January, London School of Economics.

31 Addis, R., 2007, POLIS Future of News seminar, 24 January, London School of Economics.

32 Murdock, G. and Golding, P., 2004, Dismantling the digital divide: Rethinking the dynamics of participation and exclusion, in A. Calabrese and C. Sparks (eds.), *Toward a political economy of culture: Capitalism and communication in the twenty-first century*, Lanham, MD: Rowman & Littlefield, p. 249.

33 Comedy Central, 2007, *The Daily Show*, television programme, Comedy Central, New York, viewed August 2, 2007, <http://www.comedycentral.com/>.

34 NPR, 2007, *Wait, Wait . . . Don't Tell Me*, radio program, NPR and Chicago Public Radio, Washington, DC and Chicago, IL, viewed August 2, 2007, <http://www.npr.org/programs/waitwait/>.

35 YouTube vs. the boob tube, 2006, Project for Excellence in Journalism, Washington, DC, viewed August 2, 2007, <http://www.journalism.org/node/4075>.

36 Hamm, S., 2007, Children of the web: How the second-generation Internet is spawning a global youth culture – and what business can do to cash in, *Business Week*, July 2, viewed July 29, 2007, <http://www.businessweek.com/magazine/content/07_27/b4041401.htm?chan=top+news_top+news+index_best+of+bw>.

37 *Newspaper economics: 2006 annual report advertiser influence*, 2006, Project for Excellence in Journalism, Washington, DC, March 13, viewed July 30, 2007, <http://www.journalism.org/node/650>.

38 Sawyers, M., 2007, Opinions on the status of newspapers, June,19, Editor's Weblog, viewed July 29, 2007, <http://www.editorsweblog.org/print_newspapers//2007/06/opinions_on_the_status_of_newspapers.php#more>.

39 Higginbotham, A., 2006, Local hero, August 13, *The Observer*, viewed July 30, 2007, <http://observer.guardian.co.uk/magazine/story/0,,1841318,00.html#article_continue>.

40 YouTube vs. the boob tube, 2006, Project for Excellence in Journalism, Washington, DC, viewed August 2, 2007, <http://www.journalism.org/node/4075>.

41 Ofcom, 2007, *A new approach to public service content in the digital media age*, Ofcom, London, January 24, viewed July 30, 2007, <http://www.ofcom.org.uk/consult/condocs/pspnewapproach/summary/>.

42 Ofcom, 2007, *UK's Ethnic Minority groups watch less TV but compare well on mobile and broadband take-up*, June 21, Ofcom, London, viewed July 30, 2007, <http://www.ofcom.org.uk/media/news/2007/06/nr_20070621>.

43 Richards, E., 2007, IPPR Media convention: remarks, January 18, Ofcom, London, viewed July 30, 2007, <http://www.ofcom.org.uk/media/speeches/2007/01/ippr>.

44 Prior, M., 2007, The real media divide, *The Washington Post*, July 16, p. A15, viewed July 30, 2007, <http://www.washingtonpost.com/wp-dyn/content/article/2007/07/15/AR2007071501110.html?sub=new>.

45 20% loss of editorial staff at LA Times. It's high noon at the LA Times, 2007, Project for Excellence in Journalism, viewed July 30, 2007, <http://www.journalism.org/node/2018>.

46 Castells, M., 2001, *The Internet galaxy: Reflections on the Internet, business and society*. Oxford: Oxford University Press, p. 191.

47 Norris, P., 2001, *Digital divide: Civic engagement, information poverty, and the Internet worldwide*. Cambridge: Cambridge University Press.

48 Mansell, R., 2004, Political economy, power and new media, *New Media & Society*, 6(1), pp. 96–105.

49 Andrews, R., 2007, Thompson-Reuters deal confirmed, Forbes.com, May 15, viewed September 12, 2007, <http://www.forbes.com/technology/2007/05/15/cx_0515paidcontent.html?partner=rss>.

50 DigitalUK, 2007, Getting set for digital, Digital UK Ltd, London, viewed September 12, 2007, <http://www.digitaluk.co.uk/en.html>.

51 Willsher, K., 2007, *Le Monde* journalists oust chief in protest at management style, *The Guardian*, May 24, viewed July 30, 2007, <http://www.guardian.co.uk/france/story/0,,2086674,00.html#article_continue>.

52 Burke, J., 2006, Has *Libération* lost its fight for freedom?, *The Observer*, September 17, viewed July 30, 2007, <http://media.guardian.co.uk/presspublishing/story/0,,1874160,00.html>.

53 Metro, 2007, Metro.us, New York, viewed July 30, 2007, <http://ny.metro.us/metro/about/>.

54 Campbell, K., 2007, POLIS Future of News seminar, January 24, London School of Economics.

55 Charman, P., 2007, POLIS Future of News seminar, January 24, London School of Economics.

56 Blair, T., 2007, Full transcript of Blair speech, June 12, Reuters, London, viewed July 30, 2007, <http://uk.reuters.com/article/topNews/idUKZWE24585220070612?src=061207_1647_TOPSTORY_blair_attacks_media&pageNumber=4>.

57 Lloyd, J., 2004, The fourth estate's coup d'état, The Observer, June 13, viewed August 1, 2007, <http://media.guardian.co.uk/site/story/0,,1237397,00.html>.

58 Habermas, J., 1974, The public sphere: an encyclopaedia article, New German Critique, 1(3), pp. 49–55.

59 Habermas, J., 2006, Towards a United States of Europe (acceptance speech at Bruno Kreisky Prize), March 27, viewed July 30, 2007, <http://www.signandsight.com/features/676.html>.

60 Keen, A., 2007, The cult of the amateur: How today's Internet is killing our culture, New York: Currency.

61 Ibid, p. 47.

62 Lemann, N., 2006, Amateur hour: Journalism without journalists, New Yorker, August 7, viewed July 30, 2007, <http://www.newyorker.com/archive/2006/08/07/060807fa_fact1>.

63 'Illustrated Books and Newspapers' Wordsworth 1846:

> DISCOURSE was deemed Man's noblest attribute,
> And written words the glory of his hand;
> Then followed Printing with enlarged command
> For thought – dominion vast and absolute
> For spreading truth, and making love expand.
> Now prose and verse sunk into disrepute
> Must lacquey a dumb Art that best can suit
> The taste of this once-intellectual Land.
> A backward movement surely have we here,
> From manhood – back to childhood; for the age –
> Back towards caverned life's first rude career.
> Avaunt this vile abuse of pictured page!
> Must eyes be all in all, the tongue and ear
> Nothing? Heaven keep us from a lower stage!
> (Wordsworth, W., 1888, The complete
> poetical works, London: Macmillan and Co.)

64 Sampson, A., 1996, The crisis at the heart of our media, British Journalism Review, 7(3), pp. 42–51.

65 Purvis, S., 2005, Is British journalism getting better or worse?, City Insights lecture, City University, March 17, viewed July 30, 2007, <http://www.city.ac.uk/whatson/dps/Transcript%2016032005_1%20-%20Stewart%20Purvis.pdf>.

66 Shafer, J., 2007, The newspaper of the future, Slate.com, July 3, viewed August 3, 2007, <http://www.slate.com/id/2169763/fr/rss>.

67 Tumber, H., 1999, *News: A reader*, Oxford: Oxford University Press.

68 Habermas, J., 1974 The public sphere: an encyclopaedia article, *New German Critique*, 1(3), pp. 49–55.

69 Ibid, p. 55.

70 Davies, G., 2005, The BBC and public value, in D. Helm (ed.) *Can the Market Deliver?*, London, John Libbey.

71 Walt Disney Home Video, 2002, *Schoolhouse Rock*. viewed July 30, 2007, <http://disneyvideos.disney.go.com/moviefinder/products/2304803.html>.

72 *YouTube*, 2006, Schoolhouse Rock – how a bill becomes a law, Google, Mountain View, CA, viewed July 30, 2007, <http://www.youtube.com/watch?v=mEJL2Uuv-oQ>.

73 Wikipedia, 2007, Schoolhouse Rock! Wikimedia Foundation, St. Petersburg, FL, viewed July 30, 2007, <http://en.wikipedia.org/wiki/Schoolhouse_Rock>.

74 Klein, R., 2006, GOP takes aim at PBS funding: House panel backs budget reductions, *The Boston Globe*, June 8, viewed July 30, 2007, <http://www.boston.com/ae/tv/articles/2006/06/08/gop_takes_aim_at_pbs_funding/>.

75 Holmwood, L., 2007, Channels rap Ofcom's PSP plans, *MediaGuardian*, June 13, viewed July 30, 2007, <http://media.guardian.co.uk/broadcast/story/0,,2102156,00.html>.

76 Second Life, 2007, Linden Research, Inc, San Francisco, CA, viewed July 30, 2007, <http://secondlife.com/>.

77 Wikipedia, 2007, Economy of Second Life, Wikimedia Foundation, St. Petersburg, FL, viewed July 30, 2007, <http://en.wikipedia.org/wiki/Economy_of_Second_Life>.

78 Sinreich, R., 2007, Hillary Clinton in Second Life, Personal Democracy Forum, March 21, viewed July 30, 2007, <http://techpresident.com/node/171>.

79 Second Life News Center, 2007, Reuters, London, viewed July 30, 2007, <http://www.secondlife.reuters.com/stories/category/second-life/economy/>.

80 Au, J.W., 2007, email to the author, July 10, 2007.

81 Au, J.W., email to the author, July 10, 2007, see also: Au, J.W. *The making of Second Life: Notes from the new world*, New York: HarperCollins.

82 Murray-Watson, A., 2007, Second Life rival seeks €1bn UK listing: Virgin-backed start-up promises to become the "iTunes for the games industry," *The Independent*, July 15, viewed July 30, 2007, <http://news.independent.co.uk/business/news/article2770935.ece>.

83 Semuels, A., 2007, Virtual marketers have second thoughts about Second Life: Firms find that avatars created by participants in the online society aren't avid shoppers, *LA Times*, July 14, viewed July 30, 2007, <http://www.latimes.com/business/la-fi-secondlife14jul14,1,3135510.story?coll=la-headlines-business&ctrack=1&cset=true>.

Chapter 2: Networked Journalism

1   Lemann, N., 2006, Amateur hour: Journalism without journalists, *New Yorker*, August 7, viewed July 30, 2007, <http://www.newyorker.com/archive/2006/08/07/060807fa_fact1>.

2   Gillmor, D., 2007, Journalism isn't dying, it's reviving, *San Francisco Chronicle*, June 7, viewed July 30, 2007, <http://www.sfgate.com/cgi-bin/article.cgi?file=/chronicle/archive/2007/06/07/EDGGTP3FOE1.DTL>.

3   Waugh, E., 2003 (New Ed. edn), *Scoop*, London: Penguin Books Ltd.

4   Frayn, M., 2005, *Towards the end of morning*, London, Faber and Faber.

5   *Citizen Kane*, 1941, motion picture, produced by RKO, directed by Orson Welles.

6   *His Girl Friday*, 1940, motion picture, produced by Columbia Pictures Corporation, directed by Howard Hawks.

7   *All The President's Men*, 1976, motion picture, produced by Warner Bros. Pictures, directed by Alan J. Pakula.

8   *Broadcast News*, 1987, motion picture, produced by American Films, directed by James L. Brooks.

9   Jenkins, S., 2007, The British media does not do responsibility. It does stories, *The Guardian*, May 18, viewed July 30, 2007, <http://media.guardian.co.uk/broadcast/comment/0,,2082508,00.html>.

10 Peacey, J., c2004, *Politicians and pamphleteers: Propaganda during the English civil wars and interregnum*, Aldershot, England and Burlington, VT: Ashgate.

11 Raymond, J., 2002, *Pamphlets and pamphleteering in early modern Britain*, Cambridge: Cambridge University Press.

12 Hubbard, E., September 30, 2006, *Pamphlets and pamphleteers*, Whitefish, MT: Kessinger Publishing; Pmplt edition.

13 Marr, A., 2004, *My trade: A short history of British journalism*, London: Macmillan.

14 Ackroyd, P., 2002, *Dickens*, New York: Vintage.

15 Wikipedia, 2007, Alfred Harmsworth, 1st Viscount Northcliffe, The Wikimedia Foundation, St. Petersburg, FL, viewed September 12, 2007, <http://en.wikipedia.org/wiki/Alfred_Harmsworth%2C_1st_Viscount_Northcliffe>.

16 Wikipedia, 2007, Joseph Pulitzer, Wikimedia Foundation, St. Petersburg, FL, viewed July 30, 2007, <http://en.wikipedia.org/wiki/Joseph_Pulitzer>.

17 Wikipedia, 2007, William Randolf Hearst, Wikimedia Foundation, St. Petersburg, FL, viewed July 30, 2007, <http://en.wikipedia.org/wiki/William_Randolph_Hearst>.

18 Welch, D., 2002, *The Third Reich: Politics and Propaganda* (2nd edn), London: Routledge.

19 Mirror.co.uk, 2007, Trinity Mirror plc, London, viewed September 12, 2007, <http://www.mirror.co.uk/>.

20   Wikipedia, 2007, CBS Evening News, The Wikimedia Foundation, St. Petersburg, FL, viewed September 12, 2007, <http://en.wikipedia.org/wiki/ CBS_Evening_News>.

21   Jarvis, J., 2006, Networked Journalism, The Buzz Machine, July 5, viewed July 30, 2007, <http://www.buzzmachine.com/2006/07/05/networked-journalism/>.

22   Ito, M., 2006, Introduction, in K. Varnelis (ed.), *Networked publics*. Los Angeles: Anneberg Center for Communication, University of Southern California, viewed July 30, 2007, <http://networkedpublics.org/book/introduction>.

23   Marr, A., 2004, *My trade: A short history of British journalism*, Basingstoke: Macmillan.

24   MyTelegraph, 2007, *The Telegraph*, London, viewed July 30, 2007, <http://my.telegraph.co.uk/>.

25   Chron Commons, 2007, *The Houston Chronicle*, Houston, TX, viewed July 30, 2007, <http://www.chron.com/commons/commons.html>.

26   Orgad, S., 2006, *This box was made for walking*, London: Nokia and London School of Economics, viewed July 30, 2007, <http://www.lse.ac.uk/collections/ media@lse/pdf/Mobile_TV_Report_Orgad.pdf>.

27   Godin, S., 2007, Non-linear media, Seth Godin, viewed August 1, 2007, <http://sethgodin.typepad.com/seths_blog/2006/01/nonlinear_media.html>.

28   Wikipedia, 2007, Walt Disney Imagineering, The Wikimedia Foundation, St. Petersburg, FL, viewed September 12, 2007, <http://en.wikipedia.org/wiki/ Walt_Disney_Imagineering#Imagineers>.

29   Richmond, S., 2007, The distributed me, Telegraph.co.uk, June 19, viewed August 1, 2007, <http://blogs.telegraph.co.uk/technology/shanerichmond/ june07/distributedme.htm>.

30   MyTelegraph, 2007, *The Telegraph*, London, viewed July 30, 2007, <http:// my.telegraph.co.uk/>.

31   Blair, T., 2007, Full transcript of Blair speech, 12 June, Reuters, London, viewed July 30, 2007, <http://uk.reuters.com/article/topNews/idUKZWE24585220070612? src=061207_1647_TOPSTORY_blair_attacks_media&pageNumber=4>.

32   Wikipedia, 2007, Citizen Kane, Wikimedia Foundation, St. Petersburg, FL, viewed August 1, 2007, <http://en.wikipedia.org/wiki/Citizen_Kane>.

33   Tracey, M., 2003, *BBC and the reporting of the general strike: Introduction to the microfilm edition*, East Ardsley, UK: Microform Academic Publishers, viewed September 12, 2007, <www.microform.co.uk/guides/R97608.pdf>.

34   Aitken, R., 2007, *Can we trust the BBC?* London: Continuum International Publishing Group.

35   McLeary, P., 2006, Katrina coverage, by the numbers, *Columbia Journalism Review*, August 30, viewed December 11, 2007, <http://www.cjr.org/behind_ the_news/katrina_coverage_by_the_number.php>.

36   Solomon, N., Erlich, R., Zinn, H., and Penn, S., 2003, *Target Iraq: What the news media didn't tell you*, Context Books, viewed August 1, 2007, <http://www. normansolomon.com/norman_solomon/2004/07/target_iraq_now.html>.

37 Schechter, D., 2003, *Media wars: News at a time of terror*, Lanham, MD: Rowman & Littlefield Publishers, Inc.

38 News magazine believability over time, 2006, Project for Excellence in Journalism, Washington, DC, viewed August 1, 2007, <http://www.journalism.org/node/1407>.

39 Tomlinson, K., and the Mann Report, 2006, *Radio public attitudes*, Project for Excellence in Journalism, Washington, DC, March 13, viewed August 1, 2007, <http://www.journalism.org/node/868>.

40 Edmonds, R., and Project for Excellence in Journalism, 2005, *2005 Annual Report – newspaper public attitudes*, Project for Excellence in Journalism, Washington, DC, March 15, viewed August 1, 2007, <http://www.journalism.org/node/1417>.

41 BBC News, 2007, BBC apologises over Queen clips, BBC, July 12, viewed August 1, 2007, <http://news.bbc.co.uk/1/hi/entertainment/6294472.stm>.

42 BBC 6 O'clock News, 2007, television programme, BBC, 13 July, viewed August 1, 2007, <http://news.bbc.co.uk/player/nol/newsid_6890000/newsid_6895600/6895658.stm?bw=bb&mp=wm&news=1>.

43 Lloyd, J., 2004, *What the media do to our politics*, London: Constable and Robinson.

44 Davis, L., 2007, *Scandal: How "gotcha" politics is destroying America*, New York: Palgrave Macmillan.

45 Staines, P., 2007, Guido Fawkes' blog, viewed August 11, 2007, <http://www.order-order.com/2006_07_01_archive.html>.

46 Little Green Football, 2007, Little Green Footballs, viewed July 17, 2007, <http://littlegreenfootballs.com>.

47 Wemple, E., 2007, The Post's 10 web "principles," *Washington City Paper*, July 5, viewed July 17, 2007, <http://www.washingtoncitypaper.com/blogs/city-desk/index.php/2007/07/05/the-posts-10-web-principles/>.

48 Jarvis, J., 2007, The 11th principle, The Buzz Machine, July 7, viewed July 14, 2007, <http://www.buzzmachine.com/2007/07/07/the-11th-principle/>.

49 Wemple, E., 2007, The Post's 10 web "principles", *Washington City Paper*, July 5, viewed July 17, 2007, <http://www.washingtoncitypaper.com/blogs/citydesk/index.php/2007/07/05/the-posts-10-web-principles/>.

50 Global Voices, 2007, Berkman Center for Internet and Society, Harvard Law School, Cambridge, MA, viewed September 12, 2007, <http://www.globalvoicesonline.org/>.

51 Alertnet, 2007, Reuters Foundation, London, viewed August 2, 2007, <http://www.alertnet.org/map/index.htm>.

52 Zkman, 2006, George Allen introduces "Macaca", *YouTube*, August 15, viewed August 11, 2007, <http://www.youtube.com/watch?v=r90z0PMnKwI>.

53 Schlesinger, D., 2007, Out of Africa, Reuters, February 26, viewed August 2, 2007, <http://blogs.reuters.com/2007/02/26/out-of-africa/>.

54 Liberia Ledger, 2007, Crappy Liberia coverage in *Time Magazine*, Liberia Ledger, Monrovia, Liberia, viewed August 2, 2007, <http://liberialedger.blogspot.com/2007/07/crappy-liberia-coverage-in-time.html>.

55   BBC World Service, 2007, BBCNazer.com is launched, BBC, April 18, viewed May 5, 2007, <http://www.bbc.co.uk/worldservice/trust/asiapacific/story/2007/04/070416_aep_website_nazer.shtml>.

56   BBC World Service, 2006, Trust launches Iran youth radio program, BBC, October 23, viewed September 12, 2007, <http://www.bbc.co.uk/worldservice/trust/mediadevelopment/story/2006/10/061020_iranyouth_radio.shtml>.

57   Gillmor, D., 2006, We the media: Grassroots journalism by the people, for the people, Beijing, O'Reilly.

58   Younkins, E., 2007, A Randian definition of the common good, Rebirth of Reason, Santa Clara, CA, viewed July 17, 2007, <http://rebirthofreason.com/Articles/Younkins/A_Randian_Definition_of_the_Common_Good.shtml>.

59   Oreskes, M., 2007, Opening remarks, World Economic Forum, Davos, Switzerland, January, viewed August 2, 2007, <http://www.cbc.ca/news/about/burman/pdf/oreskes-davos.pdf>.

60   Kilman, L., 2007, How young people use media: Youth DNA study measures trends, World Association of Newspapers, Paris, June 3, <http://www.wan-press.org/article14281.html>.

61   Sass, E., 2007, Biggest threat to newspapers is . . . MySpace?, Media Daily News, MediaPost Publications, June 18, viewed August 2, 2007, <http://publications.mediapost.com/index.cfm?fuseaction=Articles.showArticleHomePage&art_aid=62480>.

62   Wikipedia, 2007, Network neutrality, Wikimedia Foundation, St. Petersburg, FL, viewed August 2, 2007, <http://en.wikipedia.org/wiki/Net_neutrality>.

63   Rogers, R., 2004, Information politics on the web, Cambridge, MA: MIT Press.

64   Machill, M., Neuberger, C., and Schindler, F., 2003, Transparency on the Net: Functions and deficiencies of Internet search engines, Info, 5(1), pp. 52–74.

65   Luft, O., 2007, Rusbridger tells Lords "ten year act of faith" needed for digital publishing future, Project for Excellence in Journalism, July 18, viewed December 11, 2007, <http://www.journalism.co.uk/news/story3429.shtml>.

66   Thompson, C., 2006, Google's China problem (and China's Google problem), The New York Times, April 23, viewed August 2, 2007, <http://www.nytimes.com/2006/04/23/magazine/23google.html?pagewanted=1&ei=5090&en=972002761056363f&ex=1303444800>.

67   Martinson, J., 2007, China censorship damaged us, Google founders admit, The Guardian, January 27, viewed August 2, 2007, <http://business.guardian.co.uk/davos2007/story/0,,1999994,00.html#article_continue>.

68   McGuinness, B., 2007, Where have all the (marketing) leaders gone?, Below the Fold, July 14, viewed August 2, 2007, <http://belowthefold.typepad.com/my_weblog/>.

69   Rosen, J., 2007, NewAssignment.net, New York, viewed September 12, 2007, <http://www.newassignment.net/>.

70   Rosen, J., 2006, Introducing NewAssignment.Net, July 25, viewed September 12, 2007, <http://journalism.nyu.edu/pubzone/weblogs/pressthink/2006/07/25/nadn_qa.html>.

71   *The Lady*, 2007, *The Lady*, London, viewed August 2, 2007, <http://www.lady.co.uk/index.cfm>.

72   Usden, A., pers. comm., July 20, 2007.

73   Waghorn, R., 2007, Norwich City, MyFootballWriter.com, viewed August 2, 2007, <http://norwichcity.myfootballwriter.com/index.asp>.

74   Rick Waghorn, email to the author, June 1, 2007.

75   Ali, R., 2007, Local community network Backfence closing down all sites, Paidcontent.org, July 5, viewed August 2, 2007, <http://www.paidcontent.org/entry/419-local-community-network-backfence-closing-down-all-sites/>.

76   Jarvis, J., 2007, Towns are hyperlocal social networks with data (people that is), The Buzz Machine, July 11, viewed August 2, 2007, ,http://www.buzzmachine.com/2007/07/11/hyperlocal/>.

77   *Southwark Weekender*, 2007, Southwark Newspaper Ltd., London, viewed August 2, 2007, <http://www.southwarkweekender.co.uk/shopping/00,news,5124,183,00.htm>.

78   Krim, T., 2007, NetVibes, viewed August 2, 2007, <http://blog.netvibes.com/>.

79   Wikipedia, 2007, Widget (computing [sic], Wikimedia Foundation, St. Petersburg, FL, viewed August 2, 2007, <http://en.wikipedia.org/wiki/Widget_(computing)>.

80   This idea from Craig McGinty in a post on the author's blog, Beckett, C., 2007, Widget News, charliebeckett.org, Polis, London School of Economics, London, July 20, viewed August 2, 2007, <http://www.charliebeckett.org/?p=231>.

81   Michael Oreskes, email to the author, August 1, 2007.

82   Taylor, V., pers. comm., August 10, 2007.

83   Eltringham, M., pers. comm., August 2007.

84   Ofcom, 2007, A new approach to public service content in the digital media age, Ofcom, London, January 24, viewed August 2, 2007, <http://www.ofcom.org.uk/consult/condocs/pspnewapproach/summary/>.

85   Radford, S., 2007, Village rocks at Shalfest, *Newbury Today*, July 16, viewed August 2, 2007, <http://www.newburytoday.co.uk/News/Article.aspx?articleID=4718>.

86   Ofcom, 2007, A new approach to public service content in the digital media age, Ofcom, London, January 24, viewed August 2, 2007, <http://www.ofcom.org.uk/consult/condocs/pspnewapproach/newapproach.pdf>.

87   Ibid.

88   Curzon Prize, T., 2007, POLIS Future of News seminar, 24 January, London School of Economics.

Chapter 3: Networked Journalism and Politics

1   Blair, T., 2007, Full transcript of Blair speech, June 12, Reuters, London, viewed July 30, 2007, <http://uk.reuters.com/article/topNews/idUKZWE24585220070612?src=061207_1647_TOPSTORY_blair_attacks_media&pageNumber=4>.

2   McLuhan, M., 1962, *The Gutenberg galaxy: The making of typographic man*, Toronto: University of Toronto Press.

3   Wikipedia, 2007, John Pilger, Wikimedia Foundation, St. Petersburg, FL, viewed August 13, 2007, <http://en.wikipedia.org/wiki/John_Pilger>.

4   Johnpilger.com, 2007, Doward, O. ITV, London, viewed August 13, 2007, <http://www.johnpilger.com/page.asp?partID=5>.

5   Norris, P., 2002, *Democratic phoenix: Reinventing political activism*, Cambridge: Cambridge University Press.

6   Giving USA Foundation, 2007, U.S. charitable giving reaches $295.02 billion in 2006, Charity Navigator, June 25, viewed August 11, 2007, <http://www.charitynavigator.org/index.cfm/bay/content.view/cpid/619>.

7   Project for Excellence in Journalism, 2004, *2004 annual report: Newpaper public attitudes*, March 15, viewed August 11, 2007, <http://www.journalism.org/node/807>.

8   Project for Excellence in Journalism, 2007, *The state of the news media 2007: An annual report on American journalism*, viewed August 11, 2007, <http://www.stateofthenewsmedia.com/2007/narrative_overview_publicattitudes.asp?cat=8&media=1>.

9   Ibid.

10   Trippi, J., 2004, Down from the mountain, keynote speech, O'Reilly digital democracy teach-in, San Diego, CA, February 9, viewed August 11, 2007, <http://www.itconversations.com/transcripts/80/transcript80-2.html>.

11   Horrigan, J., 2004, *Pew Internet project data memo*, Pew Internet and American Life Project, April, viewed August 11, 2007, <http://www.pewinternet.org/PPF/r/121/report_display.asp>.

12   Rainie, L., Cornfield, M., and Horrigan, J., 2005, *The Internet and campaign 2004*, Pew Internet and American Life Project, March 6, viewed August 11, 2007, <http://www.pewinternet.org/PPF/r/150/report_display.asp>.

13   Sweney, M., 2007, Olympics and presidents to drive ad spend growth, *Media-Guardian*, June 27, viewed August 13, 2007, <http://media.guardian.co.uk/advertising/story/0,,2112934,00.html>.

14   Farnsworth, M. 1998, Drudge Report: Newsweek kills story on White House intern, Australianpolitics.com, January 17, viewed August 11, 2007, <http://australianpolitics.com/usa/clinton/impeachment/drudge.shtml>.

15   Black, D., 2002, Escahnton, December 6, viewed August 11, 2007, <http://atrios.blogspot.com/2002_12_01_atrios_archive.html#90023494>.

16   Rosen, J., 2004, The legend of Trent Lott and the weblogs, PressThink, March 15, viewed August 11, 2007, <http://journalism.nyu.edu/pubzone/weblogs/pressthink/2004/03/15/lott_case.html>.

17   "Buckhead," 2004, No title, Freerepublic.com, Fresno, CA, September 8, viewed August 11, 2007, <http://www.freerepublic.com/focus/f-news/1210662/replies?c=47>.

18   Abovitz, R., 2005, Easongate: The end of MSN as we know it?, World Economic Forum, Geneva, Switzerland, February 8, viewed August 11, 2007, <http://www.forumblog.org/blog/2005/02/following_eason.html>.

19   Media Matters for America, 2005, "Go ahead, Jeff": Talon News "reporter" Jeff Gannon is McClellan's lifeline during briefings, Media Matters for America, February 2, viewed August 11, 2007, <http://mediamatters.org/items/200502020014>.

20   Leibovich, M., 2006, Lieberman hopes his fate isn't sealed with a kiss, *The New York Times*, July 16, viewed August 13, 2007, <http://www.nytimes.com/2006/07/16/washington/16lieberman.html?ex=1310702400&en=b423a86bccfd09af&ei=5088&partner=rssnyt&emc=rss>.

21   DubyaD40web, 2007, Hillary Clinton Sopranos spoof, *YouTube*, June 19, viewed August 11, 2007, <http://www.youtube.com/watch?v=shKJk3Rph0E>.

22   Zkman, 2006, George Allen introduces "Macaca", *YouTube*, August 15, viewed August 11, 2007, <http://www.youtube.com/watch?v=r90z0PMnKwI>.

23   Albrekts, 2006, Rush Limbaugh trashes Michael J Fox, *YouTube*, October 25, viewed August 11, 2007, <http://www.youtube.com/watch?v=0o6yrdInw6s>.

24   Barelypolitical, 2007, "I've got a crush . . . on Obama" by Obama Girl, *YouTube*, June 13, viewed August 11, 2007, <http://www.youtube.com/watch?v=wKsoXHYICqU>.

25   Jarvis, J., 2007, Puppets aside, *YouTube* is the best forum for debate, *The Guardian*, July 30, viewed August 11, 2007, <http://media.guardian.co.uk/mediaguardian/story/0,,2137336,00.html>.

26   Huffington, A., 2007, New HuffPost project: The wisdom of the crowd hits the '08 campaign trail, *The Huffington Post*, March 26, viewed August 11, 2007, <http://www.huffingtonpost.com/arianna-huffington/new-huffpost-project-the_b_44321.html>.

27   Clinton, H., 2007, Hillary Clinton, *Facebook*, viewed August 11, 2007, <http://lse.facebook.com/person.php?id=2290827757>.

28   Edwards, J., 2007, John Edward's wall, *Facebook*, viewed August 11, 2007, <http://lse.facebook.com/wall.php?id=2352506197>.

29   Obama, B., 2007, Barack Obama, *Facebook*, viewed August 11, 2007, <http://lse.facebook.com/person.php?id=2355496748>.

30   Bai, M., 2007, *The argument: Billionaires, bloggers, and the battle to remake Democratic politics*, Penguin Press.

31   NUJ, 2006, Tony Benn pulls no punches at launch of media lectures, National Union of Journalists, November 15, viewed August 11, 2007, <http://www.nuj.org.uk/inner.php?docid=1532>.

32   Benn, T., *Covert Action Quarterly*, April 2001.

33   BBC News, 2000, Blair unveils internet plans, BBC News, September 11, viewed August 11, 2007, <http://news.bbc.co.uk/1/hi/uk_politics/919903.stm>.

34 Blair, T., 2007, Full transcript of Blair speech, June 12, Reuters, London, viewed July 30, 2007, <http://uk.reuters.com/article/topNews/idUKZWE24585220070612? src=061207_1647_TOPSTORY_blair_attacks_media&pageNumber=4>.

35 Staines, P., 2006, Something rotten in the media-politico nexus, Guido Fawkes' blog, July 12, viewed August 11, 2007, <http://www.order-order.com/ 2006_07_01_archive.html>.

36 Hencke, D., 2006, Westminster weekly, *The Guardian Unlimited*, June 29, viewed August 11, 2007, <http://download.guardian.co.uk/sys-audio/Politics/ Westminster/2006/06/29/PoliticsShow290606.mp3>.

37 Staines, P., 2006, Meanwhile, back at the ranch, Guido Fawkes' blog, July 3, viewed August 11, 2007, <http://www.order-order.com/2006/07/meanwhile-back-at-ranch.html>.

38 Crerar, P. and Cecil, N., 2006, Double blow for two jags, *The Evening Standard*, July 4, p. 16, viewed August 11, 2007, Lexis Nexis.

39 Robinson, N., 2006, Prescott for dummies, Nick Robinson's newslog, BBC News, July 5, viewed August 11, 2007, <http://www.bbc.co.uk/blogs/ nickrobinson/2006/07/05/index.html>.

40 Staines, P., 2007, Guido Fawkes' blog, viewed September 12, 2007, <http://www.order-order.com/2006/07/meanwhile-back-at-ranch.html>.

41 Staines, P., 2006, Robinson for dummies, Guido Fawkes' blog, July 5, viewed August 11, 2007, <http://www.order-order.com/2006/07/robinson-for-dummies.html>.

42 Humphrys, J., 2006, I will not quit; John Prescott gives his first broadcast interview since his political troubles began, *Today Programme*, radio broadcast, BBC Radio 4, July 6, viewed August 11, 2007, <http://www.bbc.co.uk/radio4/ today/listenagain/zthursday_20060706.shtml>.

43 Staines, P., 2006, Three shags* does not deny other affairs, Guido Fawkes' blog, July 6, viewed August 11, 2007, <http://www.order-order.com/2006/07/ three-shags-does-not-deny-other.html>.

44 Dale, I., 2007, Iain Dale's diary, viewed August 11, 2007, <http:// iaindale.blogspot.com/>.

45 Barkham, P., 2006, How the net closed on Prescott, *The Guardian*, July 10, viewed August 11, 2007, <http://media.guardian.co.uk/mediaguardian/story/ 0,,1816492,00.html>.

46 Ibid.

47 Robinson, N., 2007, Nick Robinson's newslog, BBC News, viewed August 11, 2007, <http://www.bbc.co.uk/blogs/nickrobinson/>.

48 Barkham, P., 2006, How the net closed on Prescott, *The Guardian*, July 10, viewed August 11, 2007, <http://media.guardian.co.uk/mediaguardian/story/ 0,,1816492,00.html>.

49 BBC News, 2007, Road petition breaks a million, BBC News, Feburary 10, viewed August 11, 2007, <http://news.bbc.co.uk/1/hi/uk/6349027.stm>.

50 Stiglitz, J. and Islam, R., 2002, A free press is crucial in overcoming global poverty, Global Policy Forum, November 14, viewed August 13, 2007, <http://www.globalpolicy.org/globaliz/cultural/2002/1114pov.htm>.

51 BBC News, 2005, Africa calls on G8 to scrap debt, BBC news, July 5, viewed August 13, 2007, <http://news.bbc.co.uk/1/hi/world/africa/4651337.stm>.

52 BBC News, 2005, G8 leaders agree to $50bn aid boost, BBC News, July 8, viewed August 13, 2007, <http://news.bbc.co.uk/1/hi/business/4662297.stm>.

53 DFID, 2007, Getting rid of polio and measles in Uganda, DFID, London, January 18, viewed August 13, 2007, <http://www.dfid.gov.uk/casestudies/files/africa/uganda-measles.asp>.

54 USAID, 2007, Sub-Saharan Africa, USAID, Washington, DC, viewed August 13, 2007, <http://www.usaid.gov/locations/sub-saharan_africa/>.

55 Collier, P., 2004, Development and conflict, Centre for the Study of African Economics, Oxford University and United Nations, Economic and Social Development, viewed August 13, 2007, <http://www.un.org/esa/documents/Development.and.Conflict2.pdf>.

56 Amnesty International, 2007, Africa: The state of human rights, AllAfrica.com, May 24, viewed August 13, 2007, <http://allafrica.com/stories/200705240372.html>.

57 UNAIDS, 2006, Report on the global AIDS epidemic 2006, Joint United Nations program on HIV/AIDS, May, viewed August 13, 2007, <http://www.unaids.org/en/HIV_data/2006GlobalReport/default.asp>.

58 Amnesty International, 2007, Africa: The state of human rights, AllAfrica.com, May 24, viewed August 13, 2007, <http://allafrica.com/stories/200705240372.html>.

59 CNN, 2007, African Journalist Awards, 2007, CNN, Atlanta, GA, viewed August 13, 2007, <http://www.cnn.com/WORLD/africa/africanawards/>.

60 Wikipedia, 2007, Live Aid, Wikimedia Foundation, St. Petersburg, FL, viewed August 13, 2007, <http://en.wikipedia.org/wiki/Live_Aid>.

61 Live 8, 2007, Charity Projects, London, viewed August 13, 2007, <http://www.live8live.com/>.

62 Putzel, J. and van der Zwan, J., 2005, *Why Templates for media development do not work in crisis states*, Crisis States Research Center, London School of Economics, London, viewed August 13, 2007, <http://www.crisisstates.com/download/publicity/FINAL.MEDIA.REPORT.PDF>.

63 IFEX, 2007, Uganda: Independent radio station closed, journalist charged, International Freedom of Expression Exchange, Toronto, viewed August 13, 2007, <http://www.ifex.org/en/content/view/full/44/>.

64 Beckett, C. and Kyrke-Smith, L. (eds.), *Development, governance and the media: The role of the media in building African society*, POLIS, London School of Economics, London, viewed August 13, 2007, <http://www.lse.ac.uk/collections/polis/pdf/DGMfullreport.pdf>.

65   CNN, 2007, African Journalist Awards, CCN, Atlanta, GA, viewed August 13, 2007, <http://edition.cnn.com/WORLD/africa/africanawards/winners.html>.

66   Zachary, G.P., 2007, Media and development, *Africa Works*, January 23, viewed August 13, 2007, <http://africaworksgpz.com/g-pascal-zachary/>.

67   BBC World Service Trust, 2006, *Research summary report: African media development initiative*, BBC World Service Trust, London, p. 43, viewed August 13, 2007, <http://downloads.bbc.co.uk/worldservice/trust/pdf/AMDI/AMDI_summary_Report.pdf>.

68   Nyirubugara, O., 2007, Mobile reporters in Africa, *Africa News*, July 25, viewed August 13, 2007, <http://www.africanews.com/site/list_messages/10175>.

69   Kenya Unlimited, 2007, Kenyan blogs webring, viewed August 13, 2007, <http://www.kenyaunlimited.com/kenyan-blogs-webring/>.

70   Blog Africa, 2007, Global Voices, Cambridge, MA, viewed August 13, 2007, <http://www.blogafrica.com/>.

71   *The Zimbabwean*, 2007, The Zimbabwean Limited, Hythe, viewed August 13, 2007, <http://www.thezimbabwean.co.uk/index.cfm?id=199&linkid=35&siteid=1>.

72   Bloomfield, S., 2007, Boom in blogs gives Africans a voice on the web, Independent.co.uk, August 2, viewed August 13, 2007, <http://news.independent.co.uk/world/africa/article2826183.ece>.

73   Heavens, A., 2005, African blogers find their voice, *BBC Focus on Africa magazine*, December 20, viewed August 13, 2007, <http://news.bbc.co.uk/1/hi/world/africa/4512290.stm>.

74   Sleepless in Sudan, 2007, Sleepless in Sudan. Uncensored, direct from a dazed & confused aid worker in Darfur, Sudan, viewed August 13, 2007, <http://sleeplessinsudan.blogspot.com/2005_10_01_archive.html>.

75   Kalonji, C., 2007, Cedric au Congo, Democratic Republic of Congo, viewed August 13, 2007, <http://cedric.uing.net/>.

76   Ibid.

77   Bankelele, 2007, Economic Matrix, Bankelele, July 29, viewed August 13, 2007, <http://bankelele.blogspot.com>.

78   Soremi, T., 2007, Rape of the Niger Delta, My Thots, July 26, viewed August 13, 2007, <http://titilayoobishineshine.blogspot.com/>.

79   Sarpong, O., 2007, South Africans – what are they doing, Sarpong Obed – ready to chew, July 31, viewed August 13, 2007, <http://sarpongobed.blogspot.com/>.

80   Sarpong, O., 2007, A Western evil, Sarpong Obed – ready to chew, August 3, viewed August 13, 2007, <http://sarpongobed.blogspot.com/>.

81   BBC World Service Trust, 2006, *Research summary report: African media development initiative*, BBC World Service Trust, London, p. 103, viewed August 13, 2007, <http://downloads.bbc.co.uk/worldservice/trust/pdf/AMDI/AMDI_summary_Report.pdf>.

82 McNair, B., 2007, *An introduction to political communication (communication & society)*, London: Routledge, p. 6.

83 Trippi, J., 2007, Democracy reborn, digitally, *Sunday Times* (London), June 10, p. 19, viewed September 13, 2007, Lexis Nexis.

Chapter 4: Terror, Community, and Networked Journalism

1   Khan, M., 2007, Khan's Statement, *The Telegraph*, September 2, viewed August 30, 2007, <http://www.telegraph.co.uk/news/main.jhtml?xml=/news/2005/09/02/wterr302.xml>.

2   BBC Radio 4, 2006, *Analysis: Telling Muslim stories*, radio programme, BBC, London, December 28, viewed September 13, <http://news.bbc.co.uk/1/hi/programmes/analysis/6199779.stm>.

3   Jenkins, S., 2007, The British media does not do responsibility. It does stories, *The Guardian*, May 18, viewed July 30, 2007, <http://media.guardian.co.uk/broadcast/comment/0,,2082508,00.html>.

4   BBC News, 2007, Misbah parents reach settlement, BBC News, January 18, viewed September 13, 2007, <http://news.bbc.co.uk/1/hi/scotland/highlands_and_islands/6273641.stm>.

5   BBC Radio 4, 2006, *Analysis: Telling Muslim stories*, radio programme, BBC, London, December 28, viewed September 13, 2007, <http://news.bbc.co.uk/1/hi/programmes/analysis/6199779.stm>.

6   Ibid.

7   Select Committee on Office of the Deputy Prime Minister, House of Commons, 2004, Memorandum by Nick Carter, Editor of the *Leicester Mercury* (SOC 74), Housing, Planning, Local Government and the Regions Written Evidence, May 5, viewed August 30, 2007, <http://www.publications.parliament.uk/pa/cm200304/cmselect/cmodpm/45/45we17.htm>.

8   9/11 Truth, 2007, 9/11Truth.org, Kansas City, MO, viewed August 30, 2007, <http://www.911truth.org/index.php?topic=contacts>.

9   McLeod, J., 2007, Glasgow bomber and online jihadist, *Canada Free Press*, August 21, viewed August 30, 2007, <http://www.canadafreepress.com/2007/cover082107.htm>.

10 Lammy, D., 2006, Diversity in the media – the twin challenge, POLIS lecture, London College of Communication, October 18, viewed August 30, 2007, <http://www.lse.ac.uk/collections/polis/davidlammytranscript.htm>.

11 Ofcom, 2007, UK's Ethnic minority groups watch less TV but compare well on mobile and broadband take-up, June 21, Ofcom, London, viewed July 30, 2007, <http://www.ofcom.org.uk/media/news/2007/06/nr_20070621>.

12 Munro, J. email to the author July 10, 2007.
13 Urquhart, C., 2007, The girl who urges children to fight Israel . . . with clean teeth, *The Observer*, August 26, viewed August 30, 2007, <http://www. guardian.co.uk/israel/Story/0,,2156377,00.html>.
14 Media12312345, 2007, Hamas "Mickey Mouse" wants Islam takeover, *YouTube*, viewed August 30, 2007, <http://www.youtube.com/watch?v= pCNGJtIg73s>.
15 Fouda, R., 2006, Aljazeera – a different voice in the world?, POLIS The news we deserve lecture series, London School of Economics, October 2, viewed August 30, 2007, <http://www.lse.ac.uk/collections/LSEPublicLecturesAndEvents/ events/2006/20060904t1239z001.htm>.
16 Ibid.
17 Birt, Y., 2007, POLIS Reporting Muslims and Extremism seminar, July 5, London School of Economics, viewed September 13, 2007, <http://www.lse. ac.uk/collections/polis/pdf/FINAL%20MUSLIM%20SEMINAR%20REPORT. doc>.
18 Wikipedia, 2007, Ed Husain, The Wikimedia Foundation, St. Petersburg, FL, viewed August 30, 2007, <http://en.wikipedia.org/wiki/Ed_Husain>.

Chapter 5: Editorial Diversity and Media Literacy

1 Goldhammer, G., 2007, Media must learn to think beyond the medium, Below the Fold, April 28, viewed August 30, 2007, <http://belowthefold.typepad.com/ my_weblog/2007/04/media_must_lear.html>.
2 Schlosser, E., 2005, *Fast food nation*, London: Harper Perennial.
3 *Fahrenheit 9/11*, 2004, documentary motion picture, produced by Lions Gate Films, directed by Michael Moore.
4 Armitage, T., 2006, 2007 and the "next" big media thing, *New Statesman*, July 31, viewed August 30, 2007, <http://www.newstatesman.com/200607310067>.
5 McLeary, P., 2007, How TalkingPointsMemo beat the big boys on the U.S. Attorney story, *Columbia Journalism Review*, March 15, viewed August 30, 2007, <http://www.cjr.org/behind_the_news/how_talkingpointsmemo_beat_the.php? page=2>.
6 Jarvis, J., 2006, New rule: Cover what you do best. Link to the rest., The Buzz Machine, July 5, viewed August 30, 2007, <http://www.buzzmachine.com/ 2007/02/22/new-rule-cover-what-you-do-best-link-to-the-rest/>.
7 Stephens, M., 2007, Beyond the news, *Columbia Journalism Review*, January/ February, viewed September 13, 2007, <http://www.cjr.org/feature/beyond_ the_news.php?page=5>.
8 Leigh, D. and Evans, R., 2007, The BAE files, *Guardian Unlimited*, viewed August 30, 2007, <http://www.guardian.co.uk/baefiles/>.

9   Smith, P., 2007, Guardian investigators share BAE bribery exposé on the web, PressGazette.co.uk, July 23, viewed September 13, 2007, <http://www.pressgazette.co.uk/story.asp?storycode=38280>.

10 Wikipedia, 2007, The Wikimedia Foundation, St. Petersburg, FL, viewed August 1, 2007, <http://www.wikipedia.org/>.

11 *Encyclopaedia Britannica*, 2007, Encyclopaedia Britannica UK Ltd, London, viewed August 1, 2007, <http://info.britannica.co.uk/?jlnk=hsl0010>.

12 Giles, J., 2005, Internet encyclopaedias go head to head, December 14 (updated March 28, 2006), *Nature*, viewed August 1, 2007, <http://www.nature.com/news/2005/051212/full/438900a.html>.

13 Glaister, D., 2005, LA Times "wikitorial" gives editors red faces, *The Guardian*, June 22, viewed August 2007, <http://www.guardian.co.uk/international/story/0,,1511745,00.html>.

14 Wikinews, 2007, Wikimedia Foundation, St. Petersburg, FL, viewed August 1, 2007, <http://en.wikinews.org/wiki/Main_Page>.

15 BBC News Online, 2007, US university shooting kills 33, BBC, 17 April, viewed August 1, 2007, <http://news.bbc.co.uk/1/hi/world/americas/6560685.stm>.

16 Garfunkel, J., 2007, Virginia Tech shooting: Can media get beyond retroactive response to tragedy?, Mediashift, PBS, April 20, viewed August 1, 2007, <http://www.pbs.org/mediashift/2007/04/virginia_tech_shootingcan_medi.html>.

17 Cohn, D., 2007, VA Tech and the changing role of citizen networks, Newassignment.net, April 17, viewed August 1, 2007, <http://citmedia.org/blog/2007/04/17/virginia-tech-how-media-are-evolving/>.

18 Bradshaw, P. (ed.), 2007, Wiki journalism: Are wikis the new blogs? Wikijournalism: Front Page, viewed August 30, 2007, <http://wikijournalism.pbwiki.com/>.

19 Sholin, R., 2007, Further notes on the new journalism skillset, *Invisible Inkling*, February 5, viewed September 13, 2007, <http://www.ryansholin.com/2007/02/05/further-notes-on-the-new-journalism-skillset/>.

20 Surowiecki, J., 2005, *The wisdom of crowds*, New York, Anchor Books.

21 Tumber, H., 1999, *News: A reader*, Oxford: Oxford University Press, pp. 79–81.

22 24weeks.com, 2007, ESP Metanational LLP, viewed August 1, 2007, <http://www.24weeks.com/about#Espra_–_an_Evolutionary_Tool>.

23 Hallett, T., 2007, BBC's new media boss talks web 3.0, Silicon.com, London, July 3, viewed August 1, 2007, <http://networks.silicon.com/webwatch/0,39024667,39167725,00.htm>.

24 Ofcom, 2007, *Media Literacy*, Ofcom, viewed August 30, 2007, <http://www.ofcom.org.uk/advice/media_literacy/>.

25 Ibid.

26 About, 2007, Creative Commons, San Francisco, CA, viewed August 30, 2007, <http://creativecommons.org/about/>.

27 About, 2007, Free Software Foundation, Boston, MA, viewed August 30, 2007, <http://www.fsf.org/about>.

28 Ashley, J., 2006, In defence of professional columnists, Comment is Free, *Guardian Unlimited*, May 18, viewed August 30, 2007, <http://commentisfree. guardian.co.uk/jackie_ashley/2006/05/in_defence_of_professional_col.html>.

29 Beckett, C. (ed.), 2007, The Future of News Seminar 4: The practicalities and politics of online journalism, POLIS, London School of Economics, 24 May, viewed 30 August 2007, <http://www.lse.ac.uk/collections/polis/pdf/Future%20of% 20News%204%20report.doc>.

30 O'Reilly, T., 2007, Draft blogger's code of conduct, O'Reilly Radar, August 4, viewed September 13, 2007, <http://radar.oreilly.com/archives/2007/04/ draft_bloggers_1.html>.

31 Ewan MacIntosh, viewed November 2007, <http://edu.blogs.com/ewanmcintosh/>.

32 Ibid.

33 Ibid.

34 Mansell, R., 2007, Introductory remarks, Third Informal Thematic Debate: Civilizations and the Challenge for Peace: Obstacles and Opportunities, United Nations General Assembly 61st Session, May 11, viewed August 30, 2007, <http://www.lse.ac.uk/collections/polis/crossingboundaries.htm>.

35 Lippmann, W., 1922 *Public opinion*, New York: Free Press; Dewey, J. 1927, *The public and its problem*. New York: Holt.

36 Chouliaraki, L., pers. comm., September 6, 2007.

37 Mansell, R., 2007, Introductory remarks, Third Informal Thematic Debate: Civilizations and the Challenge for Peace: Obstacles and Opportunities, United Nations General Assembly 61st Session, May 11, viewed August 30, 2007, <http://www.lse.ac.uk/collections/polis/crossingboundaries.htm>.

38 Wikipedia, 2007, John Pilger, Wikimedia Foundation, St. Petersburg, FL, viewed August 13, 2007, <http://en.wikipedia.org/wiki/John_Pilger>.

39 Johnpilger.com, 2007, Doward, O. ITV, London, viewed August 13, 2007, <http://www.johnpilger.com/page.asp?partID=5>

40 Wikipedia, 2007, P.J. O'Rourke, The Wikimedia Foundation, St. Petersburg, FL, viewed August 31, 2007, <http://en.wikipedia.org/wiki/P._J._O'Rourke>.

41 O'Rourke, P.J., 2007, *P.J. O'Rourke*, New York: Grove/Atlantic, Inc., viewed August 31, 2007, <http://www.groveatlantic.com/grove/bin/wc.dll?groveproc ~genauth~568~0>.

42 Bell, M., 1996, *In harm's way*, New York: Penguin.

43 Silverstone, R., 2006, *Media and morality: On the rise of the mediapolis*, Cambridge: Polity Press.

44 Ibid, p. 117.

45 Polis, viewed 12 December 2007, <www.lse.ac.uk/Polis>.

46 Silverstone, R., 2006, *Media and morality: On the rise of the mediapolis*, Cambridge: Polity Press, p. 162.

Suggested Reading

Chapter 1

Castells, M., 2001, *The Internet galaxy: Reflections on the Internet, business and society*. Oxford: Oxford University Press.

Keen, A., 2007, *The cult of the amateur: How today's Internet is killing our culture*, New York: Currency.

Marr, A., 2004, *My trade: A short history of British journalism*, Basingstoke: Macmillan.

Tumber, H., 1999, *News: A reader*, Oxford: Oxford University Press.

Chapter 2

Anderson, C., 2006, *The long tail*, New York: Hyperion.

Gillmor, D., 2005, *We the media*, Sebastapol, CA: O'Reilly Media.

Mansell, R. and Steinmueller, W., 2002, *Mobilising the information society*, Oxford: Oxford University Press.

Sunstein, C.R., 2007, *Republic.com 2.0*, Princeton: Princeton University Press.

Surowiecki, J., 2005, *The wisdom of crowds*, New York, Anchor Books.

Chapter 3

Armstrong, J. and Moulitsas, M., 2006, *Crashing the gate: Netroots, grassroots, and the rise of people-powered politics*, White River Junction, VT: Chelsea Green Publishing.

Beckett, C. and Kyrke-Smith, L. (eds.), *Development, governance and the media: The role of the media in building African society*, London: POLIS, London School of Economics.

Collier, P., 2007, *The bottom billion*, Oxford: Oxford University Press.

Lloyd, J., 2004, *What the media do to our politics*, London: Constable and Robinson.

McNair, B., 2007, *An introduction to political communication (communication & society)*, London: Routledge.

Trippi, J., 2004, *The revolution will not be televised*, New York: HarperCollins.

Chapter 4

Lessig, L., 2005, *Free culture: The nature and future of creativity*, Harmondsworth: Penguin.

Miles, H., 2006, *Al Jazeera*, New York: Abacus.

Price, M. and Thompson, M., (eds.), 2002, *Forging peace*, Edinburgh: Edinburgh University Press and Indiana: Indiana University Press.

Zelizer, B., 2004, *Taking journalism seriously*, Sage.

Chapter 5

Bauman, Z., 2007, *Liquid times*, Cambridge: Polity.

Beck, U., 2002, *Cosmopolitan vision*, Cambridge: Polity.

Chouliaraki, L., 2006, *Spectatorship of suffering*, London, Thousand Oaks, New Delhi: Sage.

Silverstone, R., 2006, *Media and morality*, Cambridge: Polity.

Index

LaVergne, TN USA
05 January 2010
168824LV00004B/89/P